LONDON SCHOOL OF ECONOMICS
NOGRAPHS ON SOCIAL ANTHROPOLOGY

*Managing Editor:* Anthony Forge

The Monographs on Social Anthropology were established
in 1940 and aim to publish results of modern anthropological research of primary interest to specialists.

The continuation of the series was made possible by a
grant in aid from the Wenner-Gren Foundation for Anthropological Research, and more recently by a further grant
from the Governors of the London School of Economics
and Political Science. Income from sales is returned to a
revolving fund to assist further publications.

The Monographs are under the direction of an Editorial
Board associated with the Department of Anthropology
of the London School of Economics and Political Science.

LONDON SCHOOL OF ECONOMICS
MONOGRAPHS ON SOCIAL ANTHROPOLOGY
No. 35

# THE KERESAN BRIDGE

A Problem in Pueblo Ethnology

BY

ROBIN FOX

UNIVERSITY OF LONDON
THE ATHLONE PRESS
NEW YORK: HUMANITIES PRESS INC.
1967

*First published by*
THE ATHLONE PRESS
UNIVERSITY OF LONDON
*at 2 Gower Street, London* WC1

*Distributed by Constable & Co Ltd*
12 *Orange Street, London* WC2


*Canada*
Oxford University Press
Toronto

Library of Congress Catalog Card No. 67–17557

*Printed in Great Britain by*
WESTERN PRINTING SERVICES LTD
BRISTOL

# PREFACE

'The Keresan Bridge' is a phrase which was coined by Fred Eggan in *The Social Organization of the Western Pueblos* (1950). He was attempting to account for the distribution of types of social structure among the Pueblo tribes of New Mexico and Arizona (see Map 1). Commenting on his theory in a later work (Eggan 1955) he puts the problem thus:

'The relationship between the Eastern and Western Pueblos and the considerable differences between their social structures offered a problem which I attempted to solve by an acculturational hypothesis . . . The key to this problem may lie in what I have called the "Keresan Bridge", the group of Keresan-speaking Pueblos which adjoin Zuni on the west and the Tewa and Tiwa on the east. Here there is some evidence of variation from lineage to bilateral organization, and I have interpreted it as in that direction, though further evidence may reverse it.' (p. 510.)

I have examined here the 'considerable differences' between the social structures of the Western and Eastern Pueblos, the 'variation from lineage to bilateral organization', and the role of the 'Keresan Bridge'. This is an 'ethnological' analysis in the British sense of the term; that is, an analysis of the history of a people who lack written records. Such analyses are not usual in British anthropology, and I should perhaps explain how I came to break with tradition.

In the summers of 1958 and 1959 I was able to gather some first-hand information on the social structure of the Pueblo of Cochiti, New Mexico – an Eastern Keresan Pueblo. Eggan and others regard this as one of the 'most acculturated' of the Keresans, and have used the data on its social structure to support their ethnological hypotheses.

When I first went to Cochiti I was not very interested in the ethnology of the Pueblos. I spent most of my time gathering material on language-use in Cochiti since I was primarily interested in Whorf's theories (Whorf, 1956). The information I gathered on social structure was, by modern fieldwork standards, very thin. It did not seem possible to make an ethnographic monograph out of it, so I put it on one side and began some fresh fieldwork in Ireland.

For four years after leaving America I taught sociology at the University of Exeter. I almost forgot about the Pueblos, and regarded my time in Cochiti as little more than fieldwork practice. The few short things I wrote on the subject concerned language, baseball, veterans and witchcraft (Fox, 1959, 1950, 1961a, 1961b, 1964). In these I followed Eggan's theory without thinking about it too deeply. But when I began to teach kinship at the London School of Economics (1963–4), I went back over my notes, and gradually became convinced that there was something wrong with the generally accepted ethnological theory. My analysis of the Cochiti material seemed to throw some doubt on the theory, so that even though the material was in many ways inadequate, I felt I should present it.

I started to write a descriptive article which was the basis for the present Chapters 4 and 5. I found it necessary to give some general account of Cochiti society as background; this became Chapter 3. I intended to end with some brief comments on the relevance of this for the ethnological problem, but when I began to explore all the issues this short comment expanded to become Chapters 1 and 2. I then added some notes on kinship terminology since this has been central to the debate; this in turn became Chapter 7. In trying to fit the terminological data into the ethnological picture, I found myself writing Chapter 8. If we add to these the discussion in Chapter 6 and the conclusion, we have the whole of the present book.

My main concern when I began was to show how Cochiti kinship structure could not be explained in terms of a 'variation from lineage to bilateral organization'. But as I went deeper into the ethnological issue the problem of the 'Keresan Bridge' began to dominate the narrower question of the 'true' nature of Cochiti kinship structure. The latter became evidence for an ethnological critique, rather than the purpose of the analysis. An earlier version of this book – very much Cochiti-dominated – was entitled 'Cochiti Kinship Structure and the Study of Pueblo Social Organization' (Ph.D. thesis, London University, 1965). In the present, much revised, version the problem of the Keresan Bridge is central, and this change of focus is reflected in the change of title.

These elements of intellectual autobiography are necessary in order to show how this rather uneven book 'happened'. In a sense it started in the middle and worked in both directions at once. The details of the book's composition may also help to explain why parts of it contradict certain things I have said in previous publications. This version is by no means final. My findings are at best tentative hypotheses and I hope they will be treated with great scepticism. There are many aspects of the problem that I have barely touched – the difficult archaeological issues, for example; and others I have dealt with all too briefly – for example, the even more difficult problem of the change from 'elementary' to 'complex' structures of alliance. But I have felt it best to publish now and let the arguments be ventilated.

I spent altogether five months in Cochiti itself. I visited most of the other Pueblos, and stayed for a short time in Moenkopi in the far west of Hopi country. In Cochiti my wife and I lived in the same house on each visit. On the second trip we shared it with a Cochiti family and were able to become involved in day-to-day kinship affairs. We were given an adoption into a clan (Oak), but I do not know quite how seriously this was taken. It was regarded as enough, however, to allow us to attend all the ceremonies connected with the marriage of a fellow clansman. These have been described from informant accounts, but as far as I know no anthropologist has attended them before. Most of my information on social structure came from the direct observation of interaction, and from many long conversations with the more intelligent and reflective Cochiti. These were mostly well-travelled ex-Servicemen, veterans of World War II and Korea, who were able to view their society with some objectivity. They realized that it was changing and were concerned that this change should be peaceful. Hence they were interested in understanding their own institutions in order to preserve the best in them without hindering necessary change. As long as I did not try to pry into ceremonial secrets these men were very willing to discuss social institutions with me; I take this opportunity of acknowledging my debt to them. My wife was very much involved in the activities of the women and learned a great deal from them about domestic life. Without her help I could not possibly have achieved any understanding of this important aspect of Cochiti kinship organization.

I spent a certain amount of time working on the Keresan language as spoken at Cochiti. My informant was a former War Captain of the Pueblo (see chapter 3), an old blind man with wonderful standards of accuracy in language. I must have been a disappointment to him as I made little headway. He spoke bad English and excellent Spanish, while my Spanish was rudimentary. Also the work was too disjointed. But I did master the basic structure of Keresan and learned enough to be able to initiate a simple conversation and in particular to follow kin-term usages. There was not a good grammar of Keresan available when I was there – only some texts and a grammatical sketch of the Western dialect by Boas (1938). I have written some tentative notes on the language myself (Fox, 1959), but there now exists Davis's excellent account of Santa Ana Keresan (Davis, 1964). Had this been available before I went to the field it would have made all the difference.

The inadequacies of my field material would have been a serious handicap if I had not had C. H. Lange's *Cochiti* (1959). With the help of this magnificent book I was able to fill in many gaps. Only those who have wrestled with the problems of Pueblo ethnography can appreciate just how excellent this comprehensive monograph is. Working in England has prevented me from looking at a few sources, but none important enough to be missed in terms of the total argument. A number of articles came to my attention after the manuscript was substantially completed. Of these, Ellis's (1964) on Jemez was of such significance that I have put a consideration of it into an appendix. Lounsbury's work on Crow terminology (1964) I find fascinating, but I do not feel I have really digested it. I have put in a few references to it where I could, but I have not been able to take proper note of it. (At the last moment, through the kind offices of Dell Hymes, I obtained a copy of Trager's unpublished paper on the Tanoan Settlement of the Rio Grande. I have not had time to integrate this fully into the book, but have included comments on it in square brackets to show that they were in fact added after the book was completed. I was able to modify Table 2 to bring in Trager's theory. I am most grateful to Professor Trager for rushing a copy of his paper to me. I notice from it that I have missed an article of his – Trager 1951.)

I am fairly critical of Eggan's theories, but I mean the criticism to be a compliment. Eggan was critical of Kroeber's work, but he built on Kroeber's foundations. In the same way I offer my work as constructive criticism; it is a long footnote to Eggan's analysis, nothing more.

### ORTHOGRAPHY

Where Keres words have a commonly accepted English or Hispanicized version, and where offices and institutions have a standard anthropological designation, I have given it: for example, *Kiva*, Giant Society, *Mayorli, Koshare, Katsina* (*Kachina*), War Captain, *Alguacilito*, etc. Otherwise I have rendered Keres words in a crude practical orthography. Long vowels which carry stress are marked with an acute accent. Glottalized consonants are signified thus: *t'*, *k'*, *s'*, etc. The orthography makes no pretence at phonetic or phonemic accuracy, but I have avoided the use of native terms for its own sake and this rough orthography will serve for the few words I have found necessary. There is a slight problem with the occurrence of unvoiced (whispered) vowels in Keres. Thus in the word I have rendered *s'anashtyu* ('my father'), the final vowel is voiceless. It is customary to write this either as a capital – *s'anashtyU* – or to raise the whole syllable in which it occurs – *s'anash*$^{tyu}$. I did not find that voicelessness of vowels was phonemic in Cochiti Keresan, so I have ignored this feature. But Davis does find it phonemic in Santa Ana Keresan, and it may be that I was mistaken about its status.

I should like to acknowledge the help of the following people: Evon Z. Vogt and Dell H. Hymes who sponsored my two trips to Cochiti; Charles H. Lange and Mrs Lange who showed me great kindness during my first trip; the students of Southern Illinois University in Dr Lange's archaeological field school, 1958; Mr and Mrs Nelson Jay of Santa Fé and Peña Blanca; Roy and Diane D'Andrade; the late Clyde Kluckhohn; Stanley Newman; my wife, without whose help I would have achieved nothing; Maurice Freedman and Stephen Morris who read the manuscript; Lucy Mair who did an enormous amount of work in turning my rather loose-limbed prose into something approaching decent English; the cartographic staff of the L.S.E. for their work on the figures, maps and genealogies; Elliott Leyton for research assistance.

I have gained a good deal from discussions with the following: E. P. Dozier; Raymond Firth; Daryll Forde; Anthony Forge; Edmund Leach; Rodney Needham; James Woodburn.

None of the above, I know, would agree with all my conclusions: some would disagree with most of them. Needless to say, all errors and omissions are my own.

The numerous Cochiti who helped both knowingly and unwittingly will understand why I do not single them out for mention. It would, if nothing else, be contrary to Pueblo good manners. I here thank the Governors, *Cacique*, officers and people for their tolerance and courtesy, and my friends for their loyalty and hospitality, and for the fun we had.

For fieldwork finance I am indebted to the American Social Science Research Council and the Harvard University Laboratory of Social Relations. I must also thank the British Academy for a grant towards the cost of photocopying out-of-print material, and the Radcliffe-Brown Memorial Fund for subsidizing the production of the many diagrams.

January 1966                                              R. F.

## AUTHOR'S NOTE

When this book was in page-proof stage I read Eggan's latest statement on the Pueblos in his *The American Indian* (1966). This contains no substantial change in position, and hence I have not needed to modify my argument. It should however be consulted as the most recent statement of his views.

I have also discovered, in a footnote to G. P. Murdock's review of Eggan's *Social Organization of the Western Pueblos* (*American Anthropologist*, vol. 53, no. 2, p. 250, 1951) that figures 5 and 15 were reversed. This helps to explain the curious discrepancy noted in pages 39 and 40 of this book.

# CONTENTS

## MAPS

## FIGURES

## TABLES

# PART I
# THE PUEBLOS

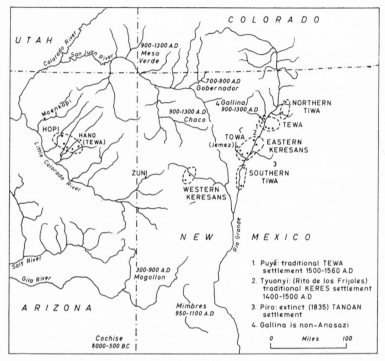

MAP I. The Pueblo Area
(Prehistoric sites and dates from Wormington 1956)

# I

# The Keresan Bridge

This book is concerned with a rather narrow anthropological problem. It can be summed up as the problem of the Keresan Bridge (see Map 1). Eggan divided the Pueblos into two types, the 'Western', characterized by a kinship structure 'based on the matrilineal lineage and household', and the 'Eastern', which lacked this as a 'basic' feature. The linguistic group known as the Keresans straddles the two types, having two Pueblos in the west and five in the east. The Eastern Keresans have a matrilineal kinship system, but it is not as dominant in their total social system as it is in the west. Eggan offers an interpretation of this situation – 'strong' matrilineal organization in the West and 'weak' or nonexistent in the East – in historical and adaptational terms. The test of this theory lies essentially in a proper understanding of the Eastern Keresan kinship system and its place in their social structure. The question what is a proper understanding of a kinship system, and how to discover the 'true' workings of such a system is anything but a parochial one. I hope that this discussion of a purely ethnological problem may also make some contribution in this wider theoretical field.

## I

There is a long tradition of anthropological study of the Pueblos, but all too little of this has been concerned with social structure. Anthropologists have been fascinated by the religious and ceremonial side of Pueblo life, and not so much interested in its kinship and social organization. In the latter sphere, interest has been largely confined to recording kin terms and clan names and worrying about their distribution. In all this, two landmarks stand out: two classics of structural analysis. The first is Kroeber's *Zuni Kin and Clan* (1917), which set the pattern for future discussion, and the second is Eggan's masterly synthesis *The Social Organization of the Western Pueblos* (1950), which changed the whole course of the debate.

Why has Pueblo anthropology been so patchy and so little concerned with social structure? Lévi-Strauss has recently complained that most of the vast amount of writing on the Pueblos is useless for sociological analysis,[1] and one is struck in Eggan's book by the very flimsy evidence with which he was forced to work. The answer is partly practical, partly theoretical. On the practical side, it is very difficult to do 'field work' among the Pueblo Indians, who are notoriously resistant to investigation. Consequently, information is largely of the kind that can be gleaned from individual informants. This method has its obvious limitations. Some information can be gained this way, but it is not of the kind that is really very much use to a student of social structure. Paradoxically, although the Pueblos are supposed to be most secretive about their ceremonies, we know infinitely more about ceremonial than any other aspect of Pueblo life! The reason is that village ceremonialists have to be word-perfect in their knowledge; hence if they can be persuaded to divulge information at all, the result is likely to be an excellent description. White has carried the art of pumping informants to a fine degree in a series of studies on the Eastern Keresans.[2] But more significant is the theoretical orientation of the investigators, which, with a few exceptions, has been towards the study of culture rather than social structure. Since culture is carried in the head, one does not have actually to observe the interactions of subjects; one simply has to ask them questions. Early studies also were dominated by the notion of 'traits' and their distribution. Parsons' compendium on *Pueblo Indian Religion* (1939) is almost solely concerned with this. To questions of this nature there are no structural answers. A further preoccupation with development led away from structural studies; this preoccupation runs through Kroeber's work, and Eggan does not escape it. This is a laudable interest, but it is largely oriented towards the past and does not seem to provide any incentive for the study of the structure as it is. Nor, for that matter, does the culture-and-personality school, which latched onto the Pueblos largely under the influence of Ruth Benedict's *Patterns of Culture* (1934), with its interesting but romanticized version of Zuni life.[3] The kind of research

[1] Lévi-Strauss, 1952 (reprinted as ch. xv of 1958).
[2] White, 1932b, 1935, 1942, 1962.          [3] See also Benedict, 1928.

needed to settle the questions raised by Benedict led off in yet another direction.

Practical problems have been less difficult among the more hospitable Hopi; consequently their social structure is better documented. It was fortunate that Eggan, under the influence of Radcliffe-Brown, took to structural studies in Hopi country, since almost anywhere else he would have been frustrated. His book is dominated by the Hopi, and his Western Pueblo type is based essentially on Hopi kinship structure. But before we can understand this fully, we have to look at the spatial distribution of the Pueblos, a little at the ecology, and at the 'structural principles' (to borrow Eggan's term) on which their society seems to work. A good deal of Eggan's argument rests on the classification of the Pueblos into Western and Eastern. Other classifications than his have been proposed, but the criteria differ in most cases. A classification is useful only in terms of the problem it is helping to solve, and we follow Eggan in looking for sociological criteria.

The aim of this exercise is to determine the distributions of 'types' of social structure within the Pueblo group of villages. We will try to test the idea that they are divided into an 'Eastern' and a 'Western' group, in order that we might examine the theories which have been put forward to account for this distribution. In particular we are looking for the 'bridge' nature of the Keresans – the link, according to Eggan, between East and West.

As stated earlier, this book is an attempt to answer some of the problems raised by Eggan's theory of the Keresan Bridge, and its place in the history of Pueblo society. Eggan sees the basic Western feature – the matrilineal clan, lineage and household complex – as 'weakening' from west to east. It is strong in Hopi and non-existent in eastern Taos. Elsewhere in the east there are 'vestiges', but the Eastern Keresans retain more of the basic feature than the other Eastern groups. As their Western cousins are thoroughly involved in the complex, Eggan deduces that the Eastern Keres have 'lost' some of the strength of this, and that the other Eastern groups have lost it altogether. This theory is what we propose to examine.

## II

### DISTRIBUTION

Maps 1 and 2 show the distribution of the various groups of villages, classed together in terms of linguistic affiliations. The main question to be discussed in this section is whether or not there is a uniform 'Pueblo' culture, and whether or not this goes with one or more types of social structure. Certainly there is a broad similarity of culture among the villages labelled Pueblo which sets them off sharply from their nomadic or scattered Apachean neighbours. The very fact that they live in settled, permanent villages of stone or adobe houses is the main thing they have in common. They all live by agriculture, only supplemented by hunting and gathering (or did until quite recently – most still do). They have all developed an intensive ceremonial organization which dominates their activities. They are all politically independent.

But beneath these broad surface similarities are very deep differences in culture and organization; differences that drive some commentators to exclude some Pueblos from the group. Taos, for example, is sometimes thought to be more Plains than Pueblo, and the Taos Indians have been referred to as 'Plains Indians living in a Pueblo'. I think it all depends on what level one is working. At a very abstract level, there is a general similarity which cancels out the differences, but in a sense each village is unique. This uniqueness stems, however, from the fact that each village puts together certain basic elements in different ways. Thus all the villages have *kivas* (ceremonial chambers), but the place of these in the organization of the society differs quite markedly from group to group, and even between villages of the same group.

In examining the distribution, we will move from west to east, following Eggan.

1. *Hopi*.[1] The Hopi belong to the Shoshonean branch of the Uto-Aztecan-Tanoan phylum, which gives them distant historical links with other Pueblos, with the ancient civilizations of Mexico and with the Ute and related tribes to the north. They live in compact villages atop three *mesas* in Arizona. There is no permanent water supply, and they depend on rain and dry farming for their agriculture, which is supplemented by a little hunting. Since the coming of the Spaniards they have had sheep and donkeys, but not in large numbers. There is no political unity among the villages, but there are strong social and cultural ties. The clan

[1] Major sources for the Hopi: Eggan, 1949 and 1950; Beaglehole and Beaglehole, 1935; Forde, 1931; Lowie, 1929, 1932; Simmons, 1942; Stephen, 1936; Titiev, 1944.

system seems to embrace them all, and they co-operate for ceremonial. Factionalism has led to the split-up of villages, and various
breakaway groups have started their own communities. Even
some of these new communities have been subject to the same
fissionary process. There is enough cultural and linguistic homo-
geneity among the Hopi to warrant treating them as a single
group. Linguistic outsiders, but cultural insiders, are the people of
Hano, on the first *mesa*.[1] These are Tewa migrants who were
given a home by the Hopi and have become fairly integrated with
their hosts.

2. *Zuni*.[2] Probably the most famous of the Pueblos. This
differs very much from Hopi, in that it consists of one village, very
large by Pueblo standards. It is an amalgamation of the previous
seven villages, and of course this affects its social structure. Its language is seemingly unrelated to any other, and so forms its own
phylum. It has mixed dry and irrigation farming, some herding,
and formerly hunting. It is a close-knit, tightly integrated village,
with an intricate mesh of ceremonial and social groups, and a
ruling theocracy of a kind not found in Hopi.

3. *Keresans*. (*a*) Western Group: Acoma and Laguna.[3] Keresan
again is sometimes classed as an independent language, but sometimes placed in the Hokan-Siouan phylum. Acoma had occupied
its *mesa*-top site since prehistoric times, while Laguna is said to
have been founded by migrants from the Eastern Keres group
after the Pueblo revolt against the Spaniards in 1680. We will
examine this contention later. Both have now split up into smaller
villages, but the old villages remain as ceremonial centres. It
appears that, until the mid-nineteenth century, farming was of the
Hopi type with little irrigation. When irrigation was introduced,
the villages split up into farming colonies which eventually
became independent. The dialect of Keres spoken by these two
villages is not readily intelligible to their Eastern relatives.

The above are classed together as the Western Pueblo type by
Eggan largely on the basis of their kinship system, which is of the
Crow sub-type of the lineage type, i.e., consists of matrilineal
lineages and clans and matri-uxorilocal households. Several other

[1] Hano is covered by Dozier, 1954, and Eggan, 1950.

[2] Major sources for Zuni: Eggan, 1950; Benedict, 1934a; Bunzel, 1932; Cushing,
1896, 1920; Kroeber, 1917; Li, 1937; Parsons, 1917, 1933; Stevenson, 1904.

[3] On Acoma, see: Eggan, 1950; Parsons, 1918, 1920a; White, 1932a. On Laguna,
see: Eggan, 1950; Parsons, 1918, 1920b, 1923; Ellis, 1959.

features are held in common, such as a theocratic system of social control, and an associational structure organized around the ceremony and its symbols with relationships to the lineage, clan and household. The interweaving of the kinship and ceremonial systems seems to be the basic characteristic. Some commentators would classify as 'transitional' the Western Keresan group because of its affiliations with the East, but Eggan regards them as thoroughly Western, and classes as transitional the next group (see Map 2 for details).

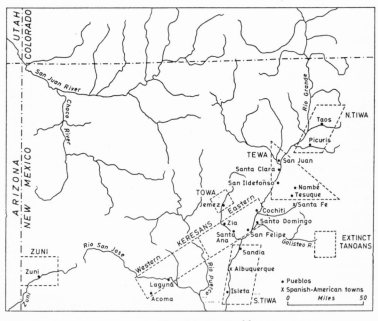

MAP 2. New Mexico Pueblos

(b) Eastern group: Cochiti, Santo Domingo, San Felipe, Santa Ana and Zia.[1] With these five villages we move right out of the 'mesa-top' complex and into the 'river-bank' area. They are built along the Rio Grande or its tributaries; the people take water from

---

[1] On Cochiti, see: Lange, 1959; Goldfrank, 1927; Dumarest, 1919; Bandalier, 1890a, 1890b; Benedict, 1931. On Santo Domingo: White, 1935. On San Felipe: White, 1932b. On Santa Ana: White, 1942. On Zia: White, 1962; Stevenson, 1889.

the permanent streams by means of irrigation systems, and so are less dependent on rainfall than their western cousins. They build their houses of adobe and not stone. Linguistically and in other ways they form a group distinct from other Rio Grande Pueblos, and they see themselves as such, but each village is politically independent. There is a good deal of intervillage co-operation in ceremonial, but not in economy. There are also some profound differences in social structure despite the overall similarity, if the somewhat sketchy reports are correct. But it is here very much a case of putting the same principles to different tasks. Apart from the basic agriculture, hunting and gathering were important in the past, but today wage labour is more important than any of these pursuits.

4. *Tewa.*[1] San Juan, Santa Clara, San Ildefonso, Tesuque and Nambé. These five villages lie to the north of the Eastern Keres and their basic economy is similar. They have other traits in common, but they differ profoundly in kinship and other aspects of social organization. In this case it is more than just a juggling of similar elements. Some of these villages seem very acculturated, but it is difficult for an outsider to judge how deep this goes. Recent work suggests that a good deal of the culture is preserved despite surface changes. Tourism plays an important part in the life and economy of the Tewa. There is a good deal of contact at present between the Tewa and the Keres, including marriage and baseball games, each of which brings its own particular problems. Ceremonial co-operation is very evident, and there seems to have been a good deal of borrowing in this sphere.

5. *Towa.*[2] This language group is represented by one village, Jemez. This village is so closely bound up with the Keresans that apart from language it is virtually a Keres village. It differs from the Keres more in degree than kind, and its economy is similarly based on irrigation farming.

6. *Tiwa.*[3] Northern group: Taos and Picuris. Southern group: Sandia and Isleta.

In many ways the Tewa, Towa and Keres form a little group which differs a good deal from the two branches of the Tiwa,

[1] On the Tewa see: Parsons, 1929; Whitman, 1947 (San Ildefonso); Dozier, 1960a, 1960b, 1961.

[2] On Jemez, see Parsons, 1925.

[3] On the Northern Tiwa: Parsons, 1936, 1939a; Fenton, 1957. On the Southern Tiwa: Parsons, 1920, 1928, 1932a; French, 1948; Harvey, 1963.

although the southern branch of the latter shows some effects of its location in the south. The northern villages are the most remote of the Pueblos in some ways and have perhaps more interaction with Plains groups like the Kiowa than with other Pueblo groups. They resemble the Tewa in some ways, though in many features they are different. Both depend on irrigation farming, but hunting used to be very important, and trips were made out to the plains to hunt the buffalo. Tourism is now a major industry at Taos. This northern group is really very much off the beaten track of Pueblo culture, and the southern group is ethnographically almost unknown. There was a migration from Laguna to Isleta in the 1870's, and there are still two groups in the latter village.

Tewa, Towa and Tiwa represent the Tanoan branch of the Uto-Aztecan-Tanoan phylum.

The Eastern or Rio Grande Pueblos[1] then have at least one thing in common: their dependence on irrigation for agriculture. They are also nearer to the old centres of White civilization (Santa Fé and Albuquerque) than are the Western Pueblos, although Laguna lies on a main highway. Santo Domingo is near the Santa Fé railway, and highways pass close to the other villages, with the exception of Cochiti, Jemez and Picuris. They all bore the brunt of Spanish domination (from the late sixteenth century) and took the full weight of American acculturative pressure (from the 1840's). The Spaniards reached Hopi and Zuni but did not remain there, while they settled in the midst of the Eastern Pueblos. Thus the Catholic religion was never established in the far west, while the east became at least nominally Catholic. All the Pueblos accepted horses, sheep, burros and metal from the Spaniards, weaving them into their own economy. The Americans brought schools, the Indian Service, medical care, Protestantism and anthropologists. The first three were reluctantly accepted or half accepted, the latter two rejected. Protestants managed to get footholds only where factional strife led to the use of Protestantism as a tool in the struggle, and in one remarkable case at Zia, well described by White, which is unique.[2] In the other Pueblos, where Catholicism was accepted, it was itself being used in the factional struggles anyway, but it also served as a kind of barrier against the new

[1] For general reviews see: Dozier, 1961 and Aberle, 1948.
[2] White, 1962.

Anglo-Protestant incursion; it acted as an outer shell behind which the essentially Indian culture could shelter – towards the Protestant Anglos they presented a solid Catholic front.

The details of distribution and history are well presented elsewhere, and there is nothing I can add to them. On the pre-history I will comment later, as the version of Pueblo pre-history that one accepts depends essentially on the version of the present structure of the Pueblos that one favours. I will now, therefore, try to give my version of the distribution of 'structural features' among the Pueblos. The 'traits' or 'structural features' that I take are the ones that are relevant to the problem I wish to solve. Other traits would give other solutions; other problems; other distributions.

## III

### DISTRIBUTION OF STRUCTURAL FEATURES

The key features that I am interested in can be simply summed up as *Kivas*, Cults and Clans. Let us take them in order.

1. *Kivas*. This is derived from a Keres word *chitya* and literally refers to the buildings or chambers used for ceremonial purposes. The first the Spanish encountered were on the Rio Grande where the actual structures reminded them of ovens, so they dubbed them *estufas*. The word is also used for the people who are members of the group which meets in the *Kiva* for ritual practices. There seem to be three types of *Kiva*: (1) square and built into the blocks of houses; (2) underground, either square or circular; (3) semi-underground and circular. They are found in the pre-historic ruins associated with the Pueblos, and it has been thought that they are a hang-over from the pit dwellings that characterized the peoples of the South-west before they took to building houses above ground. When the change to above-ground building took place, the old houses were retained as ceremonial centres. The later *Kivas* kept this form, but some were built into the house blocks to hide them from the Spaniards. They differ from group to group not only in structure, but in number and method of recruitment, and association with other groups and offices.

2. *Cults*. Most often called societies, or secret societies, cults exist for a variety of purposes such as curing, rain-making, hunting, war, and pure worship or guidance of ceremonial. Again they

are variously recruited, sometimes being strongly associated with clans, and sometimes being based on voluntary association. Particularly interesting, and the one we will fix on here, is the cult of the 'masked gods', the *Kachinas* or *Katsinas* (another Keres word), which is nearly universal. While the other societies sometimes admit both sexes, the *Katsina* cult is all-male. Initiates don the masks which represent the various supernatural beings, and perform the sacred dances. While wearing the mask the initiate is supposed to be the incarnation of the being he represents. It is primarily a rain-making cult.

3. *Clans*. Where these occur they are matrilineal, i.e., recruit the children of female members only. Sometimes they are linked into groups of related clans (phratries). They are exogamous and named after natural phenomena, and, in the Western Pueblos at least, the classification of clans also represents an interesting classification of nature. They differ primarily in their functions over and above the negative regulation of marriage. In some villages they are closely linked with cults and in others not. Likewise, some offices are associated with clans in some villages and not in others.

The 'organizational principles' in terms of which the above institutions are arranged in various combinations in the different villages may be roughly summarized as follows:

1. *Moiety organization or Duality*. There is a strong tendency to divide a tribe into two divisions for many purposes. This is stronger in some groups than in others; it can take many forms and have many functions, and the way persons or groups are assigned to the two divisions varies considerably.

2. *Space or direction*. The arrangement of people in space (for instance, on either side of a *plaza*) is sometimes used to organize them into groups. Duality is often evident here. Also, sometimes, persons or groups are classified according to 'directions', i.e., they are assigned on the basis of symbolic association to the six directions (north, south, east, west, zenith and nadir).

3. *Seasons*. The whole tribe or groups within it may be divided into Winter and Summer people, who divide ceremony and sometimes government between them according to season. This can be seen as dualism applied to seasons as opposed to, say, directions.

4. *Exogamy, endogamy, agamy*. Marriage restrictions may or may not be applied to groups arranged on the above basis.

There are enormous difficulties in the way of presenting in any simple graphic way the distribution of the above among the Pueblo groups. Relevant material stretches over a hundred years, and many changes have occurred. Some villages are virtually unknown, and material on others is contradictory. I will note these problems in their place.

Let us first then follow the varieties of the *Kiva* in the different groups.[1] *Kivas* can vary in the following ways between the villages and linguistic groupings:

(*a*) *Number:* Villages may have two or several *Kivas*, or one large one. Six or seven is the usual number if there are more than two.

(*b*) *Method of recruitment.* I have made a dichotomy between 'voluntary' recruitment (i.e., not based on kinship) which I call 'associational', and recruitment by kinship and marriage, which is either straight patrilineal or 'patrilineal-virilateral', that is, a woman relinquishes her natal *Kiva* on marriage and joins her husband's.

(*c*) *Relations to other groups, and functions.* The uses to which the *Kiva* organization can be put, and the groups with which it can be associated, vary.

(*d*) *Duality, seasonality and spatiality.* The *Kivas* can be organized in terms of these, often related, principles.

Moving from west to east again, we find that the Hopi have more than two *Kivas* per village. A boy joins the *Kiva* of his ceremonial father, but can use any *Kiva*. Thus membership is rather amorphous, but is associational in our terms. The *Kivas* are associated with cults in various ways, and it is not always clear just what the association is. The main focus of Hopi ritual life is the *ceremony* itself. This is controlled by a certain clan, and performed by a cult group or society. Each *Kiva* is associated with a clan which 'owns' it, but members of the clan will not necessarily join that *Kiva*. Some *Kivas* are associated with and named after the cult groups which perform the ceremony. Ceremonies usually take place in a specified *Kiva* – either that of the cult group, or of the clan which 'owns' the *Kiva*. But it is not at all clear exactly how this works. For present purposes it is enough to note that the *Kivas* are plural, associational and linked to cults and clans. *Katsinas* are prominent in Hopi.

[1] Hawley, 1950a, has cleared up many problems concerning the distribution of *Kivas*.

Zuni likewise has a plurality of *Kivas*, and they are likewise associational and linked to the cult groups. Particularly, they are concerned with the *Katsina* cult. Six *Kivas* each house a branch of the cult. Mostly, however, the cults are 'housed' by the clan which is most closely associated with the cult. The *Kiva* pattern is not strong in Zuni, and it might seem to be forcing the issue to wish it onto them, but *Kivas* exist and are important, although somewhat submerged in the rich complexity of ceremonial life.

Acoma and Laguna present a problem. They broke up into smaller villages earlier than other Pueblos. Since there are no *Kivas* functioning there today, it is difficult to reconstruct the older pattern. For Acoma it seems certain that there were seven *Kivas* at one time. Five of these were associated with the *Katsina* cult and the others with the chief clan and a society respectively. Children joined the *Kiva* of their father. Nothing is said about the move of the wife at marriage, but as this occurred at Laguna it is likely that it was the case at Acoma too. Laguna informants report between one and four *Kivas*. In the 1870's there were two, with the *Katsinas* and cult groups using rooms for their activities, not *Kivas*. This sounds like the Eastern Keresan pattern, of which Laguna is thought to be an offshoot, but it is difficult to assess the evidence. Children joined the father's *Kiva*, but girls transferred on marriage. A dual division of clans 'for dancing', organized in terms of directions – east and west with respect to the *plaza* – is also reported.

When we move to the Eastern Keresans the picture is still a little obscure. All the villages have two *Kivas*, Turquoise and Pumpkin (Wren at Zia). Cochiti and Santo Domingo definitely, and San Felipe probably, have the patrilineal-virilateral type of recruitment, while at Santa Ana the clans are said to be divided between the two *Kivas*. This has been also said of Cochiti, and is there considered a mistake based on a confusion of the names of the *Kivas* with the names of two clans, also Turquoise and Pumpkin. At Zia, there seems to be no regular way of organizing recruitment. Either people belong to one or other *Kiva* according as they live north or south of a line across the middle of the *plaza* or they can choose, or the War Captains can assign them to a *Kiva*. They are associated with the *Katsina* cult, but just how far this goes is obscure. They are neither endogamous or exogamous.

Jemez follows the dominant Keresan pattern in all essentials, that is, two *Kivas* recruited patri-virilaterally.

The Tewa present an interesting variation on the *Kiva* pattern, in that non-exogamous moieties in these villages do not seem to be associated with *Kivas*. Parsons thought each moiety had a *Kiva*, but it seems that this was a mistake. Each moiety had a house for meeting and practising etc., but there was only one large *Kiva*, which was used by both moieties for dancing. Certain Pueblo ruins show a pattern of two or more small *Kivas* and a particularly large one, and this may be a survival of that pattern, except that moiety houses are not *Kivas* amongst the Tewa. The word *Kiva* has the same overtones as 'Church' or 'Temple'. It suggests a high degree of sacredness and secretness. The *Kivas* amongst the Keres also have community or practice houses. I was quite free to visit these, and did so. But I would not, nor would any white man, have been allowed in the *Kivas* proper. (The present community houses in Cochiti were built recently – 1925 and 1938 – but I was told that the moieties had 'practice' houses before these.) Thus the Tewa have only one *Kiva*, used by both moieties. These moieties are divided on a seasonal basis between Summer and Winter people. Recruitment is patri-virilateral as with the Keres. There are two chiefs, one from each moiety, and power and responsibility are rotated between them seasonally. There is a village-wide *Katsina* cult.

Individual villages show some variants. Factionalism at Santa Clara has recently led to the building of a second *Kiva* there, thus making it technically a two-*Kiva* village in the same way that factionalism at Zia reduced it to one *Kiva*. At San Ildefonso there was one 'Old' *Kiva* used by both moieties, but the Summer people had a rectangular moiety house that has been reported as a *Kiva*. Since 1938 factionalism has led to the building of two *Kivas* here also. There are now two *plazas* divided between the two factions who identify themselves on a spatial basis as the North people and the South people. Within the moieties there seem to be smaller ceremonial units which Whitman calls 'clans'. As the moieties recruit patri-virilaterally, these must be basically patrilineal units of males. This observation of Whitman's will take on greater significance when we come to discuss kinship groups and *Kivas* in Cochiti.[1]

[1] Whitman, 1947.

The seasonal dual division of the Tewa has its echo among the Keres in the shape of the two 'clown' groups, *Koshare* and *Kwirena*, who are responsible for the spiritual welfare of the community in Winter and Summer respectively. Although these two groups are sometimes found in association with the *Kivas* – one being linked to Turquoise and the other to Pumpkin – the *Kivas* as a whole do not alternate between Winter and Summer. The more usual pattern is for the *Kivas* to alternate annually in, for example, providing the Governor of the Pueblo. The clown groups, too, take turns annually in arranging the Summer corn dance.

The underlying pattern here is similar. The year is divided into two periods and time into two-year periods, and various groups alternate responsibility on an annual or seasonal basis. The actual distribution of this responsibility is what differs. The Tewa pattern is of a comprehensive seasonal alternation: the Keresans go in for a more complex pattern of longer runs as well as the seasonal shifts. (See Fig. 1.)

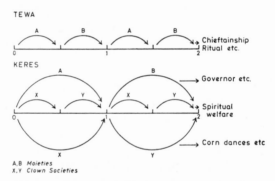

FIG. 1. Temporal sequences in Tewa and Keres
social organization

The Tiwa show some internal differences. In the north, Taos has six small *Kivas* in which membership is not determined by kinship but children are 'dedicated' in youth (a pattern which amongst the Keres pertains to the medicine societies but not the *Kivas*). There is one large *Kiva*, but its function is not clear. The six *Kivas* are arranged into two groups of three in terms of a north-south division. There are two chiefs associated with this division. There are offerings to *Katsinas* but no masked imitations of them, and medicine societies do not seem highly developed.

Similarly at Picuris there are six *Kivas* arranged on a north-south basis and membership is reported to be patrilineally determined (as for Acoma). Here again, there is a dual chieftaincy, which is probably seasonal. Information is poor. There seem to be no masked *Katsinas*, but probably offerings are made as at Taos.

Among the southern Tiwa the picture is again confused. At Isleta two *Kivas* have been reported, but these again are probably community houses. There is only one round *Kiva* used by the two moieties. Interestingly enough, each moiety uses a different name for this *Kiva*. At Sandia there is reported only one 'round house for dancing', so again the single *Kiva* pattern is suggested. There is no masked *Katsina* cult, but an unmasked dance connected with the *Katsinas* is reported. The Laguna colony at Isleta maintains its masked *Katsina* dances.

The assignment of children to the moieties here presents a puzzle. It is reported that children join the moiety of the parents if both come from the same moiety. If they come from different moieties, then children are assigned alternately, the first to the father's, the second to the mother's, and so on. I am a little at a loss to know what to call this, but I will try 'alternating' recruitment.

Amongst the Keres, both moieties sometimes use the same *Kiva* – the 'senior' of the two – for combined dances. (At Cochiti the important *Ouwe* or Spring dance is held by both groups in the Turquoise *Kiva*.) This might suggest that the one-*Kiva*-plus-moiety-houses pattern is the archaic one and, as we have seen at Santa Clara and San Ildefonso, the building of a second *Kiva* resulted from a dispute over the use of the first.

The important thing is to note that *Kivas* and moieties are not necessarily tied to each other.

I have chosen to take *Kivas* as a point of reference because they are universal. All the villages have these ceremonial chambers (underground among the Hopi and Northern Tiwa; in the house blocks at Zuni and Acoma; semi-underground elsewhere), but as we have seen, the use made of them differs and so does their recruitment and organization. Hopi and Zuni are uniform with their plural *Kivas* and associational recruitment. The Western Keres share the plurality (with Laguna doubtful) but depart from the method of recruitment, sharing this with their eastern cousins who, however, follow a two-*Kiva* system as does Jemez. In method of recruitment the Eastern Keres follow the Tewa, but the latter do not associate moieties with *Kivas*, having a single *Kiva* pattern. The Northern Tiwa have plural *Kivas*, as in the west, but organize them on a north-and-south moiety basis. Taos shares associational recruitment with the west, but Picuris follows the Tewa method. The Southern Tiwa have a single *Kiva* but two moieties like the Tewa. Their method of recruitment, however, is unique.

The several 'deviants' show some interesting features. Thus Santa Ana in the east differs markedly from its neighbours in that its dual division consists in two groups of clans, each attached to a *Kiva*. I view this report with some suspicion, but if it is true then it shows an interesting parallel with the western deviant Hano which also organizes its clans into a dual *Kiva* system. The same dual division of clans is reported for Laguna, this time *not* linked to the *Kivas* but organized spatially. Zia, according to some informants, recruits *Kivas* according to a spatial division (north and south of the *plaza*) but does not so organize its clans.

Thus, in terms of *Kivas* and the principles of dualism, space and season associated with them, we can see only a strong tendency to dualism in the east which is weak or lacking altogether in the west. (Hano is a hybrid, of course.) Also, the east is more given to kinship-determined recruitment than the west. In these matters, the Western Keresans are definitely transitional.

What emerges most strongly for the east is the fundamental nature of the moiety principle, which may or may not find expression in a dual *Kiva* arrangement. It is the tendency to divide the tribe into two complementary halves that is constant, although the content of the two moieties seems to run through all possible combinations. Thus one can take any of our 'principles' and see how it embraces others:

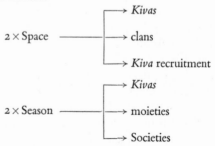

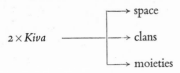

and so on.

From this examination I think it is safe to conclude that the Pueblos can be validly divided into Eastern and Western. However, the Western Keres are transitional, and the Eastern Keres should themselves be broken down into an eastern group (Cochiti, Santo Domingo and San Felipe) and a western group (Santa Ana and Zia).

## IV

This is, however, a narrow basis for classification, and we must press on to look at kinship organization. Here the picture is superficially simple.

Hopi has matrilineal named exogamous clans, organized into phratries. As we have seen, these are linked to *Kivas* and to societies. In Zuni, there are also clans, and these have at one time been organized on a phratral and maybe even on a dual seasonal basis, but this had faded into myth even in the 1880's. It is not even certain whether these phratries were exogamous. They were organized by directions, but this seemed in many ways a matter of cosmology rather than of practical activities.

The Western Keresans are as problematical in this context as they were in that of *Kiva* organization. They have the matrilineal clan system, but not seemingly any development of phratries. The clans are not linked to cults as closely as in Hopi and Zuni – and we should note that Zuni is less thoroughgoing than Hopi on this too. At Laguna there is a dual division of clans for ceremonial purposes, which is said to be in terms of their location 'with reference to the plaza'.

Among all the above, some ritual-political offices are the property of particular clans. Thus, for the Western Pueblos, clan and office and ceremony are linked, but in decreasing degrees from west to east. In all the western villages, the household unit is an extended matri-local household.

The Eastern Keresans also have the matrilineal clan, but this is not associated with office or ceremony or cult-group. As at Acoma and Laguna, there is no phratry organization, or even a hint of one, as at Zuni. The alleged division of the clans between the *Kivas* at Santa Ana has been mentioned. This resembles Laguna's spatial division, but is definitely said to be *Kiva*-based. Jemez also has the clan, and it seems to have the same status as with the Keres. The matri-local household seems less prominent here, though it may once have been important.

When we move to the Tewa we find a radical change. There are no clans. The basic kinship group seems to be the bilateral kindred, an ego-centred group, quite at variance with the clan principle. The household group is an extended family, but not a maternal extended family as in the west. There are 'clan' names which are variously inherited, but these seem only to have a limited ritual significance – a kind of honorific title. The Tiwa likewise do not have clans. Actual details are scarce, but the kinship system seems to be like the Tewa but perhaps without a formal kindred. The southern Tiwa have five 'corn groups' which inherit names matrilineally, but these seem to be of the order of the Tewa 'clan names'. In neither case do the holders form a social group any more than the holders of the same surname in our society.

## V

This absurdly sketchy outline is merely intended to indicate the gross distribution of 'clans' versus 'not clans'. Table I is an attempt to show in a simple manner the total distribution of the features we have been discussing.

In the first column M indicates the existence of a dual division; if this is associated with a *Kiva* arrangement this is indicated in brackets after the M. The letters following the brackets indicate the mode of recruitment to the moiety. Thus for Hano there is a dual division associated with two *Kivas* and recruitment is 'phratral', i.e., the *Kivas* are formed by grouping clans. With the Tewa, for example, the dual division is not associated with the *Kiva* system but is patri-virilateral in recruitment and organized seasonally. Where the *Kivas* are not incorporated into a moiety system, they are shown in the second column. The third column indicates the presence of the *Katsina* cult, and whether or not masked impersonations occur. The fourth column gives the presence or absence of clans. It must be remembered that much of the information is

TABLE I. Distribution of traits in the Pueblos

| | Moiety | Kiva | Katsina | Clan |
|---|---|---|---|---|
| Hopi | — | (KP)An | Kt.m | C |
| Hano | M(K2)Ph | — | Kt.m | C |
| Zuni | — | (KP)An | Kt.m | C |
| *Western Keres* | | | | |
| Acoma | — | (KP)Pt | Kt.m | C |
| Laguna | [M( )Ph:Sp]? | [(KP)Pv/(K2)Pv]? | Kt.m | C |
| *Eastern Keres* | | | | |
| Eastern three | M(K2)Pv | — | Kt.m | C |
| Santa Ana | M(K2)Ph | — | Kt.m | C |
| Zia | M(K2)An:Sp | — | Kt.m | C |
| Towa (Jemez) | M(K2)Pv | — | Kt.m | C |
| Tewa | M( )Pv:Sn | (K1) | Kt.m | — |
| *Northern Tiwa* | | | | |
| Taos | M(KP)An:Sp | — | Kt. | — |
| Picuris | M(KP)Pt:Sp | — | Kt. | — |
| Southern Tiwa | M( )Al:Sn | (K1) | Kt. | — |

| | | | |
|---|---|---|---|
| M | Moiety or Dual Division | Pv | Patri-virilateral recruitment |
| K | *Kiva* (1 or 2; or P = Plurality) | An | Associational recruitment |
| C | Clan | Al | Alternating recruitment |
| Kt. | *Katsina* cult | Sp | Spatial arrangement |
| | (m = masked impersonations) | | of groups or recruitment |
| Ph | Phratrality (grouping of clans) | Sn | Seasonal arrangement |
| Pt | Patrilineal recruitment | | of groups |

doubtful, and some of it pertains to a traditional system now no longer operative. However, it does give some idea of the spread of these traits and organizational principles. In a sense these represent a minimum set of components for distinguishing between types. What they enable us to see is that there is no clear-cut dividing line between east and west, but a gradual shading off, some traits being virtually universal. Remembering that Hano is a hybrid, and ignoring most of the finer details of 'deviant' villages, we get a rough distribution of features as follows:

| | Moiety | Katsina | Clan |
|---|---|---|---|
| Hopi/Zuni | − | + | + |
| Western Keres | − | + | + |
| Eastern Keres/Towa | + | + | + |
| Tewa | + | + | − |
| Tiwa | + | + | − |

This illustrates the 'bridge' nature of the Eastern Keresans. They intrude their 'Eastern' clanship into an area where this is lacking, but share with it the moiety principle lacking in the west. If we add more details, such as the patrilineal tinge to *Kiva* recruitment in the Western Keres, married to the 'Western' trait of plural *Kivas*, then the bridge nature of the Keres becomes plain.

Explanations of the place of the Keresans in the total Pueblo picture have been various. Eggan found those phrased solely in terms of 'borrowing' inadequate, and offered his own interpretation of the prehistory and history of the area to account for the present distribution of traits. It is to this that we must now turn.

# 2

# The Theories

## I

To the non-archaeologist the prehistory of the South-west is a puzzling array of theories and counter-theories based on curiously elusive evidence. While it is fairly easy to dismiss ridiculous theories, it is difficult to choose between the plausible ones. Most reconstructions are concerned with the Eastern Pueblos, since they present the biggest problem. Zuni is largely disregarded. Its linguistic and cultural affinities are unclear, but Newman is working on the theory that the Zuni language is related to Penutian, which would probably suggest a westerly origin.[1] Eggan derives the Hopi from a mixture of original people living in the Hopi area, and certain influxes of people from (a) the western San Juan – a product of the Anasazi culture (see Map 1); – and (b) Shoshonean speakers living near the Hopi country who contributed at least their language to Hopi development. There were also probably 'influences' from the Mogollon culture farther to the south-east. He leans on Steward's theories of the development of matrilineal bands for the base-line of Hopi development.[2] In this general region, it is argued, there was a preference for matrilocal residence connected with female ownership of seed plots. This, according to Steward, 'tended to convert small villages into female lineages which approximated to, but failed actually to be exogamous matrilineal bands'. This is extraordinarily vague. Matrilocal residence does not of itself produce 'matrilineal bands', and I cannot imagine what the latter would be. They would have to consist of 'brothers' and 'sisters' and the children of the sisters to qualify as 'matrilineal'. Matrilocal residence does not produce this – far from it; it disperses the 'brothers' to the various villages of 'female lineages'. A 'unilateral group living on its own land' is *not* produced by

---

[1] See Dozier, 1964.      [2] Steward, 1937, 1938, 1955.

matrilocal residence. Matrilocal residence may be an indispensable first step in the development of certain types of matrilineal organization, but Steward seems to think it 'almost' produces matrilineages. I do not follow this reasoning. The members of the matrilocal residential group are not a matrilineage. If this residential group is the autonomous unit from which 'multiband villages' are produced, then the unit is not a matrilineage. I cannot imagine how an autonomous relatively isolated 'matrilineal band' could function. Kroeber thought the same and Eggan disgrees – but he disagrees on the basis that Steward has shown that such bands did exist in this area.[1] What probably did exist were groups of houses with female residents all related and owning the seed plots, and the husbands of these women who joined them at marriage. (This is like the pattern amongst some Apachean 'bands'.[2]) If these then amalgamated as a result of increases in population and improved food techniques, then the 'multiband villages' that arose would have the basis for a matrilineal organization, because the natal home of the men would be near at hand. The 'brothers' could then associate with the 'sisters', whose continued residence in the house would provide a 'base' for the lineage. But on definition alone, the existence of 'matrilineal bands' could not have antedated the growth of large villages.

Be this as it may, the Hopi developed an organization of matriclans in the valleys, and then, in the historical period, on the *mesa* tops. Zuni had meanwhile gone the same way in its seven villages.

Turning to the eastern San Juan we find what has been suggested as the original home of most of the Eastern Pueblos. This is a continuation of the Anasazi culture which contributed to the Hopi development. Sometime in the twelfth and thirteenth centuries, the inhabitants of the eastern San Juan area began to leave their cliff houses and move south. No one knows quite why – it may have been drought or marauding Apaches or civil strife. The Pueblos, for all their sedentariness, seem to have been bitten by something of a wanderlust, and in prehistoric times at least were probably a unique social type – urbanized nomads. Now Eggan argues that the eastern San Juan culture was similar to the western and its basic social unit was the matrilocal household with the attendant lineage and clan organization. There is, of course, no direct evidence of this at all, but on the basis of the present dis-

[1] Kroeber, 1938.          [2] See Opler, 1941, 1955.

tribution, the evidence of movement, and Steward's matrilineal band theory, Eggan makes out a plausible case for it. His theory is essentially a survival theory – one might call it the 'Time of arrival: Length of survival' theory. Thus, the groups that arrived on the Rio Grande first were the first to 'lose' their clan organization and take up moieties. They did this in response to the irrigation problem posed by life on the big river and its tributaries. A federation of autonomous clans was no use in integrating a large population that had to be communally organized. In this he follows the theory of Wittfogel and Goldfrank on 'hydraulic' societies.[1] The evidence of movement is both archaeological and linguistic. On the archaeological side, he turns to Reed's reconstruction which suggests that the Rio Grande had experienced four invasions.[2] The first was from the Anasazi area before the twelfth century: the second was from the eastern San Juan (Chaco) area during the twelfth century; the third was from Mesa Verde, also in the San Juan area, about 1300, and the fourth was from the Zuni area, around 1350. These last, Eggan thinks, are the Keresans, which fits both his Western-Pueblo-type theory and his length-of-survival theory. They were originally Zuni-like Westerners and they arrived last, thus retaining their Westernness until today. The original inhabitants of the Rio Grande were the Tiwa; the Towa (Jemez) came in from Chaco, and the Tewa from Mesa Verde, in that order. Thus the Tiwa have lost their clans altogether, and the Tewa have only 'vestiges' of them in the ceremonial names. The Towa, however, have clans and a two-*Kiva* system. (There were, of course, two 'great *Kivas*' in the large Chacoan towns as well as many small ones.) They therefore present a problem for Eggan because they have stubbornly 'retained' their clans, irrigation or no. He puts this down to conservatism and isolation, and Keresan influence, although the argument is never fully worked out.

Eggan finds excellent confirmation of his views in lexicostatistical dating by Whorf, based on the work of Whorf and Trager.[3] Tiwa is the most archaic dialect, diverging from the others about A.D. 800; Tewa and Towa separated about A.D. 1000; and the Tewa dialects began to diverge around A.D. 1300. This correlates more or less with the dates suggested by Reed for the various excursions of each of these groups out of the San Juan area.

[1] Wittfogel and Goldfrank, 1943.     [2] Reed, 1946, 1949.
[3] Whorf and Trager, 1937 – quoted in Eggan, 1950, p. 312.

Since the Upper Rio Grande population and culture expanded at the same rate as the Anasazi waned, and at the same time, the hypothesis – backed by the evidence of pottery – that the San Juan was the source of the Rio Grande Pueblos (except the Keres), is plausible. But there are other theories. Given Eggan's notion that in prehistoric times *all* the Pueblos were basically western in type (if they came from the San Juan they would have to be on his argument – Zuni and the Keres excepted), and that some groups 'lost' the Western traits in the process of adapting to the Rio Grande, then the present distribution makes sense and the traits as distributed 'fit' Eggan's theory.

Objections, however, pour in against this most ingenious and well-worked-out theory. The Keres themselves resist the idea that they come from the west. Their tradition is that they come from the north, from 'White House' – i.e., Mesa Verde. Their traditional route and the towns they built on the way are remembered. As they have been settled in the area for the shortest time, their memory of such events is likely to be freshest, and although one should treat oral traditions sceptically, one so strongly rooted has to be treated with some respect. This would not destroy Eggan's theory altogether but he would have to find a home in the San Juan for the Keres, which might mean ousting the Tewa from Mesa Verde. All this runs against the pottery evidence which Eggan cites, but pottery evidence is at best indecisive, and at worst downright misleading.

Dozier thinks it unlikely that the Tewa, at least, ever had clans:[1] the evidence offered for this he dismisses as misconceived. If not the Tewa, then certainly not the Tiwa. Dozier does not think that the absence of clans can be explained by a degeneration of groups of Western type.

Hawley, on the basis of the relation of Kiowa and Tanoan, posits the Plains as the original home of the latter.[2] This would perhaps explain the bilateral-kinship/patrilineal-moiety aspects of the social structure. The Plains origins of the Tanoans, though not perhaps a very convincing theory, would certainly fit Taos better than a 'degenerate Western' explanation.

Wendorf and Reed, in an article which re-examines Reed's theory,[3] offer an alternative reconstruction. In this there is 'a

[1] See especially, Dozier, 1961.          [2] Hawley, 1937.
[3] Wendorf and Reed, 1955.

broad correlation of Keresan language with San Juan Anasazi culture and of Tanoan dialects with Rio Grande Anasazi culture, prior to 1300'. This is more in line with the Keresans' view of themselves, and with the developments envisaged in the next theory to be dealt with.

TABLE 2. Theories of Tanoan language relationships

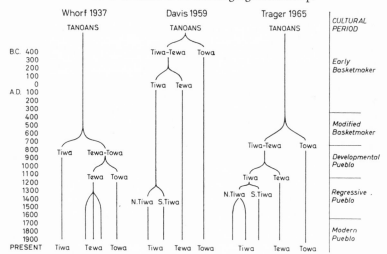

The most comprehensive counter-argument to Eggan's that I have seen never even mentions him. It is based almost solely on linguistic evidence, and has all the inherent problems of glotto-chronology. However, its author, Irvine Davis, proposes an equally plausible sequence.[1] He is mainly concerned with linguistic relations among the Aztec-Tanoan groups, and it is these that run counter to Eggan's notions. For a start, he claims that if the Tanoans were ever in the Rio Grande area as an undifferentiated group, then they must have been there *for at least 2,000 years*. This immediately renders the San Juan evacuation theory out of the question. Also, on his dating, the Tiwa are by no means the most archaic of the Tanoans. Tiwa-Tewa, he calculates, broke off from Towa about 400 B.C., and the latter two split about 100 B.C. The northern and southern branches of Tiwa split about A.D. 1300. This picture is wholly at variance with Eggan's theory. (The conflicting evaluations of the linguistic evidence are shown in Table

[1] Davis, 1959.

2.) What is more, Davis is inclined to attribute to the Tanoans an origin in the South-west rather than either in the Plains or on the San Juan. He sees the Tanoans as originating in the Cochise culture (which lasted from about 8000 B.C. to 500 B.C.) and suggests they moved north-westwards via the Mogollon of south-western New Mexico to become the Kiowa-Tanoan upper-Rio Grande-and-Plains culture. If the Cochise was indeed the origin of all the Aztec-Tanoans, as Davis suggests, then the Hopi may well have been a divergent group that moved north very much earlier, instead of north-east. (The matter is complicated by the fact that the Mogollon is supposed to have some connection with Zuni and Hopi.) But this argument takes us back beyond 2000 B.C., and, to say the least, no inferences about social structure make much sense over such time spans as this. Suffice it to say that Davis regards the Tanoans as a group, undifferentiated up to 2000 years ago, who came from the south-east of Arizona and whose dialects diverged before they reached the Rio Grande; while Eggan regards them as having been undifferentiated up to only 1000 years ago and as having come from the San Juan in the north – their dialects diverging as they moved southwards.

[Trager (1965) has recently put forward a comprehensive re-construction of linguistic and cultural affinities in the South-west which disagrees with both the foregoing theories. With Hawley he attributes a north-eastern origin to the Tanoans. According to his chronology, Kiowa broke off from Tanoan between A.D. 1 and A.D. 500. Towa split off from Tiwa-Tewa between A.D. 500 and 750. Tiwa and Tewa split about A.D. 1050 +, and 'not much later' Northern and Southern Tiwa diverged. (See Table 2.)

Those Tanoans who left Colorado first, and who by A.D. 750 were settled on the Rio Grande, were the ancestors of the Towa (Jemez). They settled among the Keresans – who had been there since A.D. 700 – and adopted many Keresan traits. The undifferentiated Tiwa-Tewa stayed farther north and probably 'adopted the pre-Pueblo and the developing Pueblo culture, it being likely that they took over the places and the houses, and everything else; but in doing so they retained un-Pueblo features of social organization'. In about A.D. 900 or 1000 some of these undifferentiated Tiwa-Tewa moved south and assimilated some Towa-Keres villages, producing a 'pidginized' Tanoan language – Tewa. Yet others skirted this area and settled farther south, becoming the Southern Tiwa.

Trager says, 'The chronology fits, the linguistic distances fit and, we venture to say, the total cultures – if we but knew them well enough – probably fit also.'

His theory raises an interesting problem, roughly illustrated in Table 2. He agrees with Whorf on the time-depths, an agreement we might expect, since they collaborated in the pioneering work on Tanoan. He disagrees violently with Davis, describing the latter's dates as 'utterly misleading'. However – and this we would not expect – when it comes to the order of segmentation he agrees with Davis as against Whorf. Trager and Davis have Towa splitting from Tiwa-Tewa; Whorf has Tiwa splitting from Tewa-Towa. If Trager is correct – and no one knows more about the Tanoan languages than he does – then Davis's segmentation-order is right but his time-depth is wrong, whereas Whorf is more or less right as to time-depth but wrong as to the order of splitting.

Thus we have really four theories: the original Eggan-Reed-Whorf theory, which brings in the Tanoans from the San Juan and the Keres from 'the west'; the revised Wendorf and Reed theory, which has the Tanoans as indigenous to the Rio Grande and brings in the Keres from the San Juan; the Davis theory (accepted latterly by Florence Hawley Ellis), which brings in the Tanoans from the south-west and the Keres from the San Juan again; and the Trager-Hawley theory, which derives the Tanoans from the Plains in the northeast, and which, in Trager's version, has the Keresans as the indigenous inhabitants deriving from the general Anasazi culture.]

I will not attempt to judge between these and other theories. I present them partly to illustrate the possible diversity of views, because we are considering Eggan's theory, which leans heavily on linguistic and archaeological evidence. To round off the pre-history, then, I will outline Davis's view of the Keresans, since this will be relevant later on. He cannot link them with any other language group but his evidence on the distribution of dialects within Keresan is interesting. They are grouped as follows:

(a) Cochiti;
(b) Santo Domingo and San Felipe;
(c) Santa Ana and Zia;
(d) Acoma and Laguna.

According to his calculation, these groups diverged some 700 years ago. Santo Domingo and San Felipe split about 400–500 years ago and Zia and Santa Ana at about the same time. Acoma and Laguna divided about 500 years ago. (It is obvious that this casts doubt on the historical founding of Laguna, a point to be discussed shortly.) Davis supports the theory of a northern origin, and derives all the Keres from Mesa Verde.


## II

In the historical period we find the Pueblo groups distributed more or less as we have seen, however they came to be there. The rebellion sent some of them wandering again, but after about 1700 they settled down in their present positions. The Spaniards dominated the east and left the west largely to its own devices. Now it is Eggan's contention that the Spaniards, and after them the Americans, finished off what the irrigation conditions of the Rio Grande had started. Thus traces of clanship which were already disappearing under Tewa influence in the east were gradually eroded as the Keresans became 'acculturated towards Spanish models'.

In all this Laguna is an important clue. It is supposed to have been founded by refugees from Cochiti, Santo Domingo and San Felipe, and possibly some others. Hence in Eggan's view it should provide a better example of the aboriginal Rio Grande Pueblo culture than do its related villages in the east. It preserved its pristine culture while the other Pueblos on the Rio Grande were falling under the influence of the Spanish and the Tewa. Thus it becomes the key point of his theory of the Keresan Bridge. Laguna is the 'true' Eastern Keresan Pueblo, uncorrupted (until the turn of the century) by the influences that had led to the degeneration of the others.

But this is not entirely clear. The very close relation of the dialect of Acoma to that of Laguna suggests an association going back well beyond the rebellion. We also know of a colony of Acoma people that 'welcomed' the immigrants and joined them at Laguna. We also know – although Eggan relegates this to a footnote – that a wandering priest is said to have gathered up many people from non-Keresan-speaking groups and brought them to Laguna, where they learned Keres. Also, it seems that Zia *and* *Acoma* are mentioned as co-founders in another source. It seems that heterogeneous, and probably disorganized and dispirited, groups of Keres and non-Keres could have arrived in the Laguna area and been absorbed by the Acoma colony. Florence Hawley Ellis, in fact, is adamant that the idea that Laguna was founded after the rebellion is a complete mistake.[1] It existed, she says, *for at least two centuries before the rebellion*. The refugees gathered first at Acoma, and then settled 'a cannon's shot' from Laguna, later joining forces with the latter. She presents conclusive evidence, which accords excellently with Davis's linguistic time-scheme. According to this, the Keres left the San Juan 700+ years ago, and Acoma and Laguna split about 500 years ago; that is, roughly two centuries before the rebellion.

This effectively disposes of the theory that Laguna has preserved the 'basic' Eastern Keresan type of social structure; that is, a slightly watered-down version of the Western type.

Eggan's theory, in brief, is that all the Pueblos were once of the Western type, however developed and derived. The divergencies in type that we now notice amongst the Pueblos represent a gradual running-down of this Western type amongst the Rio Grande groups in response to irrigation conditions, a development which was accelerated by the Spanish and Americans. The Keres, coming last to the Rio Grande, preserved their Western structure the longest and this is evidenced by the existence of clans – although these are practically functionless now. Laguna is the key to this, as it represents an offshoot of the Eastern Keres preserved in the west, and it is Western with Eastern connections.

The contrary evidence quoted suggests that the Rio Grande was originally inhabited by Tanoans of a non-Western type, lacking clans and *Katsinas* and the rest of the Western paraphernalia, but having the moiety system. The Keres invaded this area from somewhere – probably west, but they themselves think the San Juan – bringing with them clans and *Katsinas*, which they passed on in an imperfect form, receiving in return the moiety system. [Or, alternatively, the Keresans were the indigenous inhabitants who influenced the incoming Tanoans.]

Even if we grant that the Keresans came from the San Juan – which I am inclined to believe since it is their own tradition – this does not rule out the possibility that they came equipped with moieties as well as clans and the rest. The Anasazi peoples

[1] Ellis, 1959.

practised irrigation and built huge communal houses. Chaco towns have two large *Kivas*. It is not impossible that a moiety system was some sort of response to these conditions. Reed notes the 'pairing' of *Kivas* in the San Juan Anasazi,[1] as Eggan himself does, suggesting that conditions on the Rio Grande could have 'accelerated' the development of moieties. After all, Jemez, which on Davis's theory is the most 'archaic' and oldest, as well as the most isolated, of the Tanoans (in the Rio Grande area), has the same loading as the Keres. If the Jemez in fact came from the Chacoan area, could they not have brought this complete, and the Keres coming afterwards from Mesa Verde have brought it also? Even if the Jemez did come up from the south-west with the other Tanoans, as Davis suggests, they could have moved first to the Chaco area, and then down to the Rio Grande basin. [If they came from the north-east – the Trager-Hawley theory – the same conclusion would apply.] This would reinforce their likeness to the Keresans, as, despite their different origins, they would have 'shared' the Anasazi culture with them. Perhaps Jemez, and not Laguna, is really the crucial Pueblo for the reconstruction of the Keresan past.[2] Again proof is impossible, but this version fits the prejudices which lead me to view the Keres system – or at least the version of it which I know best – as a fairly self-contained system which is not a run-down, semi-acculturated version of the Hopi. But before we go on to ask what Keres social structure is really like, and whether or not it is a degenerate version of the Western system, we have to ask just what the latter really is, and this is not as clear as it might seem.

### III

#### THE WESTERN PUEBLO TYPE

As we have seen, Eggan sees the Western Pueblos as being characterized by a type of kinship system in which the 'basic' unit is the matrilineal lineage, and the 'basic' organizing principle is the 'lineage principle'. Associated with this is a matri-uxorilocal household system in which women own the house and the land that goes with it, and their husbands join them in the house and work the land.

Eggan treats all this at the level of 'custom' and at a high level

---

[1] Reed, 1946.                    [2] See Appendix.

of abstraction. He presents no data on household composition; no examples of lineages in action. His evidence is primarily linguistic, in terms of the distribution of kin-terms, and 'customary' in that he outlines the various customs involving kin. (These customs, it is worth noting at the outset, do not seem to involve the 'lineage' as such. They involve specific relatives of the person concerned. Thus, for example, it is the father's sister who has certain duties towards her brother's son, not the father's lineage as a whole: likewise, the mother's brother to his sister's children.)

Eggan disagrees with Kroeber's view that 'kinship' in the Western Pueblos (Zuni in particular) is essentially 'bilateral' and that matrilineal clans and sub-clans are luxuries that could be dispensed with. Kroeber thought that these were really aspects of the ritual side of Pueblo culture, while kinship was based on the household and the family.[1] 'The clans give colour, variety and interest to the life of the tribe. They serve an artistic need of the community. But they are only an ornamental excrescence on Zuni society, whose warp is the family and whose woof is the house.'[2]

Against this Eggan argues that the kinship system is 'based on the lineage principle'. He sees the elements of it as:

(a) the matrilocal household
(b) the matrilineal lineage
(c) the matrilineal clan.

(b) and (c) can coincide. (b) is the essential 'feature' which 'organizes' everything else, other 'principles' being 'subordinate' to the 'lineage principle'. It stands intermediary between household and clan. The purpose of the lineage principle is to provide 'integration through time', or 'vertical integration'. The clans, linking together various lineages and themselves linked in phratries, also serve this integrative purpose. The household and family alone could not manage this essential task, Eggan maintains.[3] One

[1] It is a moot point as to whether they were really arguing about the same thing. In a sense, as we shall see in later chapters, all 'kinship' is 'bilateral'. This does not mean that lineages may not be important elements of the social system. The issue of whether or not a kinship grouping we can describe as a lineage is important in the social structure is a real issue; but the argument that 'kinship' is not 'bilateral' but is 'organized on a lineage basis', seems to rest on a semantic and analytical confusion.                                   [2] Kroeber, 1917.

[3] Eggan makes many statements of the kind quoted in this paragraph in each chapter of his book, so I have refrained from giving a long list of page references each time I quote.

can see his point, but it does not follow that one must accept his solution.

Let us first accept the following interpretation of the 'principle of grouping *on a lineage basis*' in a matrilineal society: that for some (or all) social purposes corporate or near-corporate groups are formed on a basis of common descent in the female line from a known ancestress through demonstrable links; that is, that this *claim to common descent* through known links is the basis of their being a group. I am prepared to waive the 'known links' clause, since few societies are that rigorous. But even if the exact link is not known, members of a lineage can usually state the degree of relationship in terms of presumed generation depth etc. We need to enquire exactly what can be meant by saying that the lineage principle is the basic organizing principle of Western Pueblo society, and a 'bridge' between household and clan.

Let us then look at the relation between household and lineage. Common to both is the 'core' of women who reside in the house. These are the female members of the lineage. The men married to these women are, with their unmarried children, the other members of the household. The men born into the house marry out of it, but on divorce or on ritual occasions they return to it. This can be visualized quite easily. (See Fig. 2.)

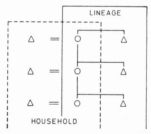

FIG. 2. Relation between household and lineage
in the Western Pueblos

Now if the dispersed male members of the 'lineage' have to return for ritual occasions to their natal home, and if ritual continuity through time is important, then Eggan is right that 'household' alone is insufficient to cover all forms of social grouping and continuity. Let us not, however, beg any questions at the moment and, for the time being, call the group of people born into the house the 'house-group' as opposed to the permanent residents, the 'household'. On this definition, and on Eggan's own description, 'lineage' = 'house-group'. He sometimes speaks of the women of the house as a 'segment' of a lineage, but it is not clear whether by this he means that they are related to women in other houses or that the men of the lineage are the other 'segment'. Also, one might note, the 'lineage' has no name.

The matrilineal clan consists sometimes of only one lineage (house-group), and sometimes of more than one. There is in fact no segmentary organization of lineages. They are a 'linear series' as opposed to a 'merging segmentary series'.[1] In fact, and this is very important, there is no reckoning of genealogy beyond at best the third or fourth ascending generation. This makes segmentary organization of lineages within a clan impossible. If lineages are not named, and if genealogies are not kept, then how does one know who is *in* the lineage? This casts grave doubt on Eggan's contention that the 'lineage principle' *per se* is the mechanism of 'vertical integration'. Clan membership is thus not an extension of lineage membership. It is a kind of nationality; one takes one's mother's clan.

The picture we get, then, is of a number of houses, whose natal members, the house-group, are members of a clan. One of these house-groups may in fact possess fetishes or rights to an office associated with the clan; that is, the house-group must provide a member to take a particular office, and the house-group as a whole must care for the fetish. This ties up with Strong's picture of the Western Pueblos as a part of the group-house, priest and fetish complex of the greater South-west.[2]

Now it is clear that in a technical sense the members of the house-group do in fact constitute a lineage. What I am questioning is Eggan's contention that the 'principle of lineage grouping' is 'basic' and 'organizing'. If, then, the 'lineage' is in fact not distinct from the house-group, and if the workings of the system can be readily understood in terms of the dichotomy between household and house-group, then the concept of 'lineage' as an organizing principle is superfluous. Lineage grouping is not basic; it results from the residential system, and the 'sacredness' of the house. If the lineage principle and the concern for vertical integration were really what 'articulated' the kinship system, then we would find

[1] Goody, 1962.     [2] Strong, 1927.

either named lineages or remembered genealogies. Failing these, what we have are houses and clans. The clan, it is true, is recruited unilineally, but I do not see what sense it makes to say it is 'organized on the *lineage* principle'. Only the children of Jewish mothers may be members of a synagogue, and only the children of British fathers may be British citizens, thus both synagogues and Great Britain recruit members 'unilineally'. But no one would want to say that they were 'organized on the lineage principle'.

If then the 'lineage principle' does not provide the continuity through time that Eggan wants, what does? I think the answer is very simply, *the house*. This is fixed and continuous, as is the line of women in it. One does not need to remember genealogies, one simply remembers the house one was born in, with its fetish and its offices. Eggan does not consider the possibility that women may leave the house in which they were born, but Kroeber's work on Zuni shows that they sometimes do. What happens then, and this is clear from Kroeber's account, is not that the members of the 'new' house remember genealogical links to their consanguine females, but they remember their house of origin. Thus Kroeber gives examples of house-groups and their linkage to other house-groups in terms of the 'original house' from which they hailed. Now again, these constitute a lineage. This is the equivalent of a lineage name. But it is not 'based on the lineage principle'. It is based on the permanence of the sacred house. If these links were ever forgotten, then only membership in the clan would be left to link the 'houses' together, and, as I have argued, while membership in the clan is unilineally determined, it is not based on the lineage principle. What is at stake here is not the existence of lineages (although the lack of a name, a known ancestress and known genealogical links might disqualify some of these groups), but whether or not these are the basic articulating principle or whether they are the product of some even more basic process. The more basic process I am suggesting is that of association with a 'sacred' house. It is house-group membership that creates the lineage and not vice versa. If one accepts the distinction between the 'ritual household' and the 'domestic household', then I think the dispute between Eggan and Kroeber becomes insubstantial. *One cannot explain the workings of the kinship system in terms of the domestic household alone, one has to include the ritual household.* Clans, then, are not 'expansions of the lineage system for integrative purposes', they are expansions, if anything, of the ritual household system. Historically, they may originally have been simply named households, each with its office and fetish. Time, migration and fission have rendered them more diffuse. But still one's membership in the clan does not even depend on one's membership in a 'lineage'. One could presumably be lineageless (an immigrant, for example) and still be a member of a clan.

The confusion stems largely, I think, from the fact of matri-uxorilocal residence. If the natal males of the house never left it, as with the Nayar for example, then the correlation of house-group with lineage would be obvious.[1] No one would, I think, want to claim that the Nayar *taravad* (at the level of the property-owning, commensal unit) was based on some mysterious 'lineage principle', but it does technically constitute a lineage, as does the Hopi house-group. The part-time nature of the natal male's association with his house in Hopi leads us to look elsewhere than the house itself for the 'basic' organizing principle, because the house itself is populated by non-natal males. But the Hopi lineage is purely a ritual group, while the *taravad* is a ritual-domestic unit. Once the ritual/domestic dichotomy is understood for Hopi, the confusion should disappear.

Regarding 'integration through time' in Zuni, Eggan says this is 'carried out through the lineage principle in large measure'. This principle 'underlies the kinship system and furnishes the core of the clan organization'. It also 'provides a mechanism for the inheritance of ceremonial duties and obligations and the transmission and preservation of fetishes and other ceremonial paraphernalia'. Now note that, 'In Zuni this inheritance is phrased in terms of the household' – that is how the Zuni see it, although I suspect that it is in fact phrased in terms of the house. Eggan continues, however, 'but it is clear that it is the lineage segment born into the house-hold that is important. This lineage segment, *or at least the female line* thereof, also owns land and holds it in trust for succeeding generations, to be worked by the men who marry into the house-hold'[2] (italics mine). This is equivalent to saying that paraphernalia and land are associated with a house and looked after by the women of the house, and the men of the ritual household, when they return there for ceremonies, do their share of coping with the ritual duties. As respects the land, the men of the ritual household

[1] Gough, 1961.  [2] Eggan, 1950, p. 217.

(house-group) neither own it nor work it. It is forcing the evidence to say that 'the lineage' owns or inherits the land. The land goes with the house and the women live in the house. That is all. Hence Eggan's cavil which I have put into italics.

When questioning the possibility of 'borrowing' the lineage principle of organization Eggan says, '. . . matrilocal residence can be comprehended readily, but the principle of grouping on a lineage basis is not easily formulated.'[1] However, on my argument, if one borrowed matrilocal residence, *and* the sacred house principle (not difficult), 'grouping on a lineage basis' would automatically follow. Again he says, 'It is clear that the kinship system is organized in terms of the lineage principle rather than in terms of residence.'[2] But the 'lineage principle' in the Western Pueblos *is*, as I have shown above, a principle of residence – ritual residence. The men of the house-group continue to be residents of the house for ritual purposes, they only leave it for domestic purposes. 'Lineage' thus becomes a way of describing certain facts about residence and not a thing in itself; not an organizing principle; not basic.

Against this Eggan might put the terminology, to which, following Radcliffe-Brown, he gives such weight. It would be strange if this were 'organized on a lineage basis' while nothing else was, and of course it was Radcliffe-Brown's opinion that it was so organized. This may be, but I suspect that the 'lineage' arrangement of the terms is more or less a matter of presentation. The same terms could be arranged differently to bring out different principles, and Schneider and Roberts have shown that the Zuni system accords more with Kroeber's interpretation than with Eggan's.[3] Eggan explains this by acculturation.[4] But even if we agree that the terms are arranged as he shows them, this does not alter the argument. The terms of any 'Crow' system can be conveniently shown on 'lineage' diagrams of the kind popularized by Radcliffe-Brown and adopted by Eggan, but there is no reason to infer from this that 'lineages' are basic units in the society. Lounsbury (1964), in his remarkable study of Crow systems, makes this point and also notes that Tax (1950) made it earlier. One cannot even infer from the Crow-type terms that the society is matrilineal, let alone based on matrilineages. But even assuming that

[1] Eggan, 1950, p. 319.
[2] Eggan, 1950, p. 133.
[3] Schneider and Roberts, 1956.
[4] Eggan, 1955, p. 511.

the society is matrilineal (as indeed it usually is), the terms can as easily be taken to refer to 'men born into my father's house' as to 'men of my father's lineage'. But they may have a different referent altogether. Eggan shows that some of the terms can be arranged on a lineage basis, and then argues that they are 'extended' to clansfolk. But by what evidence do we *show* that they are extended? All we know is to whom they are applied; the terms for clansfolk also apply to one's house-group – which is not surprising.

It is worth noting that organization on a lineage principle is not thoroughgoing. (Fig. 3 shows some typical distributions of terms in Crow-type systems, and it may help the reader to refer to this

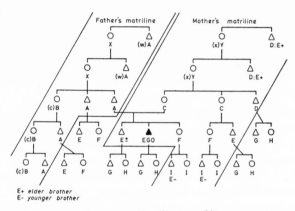

FIG. 3. Crow-type distribution of kin terms

throughout the various discussions on terminology.) Eggan notes with a little surprise that grandparents are not differentiated in Hopi. The Hopi have 'ignored these differences and classified them together', although one would have 'expected' them to be terminologically separate.[1] (It is perhaps significant that Eggan is unwilling, albeit unconsciously, to accept the Hopi terms at their face value. He shows (1950, pp. 20, 21) that for either a male or female ego no difference is made between father's mother and mother's mother; both are *iso'o* which he symbolizes as GM – grandmother. Yet on page 24, in his 'lineage diagram' of ego's father's lineage, he distinctly lists father's mother and father's mother's mother as FM, to distinguish them from mother's

[1] Eggan, 1950, p. 39.

mother and mother's mother's mother who stay GM. The Hopi refuse to make the 'lineage' distinction, so Eggan makes it for them. It may have been a typological error, or maybe even sub-conscious guilt that caused him to do the reverse for Zuni. The Zuni *do* differentiate between the two grandmothers, but Eggan lumps them together in his diagram, with a note correcting the error (1950, p. 184).) However, for the Hopi, after the first ascending generation, lineal relatives are merged.

This is not the place to try to pick our way through the intrica-cies of detail in the terminologies of all the Western Pueblos. It is sufficient again merely to question that the lineage principle is the 'basic organizing factor' of the terms[1] and to question the infer-ence from terms to social groupings. It is quite possible that 'line-age' is a factor in the generation of terms for kin amongst the Western Pueblos, but as with the kinship system proper, is there any warrant for calling it the *basic* organizing factor? In so far as unilineality is important in the system it will affect the classifica-tion of kin. Eggan criticizes Kroeber for saying that the Zuni 'ignore' generational differences, when in fact what they are doing, he says, is to 'recognize' the unity of the lineage group. Equally we can criticize him for saying that the Hopi 'ignore' lineage differences and accept his logical alternative – that they are 'recognizing' generational similarity (unity?). When dealing with Zuni, Eggan always gives the benefit of the doubt to alterna-tive usages which favour his lineage interpretation. Schneider and Roberts have called this into question. For example, Zuni usage clearly alternates between 'sibling' terms for cross-cousins, and 'proximate generation' (Crow-type) terms. The former stress generational 'unity', the latter, lineage 'unity.' Eggan, however, opts for the lineage usage as 'basic', in Zuni, as he does also for Acoma and Laguna.

The issue here is whether the Western Pueblo kinship-term systems are basically organized on a lineage basis or whether other principles are involved, and whether, even if they are so organ-ized, one can infer from this that matrilineal lineages are the basic organizing features of the social structure. It will by now be super-

---

[1] An equally basic factor in Zuni, Acoma and Laguna is self-recipocal termino-logy, and in Acoma and Laguna of alternating-generation terminology. Eggan dismisses these as 'features which, in the perspective of the total kinship systems, are relatively minor in importance'. This may be, but it is not something that can be settled by fiat. (See Eggan, 1950, p. 285.) I will take this up in Chs. 7 and 8.

fluous to say that I would feel doubtful of confident assertions on either count.

## IV

Before summing up on the Western Pueblo type, we must consider two of the most important recent studies of Western Pueblo kinship. These are Titiev's *Old Oraibi* (for the Hopi) and Schneider and Roberts' *Zuni Kin Terms*.

Titiev's most perceptive discussion of the relations of lineage, household, clan and phratry, supports, I think, the above analysis. He shows clearly how the different definitions of 'lineage' and 'clan' used by Fewkes, Stephen, Lowie and Parsons, make it difficult to reconcile their statements. He stresses the point that Hopi genealogies are 'untrustworthy' and do not seem concerned with 'accurate lists of supposed blood relatives'. Lines of descent are 'confused', though there is still a feeling that within the clan there exists a smaller unit of consanguineous kin. This 'narrow circle of blood kin' (Lowie) is, says Titiev, 'none other than that segment of a matrilineal lineage which I have termed a household'. (In my definition a house-group or ritual household.) 'The basic feature of this grouping is the fact that a mature woman, her daughters, and occasionally her grand-daughters, occupy a common residence through life and bring up their children under the same roof. It should be noted that *this definition of a household group conforms equally well to what some anthropologists call a matrilineal lineage ...*' (My italics).[1] Indeed it does, as long as there is some provision for a regular or jurally important association of the males of the group with the 'core' of resident females. Titiev then suggests that the origin of clans lay in households which split up. The links between these households were forgotten, but they kept their 'clan' identity. As long as the links were remembered, the different households constituted a 'lineage'. However, as we have seen, the links are forgotten or 'confused' very quickly. What remains intact is the house.

Following Titiev, then, we can keep 'lineage' to refer to those houses between which links can be remembered and, of course, as he sees, *technically* it can be applied to the house-group itself. But he fails to distinguish between domestic and ritual households, and

[1] All the Titiev quotations are from 1944, p. 46.

so compounds the confusion that Eggan tried to dissolve by distinguishing household and lineage. Eggan was right to insist on this distinction, but he over-emphasized the importance of the 'lineage principle' as the determinant of it.

Titiev sums up his views on the Hopi lineage thus:

2. *Lineage*—an exogamic, unilateral group of matrilineal kindred, demonstrably descended from a common ancestress. Since such demonstrations cannot always be made among the modern Hopi, and since the lineage lacks both name and *wayu* (fetishes) and may be scattered over several households, it is the vaguest of Hopi divisions. Its importance lies primarily in its theoretical implications as a nascent clan, and in the tendency for inheritance to follow a lineage pattern.[1]

(The last point is not elaborated.) This does not suggest that there is anything very basic or 'organizing' about the Hopi lineage. It underlines my argument that, far from being the basic organizing unit, it is a product of something other than 'the principle of grouping on a lineage basis', this 'other' being the ritual household.

Schneider and Roberts are primarily concerned with kinship terms, but here I want to take account of their views on the Zuni lineage, since it was from Kroeber's assertion of the primacy of household and family in Zuni that Eggan took his departure. Schneider and Roberts manage to find support for both points of view, while being more sympathetic to Kroeber's. It is not so much, they argue, that Zuni has a 'bilateral' kinship system, as that the 'mode of integration' in Zuni is 'bilateral'. This stems from the fact that lineages and clans are not multifunctional corporate groups, and that each ego has a set of allegiance, possibly peculiar to himself, to other associations than clan and lineage. The network of relations thus set up is primary in value to the individual and over-rides allegiance to any one group. Hence Zuni society, although possessing the clan as a corporate group, is not composed of clans which perform the majority of functions for the individual. A man's clan is only one of many groups with which he is affiliated, and his concern is with keeping up membership in all these groups. 'Basic in Zuni integration, then, is the individual as the nexus of a pattern of relationships and not monolithic corporate descent groups balanced one against another. Zuni

[1] Titiev, 1944, p. 58.

social structure, like Zuni kinship, is "Ego centred", not group centred. It is this fact which Kroeber saw so clearly and from which we suspect he drew his conclusion that Zuni "kinship is thoroughly and equally bilateral".'[1]

Kinship 'extensions', the authors assert, ramify along these lines of bilateral integration – a situation which no fully developed lineage system with strong corporate descent groups could tolerate. What is left for the lineage? 'The Zuni lineage takes its place, then, among the groups with which Ego is affiliated. Although it is important, the lineage is still one group among a number and it does not invariably outrank all others in the strength of Ego's commitment to it. The Zuni lineage is, as it were, frayed at the edges and limited when viewed from the perspective of what the lineage would have been if the lineage principle had been the *dominant* principle. Since the lineage competes with other groups for Ego's allegiance and since the lineage has relatively few rather than many functions in Zuni, the lineage cannot be a strongly corporate group. Its weak corporate character is reflected in the failure of the Zuni terminology to segregate and lump members of contiguous lineages and in the subordinate position of the ordering or classifying function of kinship terms.'[2]

Thus they agree that although Eggan overstressed the importance of the lineage, it was necessary to recognize its existence if only to understand the full range of groups of which ego could be a member. They accept rather uncritically the whole concept of the lineage as Eggan phrases it, and their answer to the question why the lineage is not in fact the 'basic' group is a reassertion of Kroeber's position on 'bilateral' integration as 'basic'. While I entirely agree with this interpretation, I offer my own argument on the 'nature' of the lineage as a supporting reason for its lack of dominance; that is, that the 'principle of grouping on a lineage basis' is not an independent but a derivative principle. What Schneider and Roberts do show with beautiful clarity is the reason for the lack of concern with exact genealogy and genealogical position noted by Titiev, which is destructive of any real depth in lineage reckoning. Where integration is achieved by the relations between strong corporate descent groups, they argue, then most of a person's rights and privileges are in fact defined by genealogical position. Where this is not so and a 'bilateral' pattern of

<hr />

[1] Schneider and Roberts, 1956.  [2] *Ibid.*

integration predominates, as at Zuni, then genealogical position is only one of many facts determining ego's status, and it will consequently fade in importance.[1]

## V

To sum up, then, in my view the Western Pueblo kinship system is composed of the following elements:

(a) The house, occupied permanently by a line of women who have their husbands join them. The house may have certain paraphernalia and offices associated with it. It is sacred in various ways. It may hold a fetish, and, in Zuni particularly, be the place for priestly retreats. In Hopi, babies which die uninitiated are buried in various places, but their souls return to their mother's house, where they linger under the roof to be reborn in the next child born there.[2] Thus reincarnation is phrased in terms of the house itself – not the lineage or a segment of the lineage, or the clan. Land goes with the house, and is worked by the husbands, but the women own the produce.

(b) The house-group, or ritual household, which may be contrasted with the domestic household outlined in (a). This consists simply of all those people born in the house. They gather together for ritual occasions in the house, and the dispersed male members of the group continue to be 'residents' for ritual purposes. (Professor Forde has described them by the beautiful phrase 'ritual drones'.) It is from the males born into the house that the priests must be chosen. In the event of women leaving the house on marriage – an event not provided for by Eggan's scheme – the breakaway house-group knows the house from which it originated and keeps up the relationship with it, although this possibly fades after a time and a new house-group is thus formed. The house-group is technically a lineage.

[1] Forde (1931) provides some data on lineages, but it is not altogether clear what he means by lineage. He speaks of the 'lineage or maternal family', and of the merging of two clans producing lineages. These latter are perhaps what later writers called sub-clans; they are also probably what he means by 'named lineages' or maternal families. In his genealogies he 'names' the lineages after the 'senior active woman', but he does not say if the Hopi do this. He includes *all* the descendants of an ancestress in the 'lineage', marking out those who belong to the same clan; he does not show to which households they belong.

Dozier (1954), in his study of Hano, promises in his introduction to discuss 'the lineage' in order that we may compare his analysis with Eggan's. But that is the last we hear of it.                                   [2] Eggan, 1950, p. 47.

(*c*) The clan, a wider association which may incorporate several house-groups and which controls exogamy and combines for ritual purposes. Should any house-group of the clan die out, then its duties could be taken over by another. Should a clan die out, then other clans of its phratry will take over its duties.

These strike me as an adequate account of the principles which organize Western Pueblo kinship as a system of corporate groupings. When Kroeber said it was 'thoroughly and equally bilateral' he was seeing it from the viewpoint of a particular ego, and one can see what he means, although it does not tell one very much.

I conclude that:

(*a*) the lineage principle is not the basic organizing principle which ensures vertical integration by providing continuity through time;
(*b*) this function is performed by the house and its ritual residents on the ceremonial side, and the house and its domestic residents on the economic side;
(*c*) the argument between Eggan and Kroeber concerning the relative weightings of 'residence' and 'lineage' is spurious. The only principle at work is the principle of residence, but this is divided into ritual and domestic as shown. The principle of ritual residence in fact produces lineages, but these are not independent of the principle, they are a way of describing it.

The question which of many kinship principles is to be regarded as basic is not meaningful. There is no criterion by which it can be answered. A group which is not in active operation throughout the year is not therefore necessarily 'secondary' or 'peripheral'. The purpose it serves may only arise infrequently, but may nevertheless be crucial. In any kinship system a number of principles will be called upon for different purposes, and what one must examine are the purposes and the groups formed to meet them.

I realize that in this discussion of the Western Pueblo type I have, like Hamlet's queen, protested far too much. I can assure the reader that the casuistry has been as painful for me as it has probably been boring for him. But I really had no alternative. If Cochiti is to be interpreted as a degenerate example of this type, we need to be sure just what the type is: – what its 'basic' features are. The facts are not really in doubt. What is dubious in my opinion is the conceptualization and explanation of the facts. Hence I had to wrangle with Eggan's contention that it was certain 'principles' that were at work. Like many others I am suspicious of this reification of concepts.[1] Social structures do not emerge as the result of the manifestation of principles, but as the outcome of the pursuit of interests in an institutional and ecological framework. Thus I contended that 'the principle of grouping on a lineage basis' was simply a shorthand way of describing a 'real' process. This is important because, as we shall see, in Cochiti I think there *is* 'grouping on a lineage basis' that has nothing to do with ritual households, but *simply* with common descent and its recognition. Thus we had to see exactly what was meant in the Western Pueblos by 'the lineage principle' in order to judge *what* it was that Cochiti was supposed to be departing *from*. On the two questions (*a*) what is the nature of the 'lineage'? and (*b*) how important is it? we can at least say that the issue is not perhaps as clear-cut as Eggan's analysis suggests.

## VI

### CONCLUSION

In this chapter we have tried to assess the theories which seek to account for the distribution of types of social structure among the Pueblos. In particular we have followed out Eggan's theory of a supposedly universal Western Pueblo type of kinship system which later disintegrated. We have seen that not only is this theory doubtful, but that the basic type may not be organized on the principles that Eggan puts forward.

With this in mind we can now return to the Keresan Bridge. Having dismissed the argument that Laguna is a fossilized Eastern Keresan Pueblo, and questioned whether the Keres are in fact a degenerate form of the Hopi and Zuni, we must look at the Eastern Keresan kinship system in the setting of the total social structure and try to ascertain just how it works. Is it in fact a disturbed and acculturated version of the Western system, with its house, and the domestic and ritual residents of the house, and the clan and phratry for wider integration? Or is it in fact a type of its own which is not to be explained by reference to some basic

---

[1] As more or less arbitrary devices for classification they are relatively harmless and even useful. See Ch. 1.

Western proto-system? I can only really answer these questions, and then only partially, for the Pueblo of Cochiti, supposedly the most acculturated of the Keresans. In the following chapters I will discuss the general social structure of the village, its kinship system, and the status terminology.

# PART II
# COCHITI

# 3

# Social Structure

As most of the cultural details on Cochiti can be found in Lange, I will confine myself here to an outline of the structure of groups and categories as I see them. Some of this is simply a re-organization of Lange's data, but where I have something to add I have done so without regard to length. The chapter is, therefore, somewhat unbalanced, but it should be read in conjunction with Lange's account.

I

INTRODUCTION

Cochiti is a relatively isolated Pueblo, built on a piece of rising land about half a mile west of the Rio Grande. Some fields lie between the village and the river, while others are some distance away across the river. To the west of the village the Jemez mountains rise in places to 11,000 feet; the elevation of Cochiti itself is 5,200 feet. The foothills of these mountains are characterized by heavily wooded canyons and steep-sided *mesas*. (To one of these the Cochiti retreated and built a town during the Pueblo revolt – 1680–92.) Between the village and the foothills is undulating country of desert scrub, cacti, yucca, sparse short grasses, juniper and piñon.

The Cochiti reservation covers some 22,000 acres, but of this only about 1,800 are irrigated, and of these only a little over 600 are cultivated. Some cattle and horses and a few sheep graze on the sparse grass of the hills. Erosion and over-grazing have ruined much of this land, but after a summer of light and persistent rain, there can be enough grass to support about 450 cattle and horses; but these climatic conditions are rare. Floodwater farming was once practised at Cochiti, but during this century it has declined and finally died out. At best it only supplemented the irrigation farming. Two large irrigation ditches from the river carried water to the fields; the ditches were cleaned and repaired by communal labour. Since 1930, when a dam was constructed by the Middle Rio Grande Conservancy District, water for Cochiti and other villages has been carried in two large canals, and the supply is regulated by the District. This has brought a larger acreage under irrigation, and has led to the extinction of flood farming.

Politically, the tribe – like other Pueblo groups – is relatively autonomous, having treaty relations with the U.S. Federal Government. The rights and privileges it retained under the Spaniards and Mexicans were confirmed by the U.S. Federal crimes, however, should be reported and tried in Federal courts. Otherwise the Pueblo government can make and enforce what laws it chooses. (A good summary of the legal position of the Pueblos and their lands is given in Aberle, 1948.) The United Pueblos Agency was created by the Federal Government in 1935, to administer health, welfare, agricultural and educational programmes for the Indians. The Cochiti have been relatively co-operative.

The population of Cochiti is difficult to estimate, because there are many non-permanent residents, and even more on the tribal roll who are permanently non-resident. I estimate that in 1958-9 there were some 300 permanent residents, and about another twenty semi-permanent (for example, those who were away at work during the week and returned at weekends). Perhaps about fifty to eighty more lived in Santa Fé, Albuquerque, and other towns, but kept up contacts with the village. These figures are very approximate, and the numbers fluctuated a good deal.

Cochiti was certainly at one time a compact village of traditional Pueblo type, with two- and three-storey house-blocks crowded round a central *plaza*. But even before the end of the nineteenth century this pattern of building declined, the village began to spread out, the houses of Spanish style, with doors and windows instead of roof-openings, appeared. Single-storey adobe houses are now universal, and many are being built to the west of the *plaza* as completely detached dwellings. Some families who own fields over the river maintain small *ranchitos*, and retire to these in the summer months. But there is a lot of coming and going between ranch and village.

Communications between the village and the outside world are not good, and in flood-weather they can be virtually severed, as the road is crossed by a number of *arroyos*. Its nearest neighbour is Santo Domingo, but relations with this Pueblo are not very intense. My impression is that closer relations are maintained with the other Pueblos, but this may be biased. It has two near-by Spanish villages, Peña Blanca and Sile. Peña Blanca is interesting in that it is largely composed of ex-residents of Cochiti. These Spanish residents in the Pueblo are a unique feature, and remain something of an enigma. Their numbers have dwindled now with the exodus to Peña Blanca and the buying up of their land, but they have been a constant feature of the village throughout known history. Their presence has been used to hint at 'influences' on Cochiti social structure, but there is little evidence of this, although their *cultural* influence has been in many ways profound. I had a survey made of Peña Blanca, and nothing in kinship, religion or politics emerged that was remotely like that found in Cochiti. It followed, in fact, the normal Spanish-American patterns. The Spanish in Cochiti are not really integrated into the 'Indian' life of the village at all, with the exception of a few women who married Indian men. They join in church worship and in the baseball, they run the two stores, and they are tolerated. They are even indulged. Lange gives examples of this indulgence, and I have witnessed it myself. But this in itself keeps them on the outside. They are merely allowed to play at being Indians.

The northerly position of Cochiti and its proximity to the Tewa has often been stressed. But this is a marginal proximity. Santo Domingo is effectively as near. There are many Tewa contacts, however, and a number of intermarriages. In 1910 three families from San Ildefonso migrated to Cochiti. But like the Hopi-Tewa, these Cochiti-Tewa have been pretty much assimilated. Certainly any influence has been from hosts to guests and not vice-versa.

The Cochiti economy has been traditionally based on agriculture and a little hunting and gathering. Many things made agriculture difficult, and yet others contributed to its decline by presenting alternative methods of subsistence. The agricultural difficulties were summed up for me by two officials as follows:

In the old days people either farmed or starved. Since 1931 (actual date given) things have been different. Since wage work was available near by, men could give up farming if they wanted to, or at least give up depending on it. They gave it up because it was hard. The hardships involved:

1. *Difficulty of irrigation.* Too much ditch work was required for

too little water. The two miles of ditch needed constant dredging and digging. This was very hard, and the return was poor.

2. *Scattered land holdings*. There was no pressure on land now, and there had never been a real shortage, but when everyone was farming there was some pressure. Inheritance of land was important, but there were no fixed patterns. Everyone tried to get land by inheritance 'where he could'. Thus a man might have land all over the place, and farming it became impossible. Travelling from plot to plot was tiring, and often the 'garden' crops were farthest from the house. Men were reluctant to relinquish their holdings, however, for fear of what might be substituted. The Indian Bureau (?) would not give them grants unless they consolidated.

3. *Crossing the river*. Most of the fields were across the river, and crossing it was a problem. If a man took a waggon he often had to go as far down as San Felipe to find a suitable ford. A ferry was built and plugged with cedar pitch made from bark gathered by the community from the hills. But this required two men to man it continuously and one to steer, and it was cumbersome and unreliable. Boat and 'pontoon' bridges were tried, but they were too light, and sudden floods could upset them.

4. *Flooding*. Lack of effective water control meant that floods could ruin carefully irrigated fields. The flood water was useless for irrigation and disastrous to crops.

5. *Drought*. During the thirties there was a drought. By this time men were making a little profit from trading surplus crops, but several seasons of drought could ruin this.

Finally, permanent bridges over the river were not built until after the war, and by that time men had got pick-ups and could commute to Santa Fé. Car pools were organized and jobs sought in town. English learned in the forces was useful in finding employment, and few men wanted to go back to the arduous unrewarding farming. Thus, farming came to be a little industry run by a dwindling number of people with larger farms. Holdings were consolidated, transport and better irrigation were provided, but not in time to induce the whole village to return to farming. Most men keep a little land for garden crops and food for cattle and poultry, but many fields lie idle.

I present this information direct from the mouths of two intelligent Cochiti men, as a supplement to and confirmation of

Lange's account of economic change. It may not always fit the facts, but it is how they saw the situation.

Wage work is now as important as farming in Cochiti, and has largely replaced trading with the trading posts. This is still done by the women who make pottery and tourist knick-knacks.

## II

### COMMUNITY

There are a number of areas of social activity in which the *community* as a whole, or its representatives, are involved. For some purposes the whole community is a recruiting ground. Thus, the chief officers of the Pueblo are chosen from the community at large, not on any principle of descent or other group membership. All these officers serve on the council of *principales*, the governing body in secular matters. This is the 'representative' body of the community, its legislature and its court. Its decisions have to be unanimous, for they are the decisions of the community. The three chief offices are Governor, Fiscale, and War Captain. Each of these has a 'lieutenant' (*teniente*). Each is nominated annually by one of the medicine societies. The Governor is the chief executive officer, who deals with all secular matters and with the outside world. The Fiscale handles the mission and all dealings with the priests. The War Captains (we should treat them as co-equals, and indeed they are named as the twin warrior gods *Masewi* and *Oyoyewi*) are the ceremonial policemen and the arbiters of religious matters. They see to the proper conduct of ceremonial and punish witchcraft. Among minor officials the most important are the Alguacilitos and the Fiscalitos. The former act as assistants to the War Captains and the latter to the Governor and Fiscale. These minor offices are used as a training ground for future major officials. Newer posts reflect changing ideas and functions – for example, secretary, treasurer, brand inspector, fence rider, governor's chauffeur, combine harvester crew, etc.

Governor and 'community' are closely associated in secular matters, in the same way as the Cacique and the community are in religious ones. The Cacique 'cares for' the tribe as a whole. He is the chief religious official, but is not, like the War Captains, a disciplinarian. In fact, dispute, quarrel and administration must be kept from him. His duties are prayer and fasting on behalf of the whole people (and, it is often stressed, of all people), who are supposed to support him by planting his fields with corn and harvesting them for him. He is chosen for life from the ranks of the *Flint-Koshare* society (see later), and must always be vigilant in the spiritual interests and education of the Pueblo. He is, in fact, answerable to the War Captains who may, in an extreme case, depose him for dereliction of duty. This has never happened. He is not a chief in the accepted sense. He is a priest. The work done for him is community work.

The cult of the masked 'gods' – the *Katsinas* – used to be a tribal-wide cult into which all the young men were initiated. It is now less universal, and is coming to be associated with the two moieties, as one cult but with two sets of performers. It was looked after by a medicine society which arranged its actual performances under the supervision of the War Captains. Ideally, it is still a tribal-wide cult, and is not officially associated with any sub-groups of the tribe.

We might pause here to note that the Cochiti hold 'community' as an explicit value. They will often say 'that's community' when referring to some activity or affair that is, say, not open to organization by individual decision. Cleaning the irrigation ditches or the village before a dance will be referred to as 'community'. A man's greatest fear is to be 'no use to the community any more'. (A young man given to too much drinking said this to me in bitter self-reproach.) The Cochiti strive to keep those activities that are 'community' pleasant and co-operative. The Governor, as Lange points out, is leaned on heavily here. He is more and more seen as the voice of 'community'. Two other aspects of community are the truck and the harvester. The truck has become a very important part of community life. It is used by anyone who pays a small sum to the Governor towards its upkeep, as is the combine harvester. Two men are detailed as 'crew' for the harvester. Much concern is shown for the truck, and there is great anxiety if it breaks down, as it often does. With respect to these two machines the Pueblo is united in concern and in use.

Two other 'alien' institutions serve as focal points for communal activity and sentiment. These are the church and the school. The church has a curious position in Cochiti. There is no resident priest – he comes from Peña Blanca – and the Cochiti maintain that the church is theirs, the priest coming, as it were, by invitation. The sacristan of the church has until recently always been a member of one of the more powerful societies, and the Fiscale is a medicine society nominee. In addition to its use for Catholic services, the church is used for some dances at Christmas, and after every service speeches are made by some official to the congregation in order, as Lange puts it, 'to have the last word'. Thus a tight rein is kept on the church. But we cannot understand its position if we assume that it is totally alien and merely tolerated. It is very much part of the Pueblo life, and there are very few who would declare themselves not to be devout Catholics. One man who does so very pronouncedly is considered scandalous by most. Some of the most conservative of the old people, if they had to choose, would undoubtedly reject the church for the native religion, but this choice has not, despite some near crises, been forced onto them. The church is used in factional disputes, and the progressive element declares its allegiance to Catholicism, in defiance of the native religion, as a counter to the influence of the ceremonial officials. But the attitude of the majority was summed up in the words of one moderate, 'I'm a good Catholic and a good Indian, and I want to be both.' Thus the two religions are seen as separate but not necessarily conflicting ways of reaching the supernatural. Two religions are better than one, but they cannot be fused. Those elements of Catholicism that are compatible with, or capable of being interpreted in terms of, basic Pueblo values and concepts, are accepted and stressed. It is only when the priest oversteps his functions, as the Cochiti see them, or when the progressives use the religion as a subversive weapon, that hostility to the church breaks out. Even then, however, the majority of Cochiti still attend and still believe. Thus throughout dispute and factional strife there was a common meeting place and a common ritual for the whole village. At the successive life-transitions of the individual, church rituals supplement native ones, but cannot be substituted for them. Thus everyone passes through the hands of the church. Baptism complements the native naming ceremony; confirmation parallels initiation; marriage is celebrated by both rites; death is supervised by societies and priest. In each of these, the rituals are parallel, not integrated, but both are considered necessary.

Everyone has also passed through the Indian Service school, except the old people, and there seems to be a good deal of common affection for it. Its buildings are now used for council meetings, and the whole village turned out for a farewell party for the schoolmistress on her retirement. (This happened during the first few weeks of my stay, and I was pointedly told several times that the reason why she was so popular was that 'she never asked us no questions about anything'!)

## III

### FACTIONS

Despite the explicit valuation of unity and harmony in the pursuit of true community, Cochiti life has suffered from various forms of factional dispute. The *factions* are referred to in Cochiti by their English names – 'Progressives' and 'Conservatives'. But this simple dichotomy does not really fit the true situation. The virulence of factionalism has now abated in Cochiti, but enough still remains for people to have to take it into account. And if the old basis has largely gone, in baseball the Indians have found another. We must first deal with the older factions.

The facts are very simple, and are summarized by Lange. At about the turn of the century several Indians who had been educated in schools away from the Pueblo returned with adopted Anglo names and proposed several changes in village life. They refused to accept the authority of the traditional officers, and repudiated the native religion in favour of the Catholic Church. They found the majority of their support in one moiety (Pumpkin). The progressives favoured adoption of Anglo ways and co-operation with the Indian service. They felt it necessary to throw over most of the traditional culture in order to achieve this. The conservatives, on the other hand, saw any intrusion of Anglo culture as a threat and wanted none of it. There were, however, a good many moderates, who usually classed themselves as conservatives, but who favoured the introduction of some Anglo features, and were not particularly hostile to the outside world. Their attitude was largely 'a plague on both your houses' – a desire to have things pleasant and normal, but they generally considered themselves conservatives because they blamed the progressives for spoiling things in the first place by trying to change them too quickly. They wanted the old ways in religion too, with the parallel and complementary system, and not the stark choice that the progressives offered them. Unlike the true conservatives, they did not put the native religion 'first' and would have been most distressed to have had to make a choice.

The Church naturally backed the progressives, as, it seems, did the Indian Service, but without much success. As the original leaders of the progressive movement died the cause lost its impetus. Many members slipped back into the old ways. At the same time some of the more obdurate of the old conservatives died. Progressives helped to organize ceremonies, even if they did not participate themselves. They saw to such things as collecting parking fees from tourists and the like. But the two poles of opinion remain, and occasionally disputes come into the open which line up the two sides again. Some progressives are still of the opinion that the native dances are the work of the devil, and they tend to lean heavily on the church. They are not numerous, since many have simply left the Pueblo.

This relatively quiet state of affairs prevailed in the late thirties, and until the outbreak of the Second World War. This event brought many changes to the village. In particular it took away a large number of young men for war service. It was followed five years later by the Korean campaign, which, again, took its toll of manpower. The figures for the two campaigns are shown in Table 3.

TABLE 3. Cochiti Veterans

| | In Service | Died | Re-enlisted | Returned to Pueblo | Returned to near Pueblo |
|---|---|---|---|---|---|
| 1940–5 | 33 | 3 | 5 | 14 | ? |
| 1951–3 | 24 (incl. 5 from 1940–5) | 1 | 2 | 12 (incl. 3 from 1940–5) | 4 |

These are necessarily approximate, as informants could not always remember all men concerned, but the general picture is clear.

The importance of these returned veterans is enormous.[1] They represent a force in Pueblo life which was absent during the days of the old factions. In 1958–9 there were still some twenty veterans living in Cochiti out of an adult population (male) of about 107. A few had returned to their previous farming occupations, but

[1] Fox, 1961b.

most were working for wages, or on their own account, in or out of the village. Some were silversmiths, others timber workers, janitors (in Santa Fé), school bus drivers, and workers on Anglo farms. One was a draughtsman at Los Alamos Atomic Energy Centre. Thus, to add to their considerable experience in the forces (including battle experience in the Pacific and in Europe with the Thunderbird Division), they had permanent contact with the outside world. This hindered some of them from active participation in Pueblo affairs, but most got around the problems.

The relation between the veterans and the earlier factions is interesting. Many were the sons of conservatives, and their early teaching has not left them. Most of the veterans of 1940–5 have returned to active participation in the ceremonial life, dancing *Katsina* and becoming members of, for example, drum cults and 'managing' societies. At the same time, they have tried to introduce many innovations into the Pueblo, often in the face of opposition from their older conservative relatives. The fact that they are themselves the offspring of conservatives helps to lessen the tension. In many ways they are a disappointment to extremists of both factions. They are avowedly nativistic, but also demand changes in material conditions and organization which are at variance with conservative notions. Their nativism antagonizes the more hard-boiled progressives, who would like to see them go all the way with the 'Anglo-cization' of the Pueblo. It is fascinating to see how some veterans treat the progressive attitude as old-fashioned. The effect has been to produce a 'third force' in Cochiti life, which seems to be providing a vigorous and positive alternative both to the old spent factions and to the rather negative moderates who sat on the fence. What is more, they have provided a reference group for younger people, who by taking their stand, can avoid being torn between the extreme demands of the old factions. The prestige of veterans as returned warriors is high, and this helps them to command respect for the new approach. I have called this 'progressive nativism' to emphasize that the veterans and their supporters have enthusiastically taken up *both* positions – or at least a good part of both. The whole picture might have been different, as it is at other Pueblos, had the medicine societies still been flourishing and in control. These societies are so implacably opposed by their very nature to innovation, that the veteran position would have been very difficult. The *Katsina* cult and the moiety rituals are not so directly opposed. They were opposed to the Catholic prohibition on such rituals, and so should have brought the veterans into conflict with the Church. But the veterans, with their wide experience, are not overawed by the church, and simply ignore the conflict that theoretically exists. They were helped also by the decline of agriculture. Their ability to earn wages makes them relatively independent, and enables them to have the benefits of a cash income while still participating in the life of the tribe to the full.

We have treated the veterans as a 'group', but they do not think of themselves as such. There is no American Legion branch at Cochiti, as there is at Santo Domingo. But there is a covert unity of attitude and action amongst them that makes them a very real force. According to a correspondent, at the changeover of officials at Christmas 1960–1 they took over all the major secular offices.

We have to consider as an aspect of factionalism the rivalry between the two baseball teams, although this is a fairly recent phenomenon.[1] The original team, called first the 'Eagles' and now the 'Redskins', was formed many years ago (no one is quite sure when), and was for a long time the only team. Support comes from all sections of the society, and even the most conservative do not regard it as an alien sport, but as part of normal village affairs. The only exception was the insistence of the ceremonial officials that the Cacique should not play once he assumed office. He had been a regular pitcher, but this was not thought to be consonant with the dignity of his office. After the Second World War and with the return of the veterans, interest in baseball grew and a second team was formed. (It was for this that the Cacique played.) This was known first as the 'Silversmiths', but is now called the 'Braves'. For some time this functioned as a 'second' team, sharing the same ball park as the 'first'. But after a while it claimed independent status, built its own park and entered the inter-Pueblo league as a rival to the Redskins. It had a flash of success and won the inter-Pueblo championship several times. But this meant that it had to play the 'Redskins', and so a potentially dangerous situation arose which soon erupted into real hostility. The village had two hostile camps of players and supporters. Why were they hostile? This is difficult to gauge, except that the two teams seem

[1] Fox, 1961a.

to be composed of rival families who use the baseball antagonism as a vehicle for long-standing feuds. It is not unknown for accusations of witchcraft to be made between the teams at the height of the season, and for a time the council banned games in the village between the two teams because of the trouble they caused. In Chapter 5 I analyse the composition of the 'Redskins', and illustrate that this is a very close-knit group. The 'Braves' are similarly kinship-based. These two opposing blocks, then, which cut across the other divisions of the society, have latched onto the baseball rivalry. The whole set-up militates against the careful balance and conscious harmony that is sought in the other institutions, but it underlines the tendency to faction, and the tendency to dualism in organization.

Baseball in Cochiti now represents a competitive intrusion into an essentially non-competitive social system. The inter-weaving of Pueblo institutions acts as a counter to competitive and antagonistic tendencies in that it prevents alignments of hostiles into nonoverlapping camps which are absolutely opposed. The baseball teams are, of course, cross-cut by the other groups, but at the height of the season they dominate Cochiti activity, and so far, though the council has tried forcible tactics, no one seems to be able to rise above the events and work out a solution.

## IV

### MOIETIES

The above groups and categories – factions, veterans and baseball clubs – represent opposition and competition as opposed to conscious 'community'. The two moiety groups, the *Kivas*, represent a ritual division of labour which serves the ends of community. While they are separate and rather exclusive, they essentially complement each other. There is nothing that one *Kiva* can do of its own initiative. They always divide a single ritual between them, each presenting its own contribution towards a common goal. They are spoken of in English as 'halves' or 'sides', and it was often pointed out to me that 'half a man can't do anything'. Specifically the *Kivas* organize ceremonials and dances. These are held either in the *Kivas* themselves or in the *plaza*. Each *Kiva* has also a 'community house' where practices are held, drums painted and social get-togethers held. Traditionally the Turquoise

*Kiva* takes precedence over the Pumpkin, but it is difficult to see what this entails, except perhaps dancing first – but this is not invariable. Each *Kiva* has a head who runs its general affairs together with a *Mayorli* who is chiefly responsible for the singing and organization of the chorus. These two officials are assisted by a small 'council'. Two members of this council are designated 'blue' and are the ceremonial painters of paraphernalia. Within each *Kiva* is a cult of drummers. The pounding of the great ceremonial drums is both a strenuous and skilled activity and requires some dedication.

Membership rules for the *Kiva* are simple. Children belong to the father's *Kiva*, but when a girl marries she joins the *Kiva* of her husband. The moieties are neither exogamous nor endogamous, so it is quite likely that a girl will marry a man of the same *Kiva* – about 50 per cent do. The kinship aspects of the *Kiva* are discussed in the relevant chapter.

*Kiva* affairs take up an enormous amount of time, especially for men. Membership can be changed, but not lightly, and allegiance is strongly felt. A *Kiva*'s songs and dance steps are its property, and often when asking a Cochiti about a particular song, I was told 'that belongs to the other side'. Kick stick races were run between the two groups, but this was a ceremonial, not a competitive game. The essence of a *Kiva* was its ceremonial functions, and these were complementary to those of the other. The 'balance' between the two groups is preserved, at the political level, by alternating the Governorship and Assistant Governorship between the *Kivas* annually.

A different 'managing' society was associated with each *Kiva* and the *Kiva* head was drawn from that society. As each of these societies was itself associated with a medicine society, a dual arrangement of *Kivas* and societies was set up. This is not, however, as dual as it looks, as we shall see.[1]

## V

### SOCIETIES

It is to the societies that we must now turn. Like the *Kivas* they are primarily concerned with ceremony, but they also play a more direct part in government. Again, they complement each other,

[1] See Lévi-Strauss, 1958, ch.8.

the managing societies dividing functions, and the medicine societies dividing the labour of curing and fasting. We will take the managers first. The most prominent of these in some ways is the *Koshare* – the clowns or 'delight makers', as Bandalier called them. They are associated with the dead and the winter. They have a licence to satirize and abuse the living, and to make fun of anyone and everything. They are considered to be very powerful, and are 'feared' because of their power. They are linked to the *Flint* medicine society and to the Turquoise *Kiva*, and are close to the Cacique. This linkage may explain why the Turquoise *Kiva* is thought to be the most important. This society assumes 'spiritual' control of the Pueblo in the winter (October–March). Both men and women can be members and it can in fact perform some cures. It has also, until recently, controlled the office of sacristan. The *Kwirena* is the twin society to the *Koshare*, but it is not a clowning society. It directs the spiritual interests of the village during spring, summer and harvest. It is associated with the *Shikame* medicine society and the Pumpkin *Kiva*, and is open to both sexes. It does not seem to have curing functions.

These two societies alternate annually in the management of ritual. In collaboration with the War Captains and other ceremonial leaders, and under the spiritual guidance of the Cacique, they must see to it that the ceremonies are properly performed and the proprieties observed. They discipline bad dancers and supervise the actual dancing, acting as 'side' dancers, that is, dancing alongside the dance lines and seeing that costumes are in place and steps correct. They are also, like all the esoteric societies, involved in fasts and retreats for the benefit of the Pueblo.

The third society which can be considered 'managing' is the *Shrutzi*. This society 'cares for' the *Katsina* cult. It looks after the paraphernalia and arranges the dances. It too is linked to a medicine society – the *Giant*. It holds retreats and fasts like the others, but its main concern is the *Katsinas*.

The three medicine societies we have mentioned are the most important. There were other medicine societies and societies for hunting and war, but they have become extinct. Indeed, all the medicine societies are on the verge of extinction, and this will raise many problems for ceremony and government, but it is contrary to Pueblo values to force anyone to join. When one society dies out, another usually assumes its functions. We are not concerned here with the curing, fasting and other functions of the societies, but must record their political functions and affiliations. The *Flint* is the most important society, and it overlaps in membership with the *Koshare*. It is specifically associated with the Turquoise *Kiva*, and has the privilege of nominating the War Captain and his assistant. From its ranks the Cacique is chosen. Next in importance is the *Giant* society, which is associated with the *Shrutzi*, and hence the *Katsinas*, and nominates the Governor. As it is not associated with either *Koshare* or *Kwirena*, it has as its special responsibility the welfare of the 'common' people – those who have no ceremonial knowledge. (This probably explains its right to nominate the Governor, who deals with secular affairs.) Some of these are selected to join it in its retreats, for example. There is a society for women, the *Thundercloud* (Shiwanna), which is associated with the *Giant*. Finally, there is the *Shikame* society, which is linked to the *Kwirena* and the Pumpkin *Kiva*, and nominates the Fiscale. The interconnections of all these groups are represented in Figure 4.

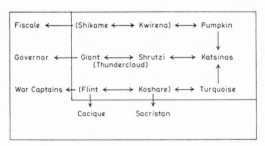

FIG. 4. Relation between societies, *Kivas*,
and officers in Cochiti

We must ask what is the nature of the 'association' between these various groups. We have already seen that the *Kwirena* and *Koshare* are ceremonially linked to the two *Kivas*, and that *Katsinas* are drawn from these moieties, which help to arrange the dances under the supervision of the *Shrutzi*. *Giant* and *Shrutzi* are linked ceremonially in that one makes prayer sticks for the other, and they join in each other's retreats and fasts. They do not overlap in membership, however, since a *Shrutzi* cannot be a member of any other society. The relation of *Shikame-Kwirena* and *Flint-Koshare* is different. They do overlap in membership, and are intimately related, sharing the same ceremonial house and many of the same duties. The two managing societies 'look after' the curing societies during their retreats, and the women of the managing societies prepare food for the medicine men. The *Thundercloud* society probably performs this function for the *Giants*, because women are not admitted to *Shrutzi* on account of its close association with the *Katsinas*. The *Flint* society also had under its wing, before they became extinct, the *Fire, Snake* and *Poshaianyi* societies, which some people think were in fact 'degrees' within *Flint*. The other extinct society which is of interest is the *Ompi*, or warriors. The head of this society was the acknowledged war magician of the tribe, and its membership was open to any man who had killed another and been purified by the society. The problem with the head *Ompi* is his relation to the War Captain. Is the latter one of the Spanish 'front' officials who took over when the warriors became extinct? Or were there two roles, that of war priest and 'General', of which only the latter has survived? There seems to be no clear evidence on this, but Lange summarizes what there is.

Recruitment to these societies, with the exception of the *Kivas*, is either voluntary, or by dedication in youth, or by curing or trapping. One can, that is, either join of one's own free will; or one can be dedicated by one's parents in childhood in return for some favour, or cure, or for the sake of one's health; or one can join in gratitude after being cured; or one can be 'trapped' into joining. The latter is achieved during society retreats, when a circle of cornmeal is drawn round the house. Anyone coming accidentally into the circle must join the society. There is a mystical rationale for this in the belief that such a person can only 'save his life' i.e., escape the effects of his ritual pollution, by joining. The factors which lead people to join voluntarily are as varied as the people themselves, but commentators agree that membership often 'runs in families'.[1] Fathers and sons, and pairs of brothers, often join the same society. This will make sense when we discuss the paternal extended family later.

The heads and senior officials of all these societies form a kind of ceremonial council, which parallels the secular council of *principales*. The great communal feasts need the co-operation of all officials and groups, and so do trials for witchcraft. This council

[1] See White, 1935.

is rather informal, but exists when the Cacique and the War Captains call together all the chief officials (including the Governor) to discuss ceremonial matters.

It is obvious that a large number of persons are required to fill all the specialized roles involved in the politico-religious system. This presents a problem now that migration, national service and schooling are draining away the necessary man-power. Up to now it has been possible, when one society ceased to exist, for another to take over its functions, but this cannot go on indefinitely. Now that the *Giant* society is extinct the Cacique names the Governor. This is not popular, since it gives even more power to the *Flint-Koshare*-Turquoise-War-Captain wing of the system. It may be that some form of election will eventually be substituted for the nomination system, although even with the latter, there is no question of a society forcing candidates on to an unwilling public. There is much sounding of opinion before the choice is made, and people usually say that it is obvious who will be chosen. In one case, however, when it was felt that the Governor and his assistant had not pulled their weight, the societies decided that they must repeat their term of office and make up for their deficiencies by doing better the second time. In this decision the people concurred. The method of officer selection bears a close resemblance in fact to the Tory party's traditional method of choosing a leader. This was done by a caucus, but not without finding out whom the party would in fact accept. As most of these positions carry with them arduous duties and responsibilities, there is no rush for them, and even a show of refusal is required of the candidates. As to the powerful position of the societies, the attitude of Cochiti seems to be that if people are willing to take on the arduous duties 'for the sake of the Pueblo', they deserve power and prestige. Indeed, gratitude was even expressed that there were persons with enough public spirit and compassion to fill the offices.

Nevertheless, the existence of the esoteric societies creates a deep division between the 'raw' people who 'have nothing', that is, have no ceremonial knowledge, and the 'cooked' who have. Lange notes that the distinction between these categories is rather vague. To be 'cooked' is a matter of ritual status, and is, of course, open only to conservatives and moderates. With the decline of the medicine societies the claim is becoming less important.

As I understand the politico-religious structure, there are two 'wings', associated with the two *Kivas* – the *Shikame-Kwirena*-Pumpkin wing and the *Flint-Koshare*-Turquoise wing. The latter takes ceremonial precedence, since it is the wing of the Cacique, the War Captains and the *Koshare*, who are the 'first men' in the origin of mankind. This is the wing of power, of death, of the winter. It is they who must turn the sun back on its course in mid-winter. The other wing takes over once things are returned to normal. The 'centre' of the system is the *Giant-Shrutzi* combination, which draws its *Katsinas* from both wings, looks after the *Crudos* (the 'uncooked' people), and appoints their Governor, the chief secular official, rotating him between the two *Kivas* along with his assistant, in the same way as the two main managing societies rotate their public ceremonial duties annually (and seasonally for that matter). I do not think this interpretation is very far from the picture of their own organization that the knowledgeable Cochiti carry in their heads. (It also corresponds quite closely to Goldfrank's analysis, allowing for changes since her time.[1]) Its ingenuity and balance are quite wonderful, but here we must note what many commentators have stressed, namely the lack of knowledge of the complexities of the system shown by the *Crudos*. 'Let the *chaianyi* get on with it, they know what they're doing' seems to be their attitude. This is, of course, disastrous when one runs out of medicine men, because then one is left with a vacuum.

The most noticeable fact to the student of Pueblo society, is the absence of any involvement of clans or other kin groups in the politico-religious system. Apart from recruitment to the *Kivas*, kinship and marriage have played no part in the exposition. We will take this up in the next chapter.

# VI

## CONCLUSION

There are a number of other groups and categories to be described. The only formal one among them is that of 'unmarried' versus 'married'. This was occasionally used for the purpose of picking teams for games, and some other purposes. Informal age groups exist as a result of non-formal circumstances. Those who have been through school together form a youth group with much interaction between members. Another division is that between the

[1] Goldfrank, 1927; also, Lange, 1959.

residents and non-residents. Many people keep their names on the tribal role but do not live in the village. They are denied certain privileges as a result (such as holding office), but many of them return quite frequently for dances, ceremonies and baseball games. A good many of those Lange describes as progressives fall into this category. Often a non-resident maintains a house in the village. Friendships are important, and amongst these we should include ceremonial relationships. The Cochiti have fully taken over the *compadre* system of sponsors for baptisms and weddings, but less formal friendships can be significant. In the old days, ceremonial friendship, such as that between two men who had killed a bear together, was very important. They would become 'hunting brothers', and regard themselves as bound by very special ties. These still exist among the older men. Finally, there are neighbours. These are important particularly in the built-up area, because where the houses are crowded together common problems arise regarding the maintenance of the structure. I heard a neighbour defined as 'someone who shares a wall with you'. This fits the *plaza* group particularly well. The village is divided into administrative districts largely for the convenience of the *Alguacilitos* and *Fiscalitos*, who take a district each for making announcements, etc.

Not all these groups and categories are of the same order. Some are formally recognized and named and given a place in the system, others are not named or even recognized, but play their part nevertheless. Most Cochiti seem to see the society as being composed of a series of opposites – Turquoise *vs* Pumpkin, Progressives *vs* Conservatives, 'Cooked' *vs* 'Raw', married *vs* unmarried, Redskins *vs* Braves, and so on. If they see any division as 'basic' it is that between the two *Kivas*, but, as we have said, this is a division of labour, radically different from the factional divisions. These two types of grouping in fact represent radically opposed principles; the two *Kivas* combine their efforts for the community, while the two factions tear the community apart.

# 4

# Kinship Structure

## I

As we have seen in the previous chapter, kinship groups are not connected in any formal way with the politico-ceremonial organization of the Pueblo. No offices are held by clans, and there is no succession to office which is determined by kinship. The *Kivas* are recruited by kinship and marriage, but they do not form kinship groups. Here there is a marked contrast with the Western Pueblos, and the usual interpretation of the difference is that 'kinship', in the form of clans and lineages, has ceased to play the part in Cochiti life that it once did. Particularly this is thought to be true of the clans. They are regarded as vestigial institutions stripped of their former functions.

It is, of course, very difficult to say anything about historical development when one does not have the data. The best that can be done is to make shrewd guesses on the basis of present-day facts. Thus Eggan says:

The kinship system of the Eastern Keresans was of the western lineage type, up to the time of the Rebellion, if our inferences from the Laguna situation are correct. After the Rebellion the Spaniards made a deliberate attempt to acculturate the Rio Grande Pueblos to Spanish models and used a great variety of means, including force, to achieve their ends. American influence in the last century has likewise been strong. As a result the Rio Grande Keresans have shifted from a lineage system to a bilateral kinship system, and different villages show various stages in that change.[1]

Cochiti, he reckons, shows the greatest degree of change.

In general, my guess is that Cochiti once had a kinship structure based on the matrilineal lineage and household, but that it has been the most acculturated (of the Keresans) toward Tewa and/or Spanish patterns.[2]

As for the question, 'was the kinship system of Cochiti ever of

[1] Eggan, 1950, p. 313.  [2] Quoted in Lange, 1959, p. 388.

the western lineage type?', this depends on what the 'western lineage type' was. As I interpret it, it was a system composed of house-based ritual groupings. There is nothing of this in Cochiti, and I do not see that we can know whether or not there ever was. There are lineages, but they do not seem to be built up from the same base as the Hopi 'lineages', and there is no evidence that they ever were. On the question of whether the kinship system (whatever it was) is now 'bilateral' (whatever that may mean), I think we can find rather conclusive evidence to the contrary.

I can speak here only for Cochiti. The other Eastern Keres villages may well have worked out other solutions. These villages are so remarkably self-contained that it would be surprising if they all produced exactly the same solution. Each has its own particular demographic and political problems which lead in different directions. There is an overall similarity of form, but about the content we are largely ignorant. What is more, we are never likely to know, which makes it all the more important to look at what material there is on Cochiti.

## II

In looking at a kinship system one wants to know what use is made of kinship ties in such matters as inheritance, succession and the determination of group membership. Succession can be easily dealt with. No succession to office or to any other status is based on ties of kinship. As regards inheritance the situation is more complex. It seems to be true that as far as house ownership and inheritance was concerned, the Western method was once prevalent if not universal, namely, that the house passed from mothers to daughters. Men had few personal possessions, and their ritual possessions were in the keeping of the *Kiva* or society. Land was held in usufruct, and on death passed back to the community for re-allocation. At some time, however, rights of inheritance must have been recognized, since all Cochiti who own land today claim to have got at least part of it by inheritance. A man could get land from any relative, I was told. Very often a man would give land to his children of either sex on their marriage, or he would indicate, before he died, to whom he wished various pieces of land to go. If he died intestate, the council would decide between his kin. There were no fixed rules except that a man's wishes should be respected. As more and more men came to build and own houses, the problem became more complex. Again there were no rules. but generally the first of a man's children to marry had a claim on his house. In effect, however, the older children often went off and built their own houses, and a much younger sibling eventually inherited the father's. The pattern now is moving towards much more individual building of houses. If a man dies without making any disposition regarding his house, the council will listen to claims from his near kin and decide between them. Individuals pursue their interests as they can. There are no hard-and-fast rules.

Marriage is, of course, monogamous, as it is in all the Pueblos. But in Cochiti the rate of marriage seems very high. There are very few bachelors, and re-marriage is the norm once a spouse has died. I recorded anything up to six re-marriages for one person. The resulting tangle of half-relatives that ensues is easy to imagine. Marriage in Cochiti is also for life. They accept the Catholic ban on divorce and Catholic rules of exogamy, and this acceptance seems longstanding (although dispensations are common and easily obtained). It may well be that marriage has always been fairly stable; it is impossible to tell. This durability of marriage is important, for reasons which will be explained.

We can now turn to the groups recruited by kinship and marriage extant in Cochiti and examine their structure and their functions. Like the socio-religious groups, some are explicitly recognized, some are not. They are the Clan; the Lineage; the Maternal Extended Family; the *Kiva*; the Paternal Extended Family; and the Nuclear Family.

### CLAN – *hánuch-hánu*

(*Hánu* is a word for 'people' in the sense of a social group. The suffix *-ch* is usually used when the word is qualified by a clan name, e.g., *t'sits hánuch* 'water clan'.)

Cochiti clans are matrilineal and named.[1] Members of clans address each other by the clan name. These names are of natural phenomena, animals, etc., but no totemic observances are connected with the names. The clans are not linked in any phratry

---

[1] There were, in 1948, ten clans ranging in size from 13 members (Pumpkin) to 114 (Oak), with an average of approx. 38. (See Lange, 1959, p. 519 for details.) The situation was similar in 1958-9.

system, nor are they localized. In theory they are not segmented, and for clan purposes no segmentation is recognized. When the clan acts as a clan it acts as a whole. The Cochiti do not see the clan as being 'made up' of lineages. There is therefore no 'merging segmentary' series of lineages in the clan, and relationships are not remembered for many generations back. The clan is exogamous, and there are few exceptions to the exogamic rule. If, however, between two members of a large clan who want to marry no possible blood relationship is suspected, the rule can be reluctantly waived. This is particularly true if one of the partners is descended from an immigrant. These cases are, however, very rare and seem to be related to clan size both in Cochiti and other Keres Pueblos.[1]

Clans have important functions in relation to marriage. When two young people wish to marry, their respective clans, and their father's clans, have to be informed, and the clans of the boy must ask formal permission from the clan of the girl. The performing of the marriage ceremony and the sanctifying of the marriage are in the hands of the clans. This is not to say that they would ever withhold their permission, but without it, the marriage is not truly valid. For second and subsequent marriages this is not so important, and nowadays the clan ceremony is supplemented by the Catholic marriage. But this comes a poor second. It simply sets the seal on an accomplished fact. The elaboration of marriage rites in Cochiti underlines the importance of the relationship.

The second major function of the clan is that of healing. This is achieved by adopting the sick person into one or more clans, which contrasts with the Hopi method of adoption by an individual 'doctor father'. Adoption is not confined to the sick. Young children are often adopted into clans other than their own in order to ensure their health and happiness, and in-marrying wives from clanless tribes are similarly adopted, both for their health and because it is unthinkable that a woman should not have a clan to pass on to her children. There is a distinction between real adoption and healing adoption. In real adoption, the adoptee becomes truly a member of the clan and passes it on to her children. In healing adoption, on the other hand, the woman will not pass on the clan to her children, and no one so adopted will be expected to keep up clan obligations or observe the rule of exogamy with

[1] See White, 1942 and 1962.

regard to the adopting clan. They may do so 'out of respect', but are not so obliged. Despite this distinction, it should be remembered that a real adoption is also thought beneficial to health. I have discussed elsewhere the relation of this form of healing to that practised by the medicine societies.[1]

The economic importance of the clan used to be greater when agriculture was more important. A man could ask the clan for help in getting in his harvest. He could also depend on it to give him corn, etc., in time of need. If the clan was too small, he could ask the village officers to muster the unmarried to help him, or he could use this as his sole source of aid. More general economic functions are hard to trace. It is often asserted that the clan would look after the interests of its members, but it is probable that this was a spiritual and not a material help. One informant described how, if a man had not enough land, his clansmen would 'speak up for him', or re-apportion theirs to give him some. As Cochiti is not short of land this must have been a rare problem. There is no evidence that the clans owned land in common. The coming of the community harvester and truck has obviated the need for clan help in harvesting. The lack of 'economic' functions of clans today is not, therefore, a result of a 'decline' of the clans, but of changes – including decline – in agriculture.

For any man, then, the clan governs his marriage choice, sanctifies his marriage and offers help and succour. It also heals sickness and provides spiritual and emotional security to those adopted into it, as well as its natal members.

There was usually, and still is for some clans, an accepted 'elder'. He would be the chief spokesman of the clan and the man to whom application should be made for harvest help, marriage arrangements and the like. One very respected man at present is regularly addressed by his clansmen and others as *shrutsuna náwa*, and referred to by others as *shrutsuna k'eanawashe* (Fox (clan), their 'elder'). He is supposed to be the oldest male of the clan, but there seems to be no regular way of deciding on the position, and there could well be several old respected men who arranged clan affairs. The oldest woman of the clan is accorded great respect and her opinion taken into account.

The clan, then, has no connection with government and public ritual. No offices are held by the clan, no land owned by it. But

[1] See Fox, 1960 and 1964.

nevertheless, it is very important to the Cochiti. Not to have a clan is tantamount to not having a mother. It is to be in a social sense 'motherless', without identity, comfort, succour and, above all, without health. The clan is all these things. Its identification with a real mother is very close, and hence it is surrounded by strong affect, which is the basis of its healing power. It is perhaps also the basis of the strong sentiment in favour of exogamy. Thus, despite its lack of connection with ritual and governmental affairs, the clan is a persistent and important element in Cochiti society. Those who see it as having 'declined' are probably according it too large a role in previous decades. Thinking that it *should* have some connection with civic and religious organization, they construe its seeming lack of connection as evidence of degeneracy. The clan is important in Cochiti, but its importance is a mystical rather than a practical matter.

## III

### LINEAGE

The word *másanyi* literally means 'leaf', and is used to refer to 'branches' of families etc., but most often to describe a lineage. The lineages are not thought of as 'leaves' of the *clan* twig however. In fact the word is not used as a name, but as a description. Various branches of a lineage can be described as *másanyi*, and indeed the word is more likely to be used for such sub-lineages than for the lineage as a whole. It simply describes a *de facto* grouping.

The lineage is all the descendants in the female line of a known (usually) female ancestress. Some younger members of the lineage may not know who the apical ancestress is, and the group is not known by her name, or for that matter by any name. When speaking of such a group, the Cochiti will name some prominent female member and refer to her 'people' (*hánu*), or 'leaf' (*másanyi*). But, as I have indicated, this is not a named group. It emerges from the fact that a group of people closely related in the female line regard themselves for many purposes as 'separate' from other similar groups. Thus, while they may know that some ultimate blood relationship exists between themselves and a similar group, they will regard themselves as separate and independent of such a group, while to other groups within the same clan they will deny any blood tie at all. The more sophisticated, if pressed, will say that ultimately all clanspeople must be related, but this relationship, while seen on the model of 'real' relationship, is not the same thing. It is a mystical bond.

This underlines my statement that the clan is not thought of as being composed of lineages. One is not a member of a clan through membership in a lineage. Indeed, it is possible to be without a lineage, e.g., in the case of an in-marrying stranger, and yet be fully and completely a member of a clan. It would be possible for the lineage to disappear completely as an effective grouping without affecting the clan. Clan membership is a kind of nationality. One takes the nationality of one's mother, that is all. The lineage is a *de facto* grouping based on interaction for certain specific purposes. The mere fact that recruitment to clans is matrilineal does not in itself produce 'grouping on a lineage basis'. What does?

In the past the household may have contributed. Its matri-local nature would provide the basis for lineage organization, as in the Western Pueblos. But it is not certain that Cochiti household organization was even predominantly matrilocal, and the 'house' as such does not seem to have had any ritual value as in the West. But even without this there was a basis in the deep and lasting bond between mothers and daughters. Whether or not they lived together, they constituted probably the most strongly knit of all Cochiti groups. This would provide the core of the lineage: the various 'leaves' would be mothers and their daughters and their grand-daughters.

We can only understand the lineage fully, however, by looking at it in action. It is, in effect, the actually operative group of matrilineal kin. The clan as such only operates in the 'formal' spheres outlined above. Any action it takes has to be initiated, and this will be initiated by an individual in consultation with his closest matrilineal kin, i.e., his lineage. It would be the lineage which actually undertook the arrangements for a marriage or an adoption – got together the food, cleaned the house, cooked the food, fixed the times, etc. The lineage would call in the clanspeople at the appropriate times and fully consult them at all stages, but the lineage would do the 'work'. There are spheres in which the lineage can act independently of the clan as a whole. These are matters which concern close matrilineal kin, such as the fate of an illegitimate child of a member, or the choice of godparents for a child and its christening, or the naming of a child, or, on some occasions, the disciplining of a young man or woman. There is no necessity to call in the clan on these occasions, although prominent non-lineage members of the clan might be consulted. These are simply matters for people of the same blood to settle. Affines, again, might be consulted – if, say, a woman of the lineage were married to an outstanding medicine man or official he might be asked to advise – but the final decision rests with the lineage itself. The outsider would be essentially a consultant: he has no vote.

Because of the respect for age, the oldest male is usually the leader of such a group, but a vigorous and important younger man might well be the effective leader. The opinions of the old ladies carry greater weight here than in clan matters. The elders of the lineage will always try to see that peace and amity prevail within it and will try to make children behave properly and married members live at peace with their spouses. Particularly are they concerned with the children. Childbirth is in the hands of the women of the lineage (with medicine society help), and the good conduct of children in the hands of the men. The lineage sees the child into the world, launches it on its way, watches over its marriage and carries a large part of the burden of seeing it into the next world. In all these things it might be aided by its affines, but the task is exclusively the responsibility of the lineage itself.

This is not a 'corporate' group in the full sense of the word. It does not own property, unless it is household-based. But even then, the men of the lineage cannot in any sense be said to own the house. They have rights in it; it could not be disposed of without their consent; but they do not have exclusive use of it and the in-marrying husband has effectively more say in its affairs than they do. If they wish, say, to leave their wives and return to the house, they must ask the permission of the head of the house, the oldest husband. He is not likely to refuse, but he has to be asked.

The position of the children of men of the lineage is interesting. While they are not members of it, they are the children of members and this gives them a special status. The Cochiti have no particular ideology of procreation. They do not see the relevance. A child belongs to its mother's clan, but it is still its father's child. Thus, when a girl gets married, her father will call on his lineage, and ultimately his clan, to help in the marriage. This is not necessary to the ceremony – illegitimate children are validly married without it – but it is always done and is regarded as the proper thing to do.

The interaction between members of the lineage is a matter of their choice. Because of the very close ties between mothers and their daughters, and for that matter, mothers and sons (not so much brothers and sisters), it is usually quite intensive. But visiting and mutual aid cannot be regarded as essential properties of the lineage; they are not activities exclusive to lineage members. If one can pin down what the lineage 'does', I think it would resolve itself into (a) initiating action that will involve a clan mobilization, and (b) looking after the welfare of its children in particular, and its members in general.

The clan-lineage relationship will vary, of course, with the size of the clan. Where a clan consists of one lineage only, the distinction obviously ceases to exist. In the large Oak clan, on the other hand, the lineages have a 'separatist' tendency which leads to the abrogation of the exogamy rule and to intra-clan healing.

I stress again that the clan is not organized as a collection of lineages. There is not, for example, any council of lineage heads running clan affairs. The lineage is not a corporation. When a lineage is organizing a wedding, it calls on other clan members as individuals, it does not simply inform the 'heads' of the lineages. In any case, these latter are not formal officials but informal leaders. The lineage is simply a close group of matrilineal kin descended from an ancestress known at least to the older members. Its members co-operate in certain matters and initiate such clan activities as they need. Its basis is the strong tie between mothers and their children, and mothers and daughters in particular, which continues to operate even after the mother's death. Its main concern is with the children of its members. It is not necessary to the clan organization, although it is an effective part of it, and shares in the strong sentiments concerning motherhood and matrilineal descent.

## IV

### MATERNAL EXTENDED FAMILY

There is no term for this grouping in Keres. It would be referred to by some descriptive phrase. (I shall call it the 'matrifamily' for

convenience.) The context would indicate what group was intended. Its core is the same as the core of the lineage – the group
of women related in the female line, usually a mother and her
daughters and daughters' daughters, with their dependent and
unmarried children. But the men of this group are the husbands
of the women. There might also be unmarried sons and brothers,
but unmarried men are rare in Cochiti. Sometimes a widower will
move back to his sister's house, sometimes not, but the main
grouping consists of women with their husbands and dependent
children. It thus overlaps with the lineage in its female and unmarried male membership, and insofar as the informal activities
of the women are concerned, it makes little sense to try to divide
them between lineage and matrifamily activities. The crucial distinction lies in the different involvement of the two sets of males, –
'brothers' and 'husbands'. For example, a woman's husband has
no particular responsibility towards her sister's child's marriage:
her brother has. On the other hand, the brother has no particular
responsibility for providing his sister's children with food: the
husband has. Nor does the brother have any responsibility for the
upkeep of his sister's house after he has married: her husband must
undertake this work.

In short, anything that concerns the house or houses of the
women of the matrifamily is the concern of the husbands. This is
the 'domestic' unit of Cochiti society. The husbands have to see
to it that the women have houses, clothes and food for themselves
and their children. The husbands market the produce of the
women's labour unless the women do this themselves. This is the
economic unit as far as houses are concerned, although each
individual family within it has its own budget for its immediate
needs. This would have been the group which occupied the house
in the matrilocal days. Hence its concern with house-building and
repairing, and with economic co-operation, is a continuance of
this tradition, even though in these days houses are rarely inhabited
by more than one family. It provides a labour force for house-
building drawn from the men who, since they live in the houses,
can be expected to take an interest in the upkeep. All the husbands
together see to it that the women of the group are properly housed.
This is their primary function as a group. The bond here is
that between a man and his son-in-law. These will be most intimately concerned with routine matters affecting the house. The

obligations of this relationship are clearly recognized by the Cochiti.

This is the most obvious of the kinship groupings in Cochiti. It is constantly in action. Its women are always visiting each other, working together, looking after each other's children, helping each other in sickness, and so on. Their husbands are drawn into the net, and form a little men's club amongst themselves. Whereas brothers and sisters are separated residentially, and are not emotionally particularly close either, husband and wife are in constant interaction, and many marriages are very close. While the lineage lies dormant most of the time, the matrifamily is in constant operation. But you will not normally find a married man plastering his married sister's house, nor a father interfering in his daughter's marriage.

These distinctions can, of course, become blurred in some circumstances. If a lineage has no males, or no active males, the husbands must take over some of its male functions. Personal differences may lead to a severance of contact which impedes lineage functioning. Often, for example, *padrinos* will be called upon to perform the roles which should fall to the brothers. But other things being equal, the distinction between lineage and matrifamily, in terms of the different functions of the respective male members, is quite clear.

V

MOIETY – (*Kiva* – *Estufa*) – *chítya, shipapu*

The ordinary Keres term for moiety is *chítya*, and the ceremonial term *shipapu*, the word for the place of emergence in Keres cosmology which is also used to translate 'heaven'. Details about the composition and organization of the *Kivas* have been given earlier. I want to consider here the question of the place of the *Kiva* in the kinship system. Despite the fact that the two *Kivas* are recruited by kinship and marriage (a man takes his father's *Kiva*, a woman her husband's), Lange will not call them kinship groups, largely because there is an optative element in membership. The number of men who actually change *Kiva* is, however, extremely small, and membership is deeply felt. Even if more men changed their *Kiva*, this would not support his point. In some patrilineal systems it is possible for a man to change his clan, but this does not alter the structure of the system. (Interestingly, I have not come across a matrilineal system with a like provision.)

My objection to calling the *Kiva* a kinship *group* would be different. It would be simply that all its members are not kin to each other either in a real or mystical sense. Members of a clan are not kin in any sense, to all other members, but ideologically they regard each other as bound together by ties of mystical relationship on the model of matrilineal kinship. This is not so with the *Kiva*. It is not then a kin group either truly or in fiction. It does not pretend to be. But it is discussed here because it *recruits* members by kinship and marriage. In a sense, then, *Kiva* membership is an exact parallel with clan membership for males at least. It is a kind of nationality. One has the same *Kiva* nationality as one's father. Like the clan it is not in theory segmented. Each member is a citizen in his own right. But like the clan it is *de facto* divided into smaller operative groups. Because the *Kiva* is highly organized and is in constant operation, the relation of these smaller groups to it is not the same as the relation of lineages to clans. They are also differently composed. While the lineage is a group of consanguines, the smaller unit of the *Kiva* includes the wives of its males. In this sense it is the opposite of the matrifamily. But the matrifamily is not a sub-unit of the clan in the way that what we shall call the paternal extended family is a sub-unit of the *Kiva*.

It is this recruitment by marriage that makes the *Kiva* interesting. Marriage is crucial both to the matrifamily and to the *Kiva*, supplying men to one and women to the other. The reasons for this are difficult to ascertain. *Kiva* affairs are overwhelmingly in male hands. Women have absolutely no say in them. Women merely serve as dancing partners and help to keep the structures in good repair. They also cook and serve food to the dancers during ceremonials. There is no reason, I suppose, why a man should not have his sister do these things, except that it would probably not be practicable. He is in constant association with his wife, not his sister, and she would be the obvious person to help out in the women's side of *Kiva* affairs. One can, I think, make too much of women's membership. The vast majority of time and effort spent in *Kiva* affairs is a man's business, but for the small amount of female help that is needed men turn to their wives. Thus, if a woman remarries often, she might change *Kiva* several times. Offices and ritual knowledge are in the hands of the men, and this knowledge passes down from fathers to sons. Women are 'helpers' in their husband's *Kivas*.

On the other hand, it would not do to underestimate their role. Some old ladies of longstanding marriages are very firmly attached to their *Kivas*. They know the songs by heart and feel very much identified with the organization. Young women, on the other hand, are often indifferent. 'You just follow the men's steps' (in the dancing), I was told, 'that's all'. However, as far as ritual is concerned, a woman is thoroughly enmeshed in her husband's moiety.

A deeper reason might be found in the fact that *Kiva* rituals are almost exclusively concerned with fertility.[1] The brother-sister relationship is 'infertile', but not the husband-wife. Hence the latter relationship is obviously the one on which to rest fertility rituals, that is, the one between the men of the moiety and the women married to them. This may, of course, involve a man and his real sister or clanswoman, as the *Kivas* are not exogamous, but the role would be different.

This interpretation, however, has not been checked against Cochiti notions of the situation.

In roughly 50 per cent of marriages a woman does not change *Kiva*. But she does change her paternal extended family, and this makes a considerable difference in her life. We shall deal with this in the next section.

As has been indicated, the *Kivas* are largely concerned with ritual. But as a result of the constant close association between the men of the *Kiva*, many other activities involve *Kiva* mates. These are, however, largely concerned with reconciling other tasks with the time demands of the ritual activity. For example, on an archaeological dig that was in progress on the reservation, one man was put in charge of recruiting Indian labour. He was in fact the head drummer of one of the *Kivas*. He did supply the labour (six men) but not always the same men. He called up his *Kiva* mates in turn so they might all have time to do their practising and preparation for the annual corn dance. Similarly, many men who hold paid jobs in Anglo towns or on Anglo farms will find substitutes from among their *Kiva* fellows when they are required for ceremonial duties. The men most likely to be chosen will be members of the same paternal extended family, but, if none of

[1] See Haeberlin, 1916.

these are available, the *Kiva* organizers will pick an unrelated member.

The above merely serves to underline the reality of *Kiva* membership for men. It is for them something as deeply felt as is membership in a clan for a woman. It expresses in its own way the attachment of fathers and sons. One of the men cited by Lange as opting out of his natal *Kiva*, in fact later returned to it. He explained that he had never been easy at his earlier move and that he would not have done it but for the extreme dictates of conscience. 'You have to feel it real deep in your heart before you change', he told me. When the dispute had cooled somewhat he returned, and was relieved to do so. The original move, while necessary, was like a denial of his father, and it hurt.

The *Kivas*, along with the *Katsina* cult, which is now largely *Kiva*-based and is another virtually all-male affair, represent the expressive side of the culture. They handle the public rituals, the dances, the singing, and even a large part of the recreation. A good deal of the knowledge of song, dance and ritual is taught to members generally by the *Kiva* leaders and societies associated with the *Kivas*. But much of it is passed down from men to their sons outside this formal instruction. The unit for this transmission is the paternal extended family, which we will now consider.

# VI

## PATERNAL EXTENDED FAMILY

There is no term for this in Keres. It might be referred to as 'the boys of so-and-so' or some similar phrase. Because of the patrilineal inheritance of Spanish surnames, it will often be referred to by the surname if this is distinctive – the *Suinas*, *Pecoses*, etc. I shall call it the 'patrifamily'. It consists of the male descendants of a common ancestor over three or more generations, with their wives and dependent children. It is, in a sense, the exact opposite of the matrifamily, but while the matrifamily is not a sub-unit of anything, the patrifamily is definitely the sub-unit of the *Kiva*. While the relationship between patrifamily and *Kiva* may seem to resemble that between lineage and clan, it is in fact different in that the *Kiva* initiates action and calls on the patrifamily to help carry it out. Also the *Kiva*, unlike the clan, is in constant action, and men will probably spend even more time with their *Kiva* fellows as a whole than with the members of their patrifamily. As with the clan, the *Kiva* is not seen formally as being composed of extended families. And much more so than the clan, it does not operate on this basis. Every member of the *Kiva* is a member in his own right. There are no offices which pass down the male line. But like the lineage it is a *de facto* grouping which the *Kiva* takes into account. For example, if a woman is asked to dance and does not wish to do so, it is considered legitimate for her to ask a sister-in-law, i.e., another female member of the patrifamily, to take her place. Usually each patrifamily is simply required to provide one or more pairs according to its size. Informants will deny this at the ideological level, stressing the individual's direct responsibility to the *Kiva*, but in fact this is how it works out. Sometimes the enthusiastic leader of a patrifamily will offer more than his fair share of pairs to the *Kiva* for a dance, and in dances with unlimited numbers his offer is usually accepted.

How does this group arise? It is not and could not be household-based, and if the *Kiva* acts in unison and as a corporation, how does this sub-group emerge? The answer lies in the aforementioned informal learning situations. As a man takes his father's *Kiva*, the father is anxious to see that he should acquit himself well in singing, dancing, drumming or whatever is his bent. Therefore, the boy will be encouraged at an early age to move his feet in rhythm to the drum, tapped probably by an old grandfather or paternal uncle, and to attempt the words and music of the simpler songs. A girl is not so much encouraged, although pleasure is expressed if she makes the attempt to dance. Many hours in the evening are spent in this activity, with male members of the patrifamily and their wives gathering at the old man's house to practise and play with the children. For his very earliest appearance in public dances ( a boy of four or five may well be allowed to dance in the corn dance) he will be shepherded by his father and older brothers and paternal uncles rather than by his *Kiva* officials. He is thought too young to be able to take the full formal education and practice and this will be arranged within the patrifamily. Thus he grows up under the nurturant gentle discipline of these male relatives and their wives. The wives will help to dress him in his costume, although his paint and feathers must be applied by the appropriate *Kiva* officials, and they will watch solicitously while he dances for any signs of fatigue and, with the approval of the *Kwirena* or *Koshare*, hustle him away to rest. Thus, each child of the patrifamily has a group of nurturant males and females anxious to see him safely through his ritual life.

Although they are basically nurturant, the old men of the group have high standards of correctness, and will see to it that the youngster lives up to them. They are immensely kind, but immensely stern. Hence the boy develops the profound identification with his male relatives which is the basis of the strong male affect surrounding *Kiva* membership. One man, who because of his position in a managing society had to take over the leadership of the opposite *Kiva* to his own, refused to relinquish his original membership. He conscientiously carried out his duties to the alien *Kiva*, but he would not take himself off the roll of his natal moiety. He could not 'deny his fathers'.

The patrifamily is concerned solely with the ritual life of its children and members, not with marriage, naming or adoption, or discipline in anything but ritual matters. If a young man gets drunk too regularly it is of no concern to the patrifamily. But if he gets drunk during a ceremony and fails to perform his part properly, then he can expect the anger of his 'fathers' and 'brothers'. In the former case, it would be for his mother's brother to chastise him, or to ask his *padrino* to do so, but the males of the patrifamily would not interfere unless it affected his ritual performance. Nor would they interfere if he ill-treated his wife, unless this prevented her from dancing.

The importance of this group, then, lies in its part in passing on the basic techniques and values which are the groundwork of adequate ritual performance. As with the lineage, other functions may accrue to it. Very often members help with each other's harvests and ploughing, or in other economic matters. But these activities are accidental features of the patrifamily and occur under special circumstances, such as when its members marry women who come from outside Cochiti, or who have no living female relatives. In such cases the men have no matrifamily to join and will tend to form an economic 'housekeeping' unit amongst themselves. There was only one such example to my knowledge.

Some of these groups are stronger than others. An important and active old man with many sons and paternal nephews will weld an imposing group of singers, dancers, drummers, pole carriers and officials out of his little extended family. Wives will be firmly bound to such a group and deeply involved in *Kiva* affairs. A weak old man, on the other hand, may not have such success and his group will be loosely knit and not important. There is more room for variation here than in the matrifamily.

The group gains its place on the basis of three factors. Firstly, there is the enormous importance of the ritual and expressive side of the culture, which far outweighs the importance of the economic or political. Second, there is the sheer fact of patrilineal inheritance of *Kiva* membership for men and the necessity of the help of their spouses. Thirdly, there is the importance of laying the groundwork of a good ritual performance and keeping young men up to scratch. This is achieved within the patrifamily rather than in the *Kiva* at large; the latter expects each patrifamily to present it with young men who can dance, sing and be conscientious in their duties.

These groups are not named and are not really corporate except in a broad sense. But in some ways this is the most important kinship group in the tribe, in that it ensures the continuous successful ritual socialization of the young, without which most that is distinctive in Cochiti culture would wither.

I have deliberately referred to this group as the patri-*family*, rather than the patri-*lineage*, although it will be obvious that it has many characteristics of a patrilineage. I have done this because I wish to reserve discussion of its patrilineal nature for Chapter 6. Also, it is not in any sense erroneous to call it a paternal extended family. Technically it is, and I think this is how the Cochiti see it. But clearly for purposes of analysis one could regard it as a patrilineage which incorporates the women marrying into it.

We are working here at two levels. On the one hand we have the view of their social groups which I assume the Cochiti to have on the basis of their statements and behaviour. On the other hand, we have the view of their society which is analytically most satisfactory. For the time being, then, I will stick to 'patrifamily', remembering that one can treat the 'line' of males as an analytically separate entity, and see the women as being merely moved about between the lines, and not in any intrinsic sense a part of them.

# VII

NUCLEAR FAMILY

Again there is no term for nuclear family. This is a somewhat submerged group tending to have few functions that are peculiar to it. It mostly acts as a unit of the matrifamily and the patrifamily. However, it is increasingly becoming the household unit, especially as men now like to build a house for independent occupation. A man will put up the money and materials, while his wife calls on her male affines to help in the labour and her female consanguines to aid with feeding them, and plastering the house. But independent housing for the family has led to the emergence of the nuclear family as a discrete unit. Each household has its own budget, and runs its own immediate affairs. The advent of television has had the same effect on Cochiti as on ourselves, i.e., of turning the family more in upon itself (although, when not all members of the matrifamily have television, this tends to be the tele-watching unit). Because of its independence in housing and because it runs most of its own day-to-day affairs, the family would appear to the casual observer to be the basic kinship unit. But in fact, except in very isolated families, it does very little of importance by itself. The men are away from the house most of the time, and the women seek company and help from their sisters and daughters married in other houses. It is a fair generalization to say that no day passes without the women of the matrifamily getting together for some function, if only to gossip. Nothing in the ritual sphere can be done by the family alone, and when it comes to weddings and healings, quite different groups take over.

Each family is, of course, the pivot of several of these groups, and each member is involved either as full participant, or helper, or observer, in everything that the others are doing. The various affairs, then, of each member of the family will bring the extended groups of the other members into play. But for many purposes the family is split, and other groups take precedence. When the children marry, the group splits along the two axes of the family, father-son and mother-daughter. Father and son remain united in ritual, mother and daughter in domestic matters. Cutting across these divisions with the family are those of lineage and clan, which unite mother and children but exclude father.

The family, then, handles all the day-to-day domestic tasks and aspects of socialization that are not the province of any of the groups previously mentioned. This in fact leaves quite a lot of informal work for the family to do, but as a unit it has no real place in the overall kinship structure except as the pivot of action for the extended kin-groups of its members. It is, however, growing in importance. Fathers, for example, are becoming somewhat more inclined to discipline their children, but as there is so little discipline of children this does not loom large. Thus, while for some purposes husband and wife are a unit (as are mother and daughter; father and son; brother and sister, etc.), the family as such can perhaps best be viewed in terms of structure as the meeting point of several kin-groups rather than a group in its own right.

This is not to overlook its importance in general as opposed to specific socialization. The sheer day-to-day business of living together will obviously have profound effects on the growing child. In terms of variables affecting personality development, Cochiti should be counted as a 'nuclear family' society. But as regards discipline, this is largely taken out of the hands of the family itself. The ritual leaders, the secular officials, the 'river men' (ceremonial disciplinarians), the *Katsinas*, the lineage and clan elders, and the paternal elders, all loom so large in discipline that there is little left for the family. This makes family relationships in the main very easy, and one is struck by the 'rather consistent respect for any individual' that Lange notes.

The family, then, as a rather submerged unit in the past, is becoming more prominent, but is still not much more than a meeting point for other groups in the structural sense. Its importance to its individual members, however, must not be overlooked.

# 5

# Genealogical Evidence

## I

In the illustrations which follow I have used a numbering system for personnel. This is for two reasons: firstly, it makes cross reference easy, and secondly, it goes some way to disguising the identity of the persons concerned.

A caution should be noted with respect to this evidence. It concerns people who were largely members of the conservative-moderate core of the Pueblo, and, of course, the veterans who belonged by birth to this section. As will be seen, progressives enter the picture at a few points, but they are not prominent. A good many progressives are, however, only part-time residents of the village, while those that are full-time tend to get drawn into kinship affairs anyway. There are represented here, however, about 200 people, and the full-time resident population of Cochiti is only a little over 300, so that two-thirds of the permanent population is accounted for. My guess is that well over half the rest fit into the picture I have outlined, and that it is the die-hard progressives and their families that have drifted away from the village in large numbers. The importance of the patrifamily in 'holding' its members is crucial here and doubles its importance as a kinship unit in Cochiti.

I have included in this evidence only assemblies and activities that I actually witnessed or investigated. The cure I report actually took place before I arrived, but it was fresh in the memory of the participants, all of whom I knew intimately, and its repercussions were still being felt.

I should stress here that these groups are not just an anthropologist's abstractions. The women of the matrifamily and lineage really are a very close, intimate and almost self-contained group, strongly attached to each other, and recognizing this attachment. The men of the patrifamily are equally intimately bound to one another and recognize their separateness from other such groups. The spouses are pulled into these groups with various degrees of intensity, particularly the men into the matrifamily. When this intimacy amongst members breaks down in a particular case, the disaster is recognized and talked about. An estrangement amongst members of such a group is discussed and its implications for the group brooded upon.

The qualitative aspects of this group feeling are difficult to convey, but it is necessary to note them. These groups are not just statistical entities, not just the results of interaction of a patterned kind. They are true groups, in that they exist in the minds of their members as groups.

It would have been possible with the aid of baptismal records and Goldfrank's genealogies to have found wider linkages for some of the groups here. But I have only taken genealogical depth as far as the Cochiti themselves reckoned and recognized it.

## II

### LINEAGE AND CLAN

Genealogy I shows a large Oak lineage and a segment of an Ivy

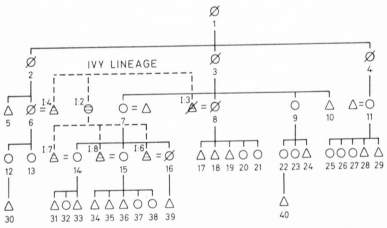

GENEALOGY I. Oak lineage A (Oa: ), and part of Ivy lineage (I: )
(Oblique lines indicate decease)

lineage with which it is intertwined in marriage. The husbands of the living female members have been added to make discussion of the matrifamily easier. This group is interesting in that in two successive generations brothers from the Ivy lineage married sisters from the Oak. The Oak lineage is itself divided into three 'leaves', the children of Oa:2, Oa:3, and Oa:4. Oa:2 and Oa:3 leaves are still very close, while Oa:4 is more distant, both in space and interaction. Other members of the lineage, who have left the Pueblo and are out of effective contact, are not represented. Oa:30 is illegitimate, while the 'husband' of Oa:9 is estranged from her. They were never married by the Catholic or native ceremonies, in any case. Oa:34 was born illegitimately to Oa:15 and reared by Oa:7 and her husband, whom he regards as his parents.

[The complete Ivy lineage is given in Genealogy II. It is an

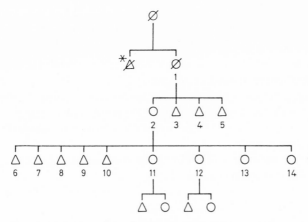

* *died in 1956, old, blind and inactive*

GENEALOGY II. Ivy lineage (I: )

interesting example of preponderance of males. The five eldest children of I:2 were all boys. Her younger daughters are now producing children, including daughters, so the lineage will continue. The Oak lineage, on the other hand, shows a preponderance of females. Such factors can strongly affect the functioning of lineages.]

The best way to see the lineage in action is to watch it assemble. While a good deal of day-to-day activity falls within the sphere of lineage affairs, it is in assemblies that we can most indisputably identify it. Three assemblies in particular involved the Oak and

Ivy lineages shown here: a christening, a wedding, and a healing.

The christening was of a child of a man of the lineage: Oa:28. He chose as *padrino* and *madrina* Oa:17 and his wife. After the actual christening in church there was feasting in the house of Oa:11, and prominent amongst the cooks and organizers were Oa:7 and her two daughters, and Oa:9. Both Oa:12 and Oa:13 helped with the general arrangements. While many people came to the feast, it was the lineage members who did the work. They were particularly important on this occasion, as the father of the baby had married a girl from outside the Pueblo, so that there was no mother's lineage to carry the major burden. Even if there had been, the father would have called on his own lineage to help, and this would have been granted. A speech on behalf of the father's lineage was made by Oa:10, and a short address by Oa:17. Oa:10 can be taken as the 'head' of this lineage, although Oa:5 was in many ways more active. Oa:10 was old and retiring. The lineage in fact did not have a strong male head, and in most difficulties turned to Oa:7, who often consulted her husband. On this occasion, the husband came along, but remained in the background, made no speeches, and did not interfere in any way. For most of the time he sat with I:4, an old blind man who had been brought along by his two daughters. Before leaving, both of them thanked Oa:11 for having them.

This christening was doubly interesting because Oa:11 is somewhat isolated from her lineage kin, and is to some extent assimilated with her husband's mother's matrifamily. But on this occasion she called on her lineage to help her son. She actually told Oa:17 first, as he was to be *padrino*, and he sent his children to tell Oa:7 and Oa:10. Also, this shows the concern of the lineage for the child of a male member.

The Oak clan at large was not specifically called upon in this event. There would have been no reason for it. Had the child been an actual child of the lineage, and hence a child of the clan, at least the elders of the clan, I was told, would have been invited individually as a matter of courtesy.

The second assembly, the marriage of Oa:35, takes us deeper into the kinship mesh. Here, as in the christening, we must remember that it is the parents of the child(ren) that are concerned in the arrangements. The child's own clan actually undertakes the main burden of the business, and its participation is absolutely necessary, but the father's clan is also involved, and the marriage is not thought to be complete (although quite valid) without their participation. At Oa:35's marriage there was some anxiety because the father of the bride was estranged from her mother. People went to great lengths to make sure that he would be there. By a coincidence, though not an uncommon one, he was of the same clan (Oak) as the prospective bridegroom. Consequently the bridegroom's lineage and other clansmen could put pressure on him. His lineage, Oak lineage B for our purposes, is shown on Genealogy III, he himself being Ob:3. The bride's lineage, Water lineage, is shown on Genealogy IV; she is W:10.

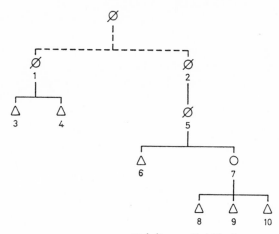

GENEALOGY III. Oak lineage B (Ob: )
(Exact connection between Ob:1 and Ob:2 forgotten; thought to have been second cousins; name of apical ancestress known to Ob:3 and Ob:4)

Once the participation of the father was ensured, the wedding went ahead in the proper manner. Oa:35 informed his father and mother that he wished to marry the girl, W:10. His mother informed Oa:7 and Oa:10, who arranged with the girl's parents a suitable time for the boy's people to go and 'ask for' the girl. The girl's parents informed their respective clan heads. In the girl's father's case this was unnecessary as he was Oak clan anyway, and this avoided involving him too closely in the arrangements and thus caused less embarrassment. The bride's mother, W:9, informed W:4, who conferred with Oa:10.

When the time was decided upon, the respective clans and lineages assembled at the house of the boy (Oa, and Ivy clan), and the girl (Ob, and Water). Oak members not of either of the two lineages concerned went to the boy's house, because it was the Oak

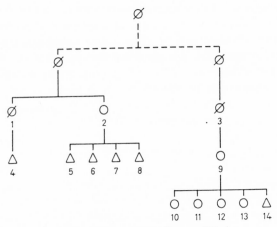

GENEALOGY IV. Water lineage (W: )
(Exact connection forgotten, but apical ancestress known)

clan that was 'asking' for the girl. At the boy's house, people sat around and smoked and talked quietly until the full complement arrived. Then, while everyone sat with bowed heads, two speeches were made in the customary rapid oratorical manner reserved for ceremonial occasions. The first speaker was the father's mother's brother, I:4, the 'head' of the Ivy clan. The second speaker was the mother's mother's brother, Oa:10, 'head' of Oak. They exhorted the boy to remember his parents and clanspeople even after he was married, and to look after his wife, be a model citizen and son. They asked him several times if he knew his mind and was sure. He nodded, but each time they repeated the question and paused a long time for him to think. Each time he nodded. Satisfied, they all put out their corn-husk cigarettes (smoked only on ceremonial occasions and provided by Oa on this one) and all set off for the girl's house.

At her house were assembled Ob: and the Water people. The Oak:Ivy contingent sat along one wall; people greeted each other quietly by clan names. There was a long silence. Then W:4 asked why they had come (addressed to *hapanyi hánuch*: Oak clan). Oa:10 replied that they had come to ask for a girl of the Water clan (*tsits hánuch*). He was, however, a shy man and did not like making speeches, so he asked I:4 to speak for him. The latter promised to take care of the girl, and to see that her husband looked after her. All the Oaks murmured approval and agreement. There was another long silence. Then W:4 said they would ask the girl and give their answer in three days. Oa:10 and I:4 thanked the Water people, and then Oa and Ivy went back to the boy's house for food and relaxed talk with a little singing.

The permission of the Water clan was finally gained, and the wedding took place, following much the same pattern, but including the Catholic ceremony and much feasting. Many more people made speeches at the actual ceremony, including officials who were not necessarily clan members of the parties concerned, *padrinos*, non-clan grandparents, and others.

The interest here lies in the fact that the all-important 'asking for the girl' was couched in clan terms and was seen as a clan matter. One clan was 'asking for' a girl of another. The fathers' clans were there to 'help' – but as clans. Here too there was a complication, in that the bride's father was of the same clan as the prospective bridegroom. Hence the lineage grouping became the operative one. This was first brought home to me when I saw I:12 at the boy's house without her husband. When we went to the girl's house, her husband was there. He is Ob:6, and hence of the lineage of the girl's father. It was by following out such clues as this that I was able to make the above observations on lineage and clan.

It should be noted that spouses of the clanspeople concerned came to these ceremonies in some cases, but only as guests. They did not speak or participate in any way. The sole exception to this rule was that the husband of Oa:7 provided the tobacco and corn husks for the cigarettes which his wife's lineage took to the boy's house, and actually made most of them himself. Both the men of the lineage were too busy with other things to go out and collect the green plant that is crushed and mixed with the tobacco, so Oa:7 asked her husband to do it for them. This lineage tends to lean on this man, as its own male contingent is small and not very active. (Oa:5, while a prominent man in the village, in fact has a daily job in Santa Fé ,which prevents him from doing all that he

would like to do.) But Oa:7's husband did this as a courtesy for
his wife's lineage and clan. He explained to me that they (Oak)
had given him a good wife, so when they were seeking a wife
themselves, the least he could do was to help in some small
way.

The third large assembly involving the Oak lineages and their
clansmen was a curing. This involves substantially the same people
as the wedding and reinforces the above analysis. The people immediately involved are shown on Genealogy v. The person to be

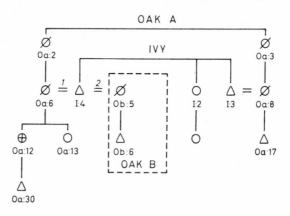

GENEALOGY V

cured was Oa:12. I have elsewhere given details of her illness, and
as they are not immediately relevant I will not repeat them here.[1]
One thing is important, however. Part of the patient's anxieties
concerned her lack of a permanent home. Her mother, Oa:6, did
not inherit the house that belonged to Oa:2 and Oa:3. The house
in fact went to Oa:8 and then to Oa:17. Oa:12 seized on this fact
to express her feelings of distress over the death of her mother. If
only she had the house that should have been her mother's, she
said, then she would not be ill. Her father, I:4, with his two
daughters and grandson, was living in a house belonging to his
stepson by his second marriage, Ob:6. Being old and blind, he
could not build a house for himself and his children, so the cousin,
Oa:17, stepped in. He gave the house to his sick relative, or rather
to her father, and in return I:4 gave him some land suitable for

[1] Fox, 1960 and 1964. See also Lange, 1959, pp. 382–5, for more details on
curing ceremonies.

building. This caused a lot of inconvenience for Oa:17, who had then to borrow a house from his stepmother, and finally from Oa:7, before he managed to complete one for himself. It should be noted here that the magnanimous Oa:17 was related patri-lineally to I:4, who was in fact his father's brother. So he was under a double obligation.

A cure still had to be arranged. In this the stepson took a hand. He approached the men of his lineage, Ob:3 and Ob:4 (Genealogy III) and asked them to help. (I have previously [Fox, 1960, 1964] referred to these men as 'mother's brothers'. The relationship is, in fact, more remote than this.) Ob:3 agreed to do so along with his wife W:9, who, as we have seen, was of the Water clan. This couple were the parents of the girl involved in the marriage cere-mony described, but at that time were not estranged. The cure is actually performed by two individuals thus, but it has to have the sanction and participation of their clans. In this case the same difficulty arose as with the marriage, namely that two people con-cerned, patient and curer, were of the same clan.

Now the whole purpose of the clan cure is to adopt the sick person into other clans than his own. The more clans one becomes a 'little' member of, the better the cure. In this case, then, half the benefit was being consciously abandoned. This arises from several causes. The Oak clan is numerically very large, and it is hard to avoid involving members of it in anything. Also, one does not want to look too far out of the immediate circle of relatives for something so important as a cure. Further, it is hard to find people who are willing to go to the trouble and expense of putting on a cure, and also know the proper ritual. Ob:6 was worried about his step-sister, particularly because of her feelings as regards the house. He saw himself as in some way responsible for her illness and was eager to help. In this he was urged on by his wife, who was the patient's father's sister's daughter. So he called in his line-age elders. The fact that they were themselves of the clan of the patient could be overlooked, because in this case there was no known relationship between their respective lineages. It did mean, however, that the burden of the cure would fall on the clan (Water) of the curer's wife. To this end W:9 informed W:4, who agreed to bring the Water clan to the cure. As W:4 was one of the most respected and knowledgeable men in the village, this was very important.

Thus the same groups assembled as for the wedding, Ivy and Oa at the patient's house, and Water and Ob at the house of Ob:3 and W:9. The relationships are sketched out in Genealogy va. They had been informed by messengers sent from the clan elders four days before, who summoned them with the ceremonial pinch of cornmeal – a summons that cannot be ignored without explanation. The Ivy and Oa contingent took the patient to the house of Ob:3, where he and his wife, with the assistance of the

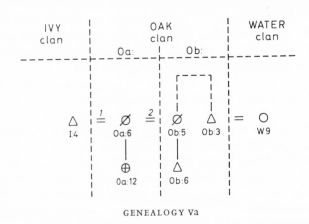

GENEALOGY Va

Water clan and Ob, washed the patient's head, gave her new names, and completed the formalities of adoption. Everyone gave her presents – mostly of food. Then she was taken back to her house by her people, who sat quietly with her for the rest of the day and most of the night.

The above three episodes show instances of lineage activity and the interaction of clan and lineage. Particularly interesting are the wedding and the curing, because they involve the splitting of the clan on a lineage basis, and show up this interaction quite clearly. They also show how important marriage is to the Cochiti, the affinal link being utilized, for example, to bring in the 'extra' clan for the cure, and the very solemnity of the wedding – or rather 'asking' – showing both the serious regard for marriage and the importance of the clan in sanctifying it. A child is the child of its clan, and can only be released by its clan in order to marry. Thus the Oak clan had to make sure that the boy really wanted to marry, and that he really wanted that particular girl. It was too important a thing to be taken lightly, as it involved the whole of his clan in a set of obligations towards the one into which he proposed to marry. When, for example, a child of his might wish to marry, Oak, as the father's clan, would be involved in the wedding. Also, if he or his wife agreed to cure anyone, then both clans would again be involved. This may explain the obvious liking in Cochiti for what Lange called 'sequential interclan marriages'. (Clans which are already linked reinforce their bonds.)

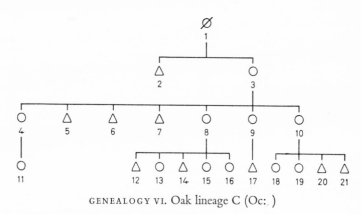

GENEALOGY VI. Oak lineage C (Oc: )

I will add details of two further lineages, again affines of Oa. The first is itself an Oak lineage – Oc. It is shown on Genealogy VI. Oc:10 is married to Oa:17. This is one of the few cases of clan endogamy, most of which occur in the over-large Oak clan. It was not generally approved, but Oc:10 was the daughter of a progressive who did not hold with the 'old ways', and Oa:17 had just returned from war service, was feeling independent, and was disinclined to listen to advice. There was no known connection between the two lineages, and once the young couple had decided on their course, it was accepted as a *fait accompli*. In fact, they threatened to go straight to the priest and miss out the native ceremony, so they were allowed to go ahead, and a hurried 'asking' was arranged to keep the record straight. I have no idea how this was managed, and no one seemed anxious to talk about it. The father of Oc:10 is W:5. He was a noted progressive, who in later years relapsed and began to practise the native religion again. At the time of the marriage, however, he was rather indifferent. He went through with the clan business at his wife's urging (Oc:3) and that of her brother, Oc:2, neither of whom were progressives. Thus the lineage took a hand in the marriage, as it should.

Another affair settled by the lineage as such was the fate of the illegitimate son of Oc:9 (Oc:17). As his mother wished to go and work in Albuquerque, someone had to look after the little boy. Oc:2, Oc:3, Oc:9 and Oc:10 conferred on this. They contemplated leaving the child with Oc:10, but as she had four already, and as the family was in transit between houses and unsure of accommodation (see the account of the cure above), it was finally decided to leave him with his grandparents, Oc:3 and W:5. Now what is interesting is that W:5 and Oa:17 did not take part in these discussions. They said quite emphatically that it was not their affair. If their wives had to look after a child of their 'leaf', this was a matter for the leaf. The fact that the husband would have another mouth to feed was neither here nor there. The fate of a child must be decided by its own people.

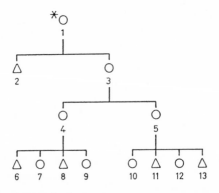

* from Santo Domingo

GENEALOGY VII. Fox (Coyote) lineage (F: )

The last lineage to be discussed is shown in Genealogy VII. This too is joined in marriage to Oa, and is therefore closely involved in its affairs. F:2 is the much-mentioned husband of Oa:7, and F:4 is married to Oa:5. F:2 is head of the Fox clan. This lineage is small, and does not function very well because of the clashing personalities of F:2 and F:3, but its women are very close indeed. F:3 is the stepmother of Oa:17, who lent him a house when he gave up his own to his sick cousin.

Having now seen the lineage and clan in action, we must turn to the matrifamily and observe it at work. We will take the same genealogies, in order to see the overlap and contrasts mentioned in the preceding section.

## III

### MATERNAL EXTENDED FAMILY

Our first matrifamily (Genealogy VIII) is based on the large Oak lineage A. It consists of six households, but household 6 is rather peripheral to the group. The male head of this household is not much involved in group affairs, but the women keep up the relationship as much as possible. Household 6 is at the extreme end

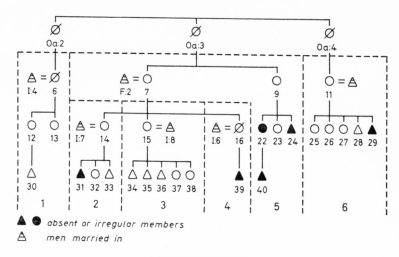

GENEALOGY VIII
(Based on Genealogy I: Oak lineage A.)

of the village, and it is quite an effort for the others to keep up the relationship. Household 5 has in fact two houses, one in the village and a *ranchito* out in the fields where it spends much of the summer. Households 2 and 3 are quite straightforward, but it should be remembered that the husbands of these two households are brothers, and that I:4 of household 1 is their mother's brother. During his lifetime, their mother's other brother, I:3, was of course a member of this group, being married to Oa:8. Household 4 has technically ceased to exist since the death of Oa:16, but

I:6 still involves himself deeply in the affairs of this matrifamily. He did not re-marry, and lives with a sister.

The clearest emergence of this group, as I have said, comes with housebuilding. The time came when Oa:9 tired of living with her sister and the latter's husband (Oa:7 and F:2). Her son, Oa:24, who was working away from the Pueblo, sent her money to buy the timber for a house. The council gave her land, and she asked F:2 to arrange the building for her. He summoned the able-bodied members of households 1, 2, 3 and 4. I:4, being blind, could not help directly, but sent his grandson, and often had himself led over to enquire about the progress. This is very interesting, as his wife was dead. That did not serve to sever his connection with the matrifamily. F:2 himself made all the bricks for the house out of mud and straw, a long and laborious business. I:8 transported them across the river from F:2's *ranchito* to the house site. They all applied for the community truck to transport the bought timber, particularly the long *vigas* to support the roof. In the meantime, the women were cooking food for them under the direction of Oa:9 and her sister. When the house was completed, the women plastered it.

This is only the barest outline of the work involved, which took over two years to complete, but what is important is the assumption of responsibility for it by the matrifamily, and the complete non-involvement of lineage males (Oa:5, Oa:10, Oa:17:18:19) who did not belong to it. They took a friendly interest, and their help would have been accepted if offered, but they had no responsibility towards the house and were not expected to contribute anything to its building.

I witnessed on two occasions each the plastering of houses 2, 3 and 5, and on each occasion the group was the same. The men did the heavy mixing, the women the actual plastering. The women alternated between plastering and cooking, taking turn and turn about. This was probably the most important regular feature of the work of the group, or for that matter for any of these groups.

An interesting case arose during the tenure by Oa:17 of his mother's sister's house (house in the village of household 5). During this tenure it was reckoned that he was partly responsible for the upkeep of the house, and his wife joined the women of this group at plastering, and whitewashed the interior by herself.

When she found the latter work too arduous, she called on her mother and sister, as shown in Genealogy IX. Her husband did his share of mixing and carrying. When, however, it came to the building of Oa:17's house, trouble arose. His brother-in-law was away from the Pueblo a good deal, and his father-in-law (W:5) was disinclined to help him. Hence he had to turn elsewhere, and asked his brothers, who gave some assistance, as did I:6 and F:2. The latter, however, complained that if the father-in-law had

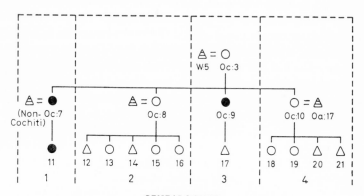

GENEALOGY IX
(Based on Genealogy VI: Oak lineage C.)

worked all summer as he should, the job would have been done. The brother-in-law was not severely criticized, since he was often out of the village. He sometimes helped at weekends.

The interesting point here is that, although the matrifamily broke down, the norms were quite clear to those involved. The father-in-law made excuses, and in fact had not been well, but he knew he should have done more. Oa:17's friends rallied round, but they knew that it was not really their job and that they were only called on in an emergency.

In the above cases, we can refer back to the activities of lineages Oa and Oc, and see the complementary activities that were carried on by 'brothers' as opposed to 'husbands' in the matrifamily. In the matters of housebuilding and repairing, the different functions, duties and obligations of these two sets of males was striking. The women, of course, are central to both units, but they too differentiated between activities that were the responsibilities of their brothers and those that fell to their husbands.

to do for one another, and this is particularly evident in childbirth. Lineage and matrifamily come into play, depending on which of the women's activities involves the brothers or the husbands respectively. But perhaps the persistent day-to-day interaction and mutual help of the mother-daughter and sister-sister groups should be taken out as a separate element in the system, the men revolving around this central core of activity and intruding into it only on specific occasions.

Having described the women's world, we must turn to the men's – the *Kiva* – to see the opposite group, the patrifamily, in action.

## IV

### THE PATERNAL EXTENDED FAMILY

For the sake of convenience, we will start with men we now know well, and look at the patrifamily of which they are members. The men are the three brothers of the Ivy lineage who married the three sisters of the Oak (Oa), that is I:6, 7 and 8. They are shown in Genealogy XII with the rest of this patrifamily of the Turquoise

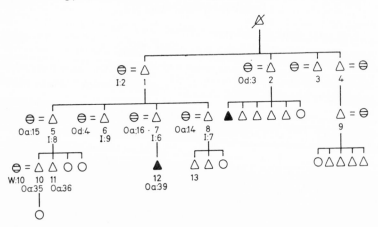

GENEALOGY XII. Turquoise A (Ta: )

*Kiva*. Their father, Ta:1, is the husband of I:2, and was the most prolific of his four brothers, but not the most influential. Ta:2 and 3 were far more important in ceremonial affairs, although Ta:1

became very wealthy as a result of cattle breeding. For some reason I failed to obtain any information about Ta:4.

To give some idea of the part this group played in ceremonial life, I list below the various offices and functions they have held at various times. Those not listed were too young to have held office, but they would all have at least danced in the corn dance, if they could walk at all.

Ta:1    Fiscale, singer. His wife (I:2) was *Koshare*.
Ta:2    *Kwirena, shikame, Mayorli*.
Ta:3    War Captain, drummer.
Ta:4    No information. His wife was *Kwirena*.
Ta:5    Fiscalito, head drummer. His wife (Oa:15) is *Kwirena*.
Ta:6    Fiscalito, dancer.
Ta:7    Fiscale, Alguacilito, Lt. Governor, singer.
Ta:8    Alguacilito, dancer.
Ta:9    Lt. Fiscale, Alguacilito.
Ta:10   Fiscalito, pole carrier, drummer.
Ta:11   Lead dancer, pole carrier.

All the older adults of this group were *Katsina*. The men listed as singer, unless they were in the drum cult, would have also danced in their youth. Some of those listed as dancers and drummers will graduate to singer when they are too old to drum or dance.

All the offices listed for this group were not within the *Kiva*, of course, but playing a full part in the *Kiva* involves also playing a full part in the tribal life generally, so I have listed the whole range of roles filled.

Insofar as this group is 'led', Ta:2 and 3 do the leading in ceremonial affairs, while Ta:1 is very much a leader in informal and economic matters. He is rather an unusual man in being something of an entrepreneur, and is reputed to be quite wealthy. He is a farmer, but mainly deals in cattle-herding and breeding, while his sons help him. Ta:2 and 3 are also farmers, but do not have cattle, and are much immersed in ceremonial affairs. The 'leaf' of Ta:4 is less closely integrated with the rest of the group. Non-resident members are not recorded. The children of Ta:3 are married away from the Pueblo, while Ta:2 married late and to a young wife, so most of his children are still very young. Ta:6 works away from the Pueblo most of the week and is only loosely in contact most of the time, but at ceremonials he joins with his brothers in the dancing.

The ceremonial activity of this group within the *Kiva* centres on drumming. Ta:3, his brother's son Ta:5, and the latter's son Ta:10 provide half the strength of the Turquoise drum cult. Ta:5 has the reputation of being the finest drum-maker not only in Cochiti, but in all the Pueblos. His drums are sought after from as far afield as Zuni and Moenkopi in the west and Taos in the north. His father's cattle enterprises are important here, since the slaughtered cattle (and horses) provide the hides for the drum-skins and the thongs. The finding of suitable trees to hollow out for drum-cases, and the killing, cleaning and curing of hides, is an arduous business in which the brothers share, calling on extra help from within the group when this is required. They also do a lot of the making of ceremonial drums for the *Kiva*. This has to be done by members of the drum cult, who observe certain rituals connected with the operation. There are clearly advantages in having this activity arranged by and largely confined to one patri-family – although for the ceremonial drums the *Kiva* heads would, for example, hire the community truck and conscript help from the *Kiva* at large in order to go for trees in the mountains. The hides, however, would be supplied by the drummers themselves.

As with the matrifamily, I could list a hundred and one cases of interaction which showed how this group came together, but this would be largely repetitive. And although many kinds of social and economic acitivity are performed within it, it is only clearly a group as opposed to other groups under ceremonial conditions – and I include making drums under this heading. You would never find this group building a house or arranging a marriage, but you would find it making ceremonial paraphernalia and arranging, for example, to obtain a Hopi dance kilt for one of its young mem-bers, perhaps in exchange for one of the drums it manufactured. The older men made rattles and tiny bows for the younger, and small practice drums for themselves and the children. The older men will listen with approval while the younger sing the dance songs, and correct them on the mistakes they make. They will encourage the children to dance and sing, and correct, gently but firmly, their efforts. In this particular group, not much in the way of discipline was needed, but one occasion brought out the dis-ciplinary functions. One of the younger members was late for the corn dance. He had gone off to spend the morning in the near-by Spanish town, when he should not have done so. He returned not drunk, but having taken alcohol and thus broken his fast. He slipped into the dance, but was brought out by Ta:3 who took him into the house. Later he came outside dressed in his ordinary clothes, looking much chastened, and the story was put around that he had a blister on his foot and could not continue. The polite fiction was adhered to, but in fact he had been told by his uncle that he could not dance because he had broken the rules and was not in a 'state of grace'. The boy was very subdued and upset. The interest in this action is that it was kept in the family. The uncle's action in fact saved the boy from public disgrace. Had he not taken him in hand, the managing society of the occasion would have been forced to discipline him, probably by making him stand for the rest of the day in a circle of cornmeal. As it was, his uncle saved him from public shame, but rebuked him severely in private. The whole conduct of the affair was considered highly satisfactory by *Kiva* and tribal officials, as it saved everyone's face and avoided a public scandal. They fully accepted the right of the patrifamily to deal with this matter itself if it so pleased. The boy's place in the dance line was taken by another member of the group.

The place of the women of this patrifamily in its affairs is typical of the place of women in all such groups. They are peripheral to most of its activities, and do not interact among themselves very much, except when the group's ritual activities demand their co-operation. They do not necessarily dance with the members of the group, the actual pairs being decided on by the *Kiva* rather than the patrifamily. But they do take an interest in the ceremonial progress of each other's children, not without a little rivalry. In this particular group several of the women were sisters and so were fairly closely knit (Oa:14, 15 and 16; Od:3 and 4). In the business, for example, of dressing the children in their ceremonial costumes, these two groups of sisters, under the general supervision of I:2, co-operated quite extensively. The women in this group, how-ever, are analogous to the men in a matrifamily. The bulk of interaction goes on between the 'natal' members of the group, the affines being involved only for specific purposes. The more ceremonious the patrifamily the more will the women be pulled into it, and the more likely will they be to join societies themselves.

On several occasions I saw these women (not including the wife of Ta:9) gathered at the house of Oa:15 for an evening of playing with the children, singing and dancing with them. Some of the men would be there too, and would generally join in with the semi-serious play, giving a good deal of attention to the children. The young children concerned were particularly those of Ta:8 and Ta:2.

I will now briefly discuss some other patrifamilies to show the general similarity of composition and function. It is nearly impossible to get details of ceremonial activities other than public ones, and this imposes a severe limit on the description. We will have to take these secret activities as read.

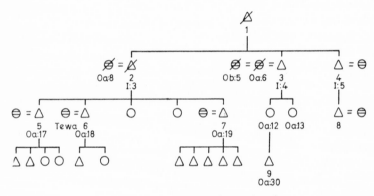

GENEALOGY XIII. Pumpkin A (Pa: )

In Genealogy XIII there are a number of men who have been mentioned before. It includes the two Ivy brothers I:3 and I:4 who married the Oak sisters Oa:6 and Oa:8. The three sons of I:3 and Oa:8 have already appeared on Genealogy I (Oa:17, 18 and 19). Below are their offices and functions. All older adults, again, were *Katsina.*

Pa:2   War Captain, *Koshare*, drummer, singer
Pa:3   War Captain, drummer, singer
Pa:4   Lt. Governor, Fiscale, Alguacilito
Pa:5   Fiscalito, Treasurer, dancer
Pa:6   Dancer
Pa:7   Fiscalito, Alguacilito, drummer

Leadership came very definitely from Pa:3, who has already figured prominently in other contexts. It was at his house that assemblies were usually held. The group of Pa:4 took less part in these; this was a 'leaf' likely to be shed in the next generation.

The members of the patrifamily were very proud of the number of songs they knew and the number of dance steps they had originated. Pa:5 and 6 were leading dancers of the Pumpkin *Kiva*, and Pa:6 particularly was proud of his skill. Pa:5's job prevented him from attending all the rehearsals of his *Kiva* for a corn dance, but he was pleased at having been able to join in, with only one rehearsal, and do even the most complex steps on the day. Pa:7, the youngest of the brothers, surprised everyone by becoming a member of the drum cult as this involves a lot of arduous restrictions and he was considered to be a bit of a gay dog. This group was noted for the fact that it had all its young children dancing in the corn and other 'unlimited' dances. They probably attained the record when they put a three-year-old boy in to the dance line. He danced throughout the period of several hours, and at the end no praise was too lavish from his doting relatives. Discipline within the group is difficult because Pa:3 is incapacitated and rather dependent, and *Kiva* officials have had to take matters into their own hands when the occasion arose. But they spoke to Pa:3 about it first. The women of this group are again fairly peripheral, and this is accentuated by personal circumstances. The wives of Pa:5 and Pa:7 are the daughters of progressives, and do not want to take too much part in their husbands' ceremonial activities. They do not – cannot – stop their children from doing so. Indeed, as we have seen, the children are noted for their participation. The wife of Pa:6 is a Tewa, who is somewhat independent, and is treated cautiously in consequence. She is 'modern' and difficult to integrate. Strangely enough it is the unmarried daughters of Pa:3 and the unmarried sisters of Pa:5, 6 and 7 who play the major part in the group's female affairs, and they are constantly trying to involve the 'wives'. These latter do the necessary minimum. This patrifamily assembles more than most, and it is noted and pointed out as a very active musical group. Both Pa:1 and Pa:2 were men of strong personality, who left their mark on their paternal descendants.

Genealogy xiv shows a small but strongly knit group, which includes two men already known to us; Pb:1 (W:4) and Pb:4

(husband of F:5). The offices held by them are shown below; again all the older males are *Katsina*.

Pb:1   Lt. Governor, *Koshare*, drummer, *Mavorli*
Pb:2   Fiscale, dancer
Pb:3   Fiscalito, singer
Pb:4   Fiscalito, Governor, drummer
Pb:5   Dancer
Pb:6   Dancer

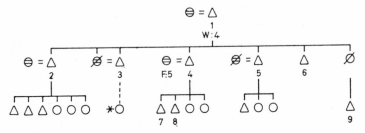

* Sister's child

GENEALOGY XIV. Pumpkin B (Pb: )

The head of the group, Pb:1, is a man of very marked ability and has the close allegiance of his sons. One of these did not marry and two others did not re-marry after the death of their wives. This is relatively unusual in Cochiti, but it has served to bind the sons even closer to their father. Pb:1 has a very active interest in his grandsons, even the youngest of whom has a considerable repertoire of songs, while all of them are prominent dancers. Pb:4, particularly, is a man of considerable influence who has risen to be Governor. The three wives of this group are not so peripheral as in the last patrifamily, but they are not society members, nor are they prominent in *Kiva* affairs. On the other hand, they take much interest in the progress of the children, particularly those of Pb:5, whose wife is dead. Pb:3 looks after his niece – his sister's child – who was given into his care when his sister died. She participates in the group as though she were his daughter. The group meets often in the house of Pb:1 for its activities, and the men make drums and ceremonial costumes.

Genealogy XV shows a group which is not quite so strongly knit. This is largely due to demographic reasons. Pc:2 married a young wife late in life, and his children are not yet of an age to take their full part in ceremonial. They do dance, however, and this branch may flourish yet. Pc:1, on the other hand, has failed to keep his sons fully under his control or even in the Pueblo. One is virtually absent all the time, while Pc:4 vacillates in his membership. He occasionally comes for a dance, but this cannot be relied on. One of the younger sons, Pc:3, seems likely to stick to the Pueblo, and has held a minor office.

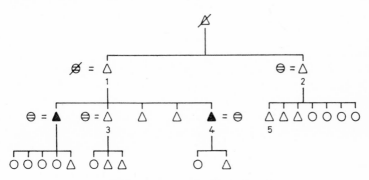

GENEALOGY XV. Pumpkin C (Pc: )

The offices etc., are listed below.

Pc:1   Alguacilito, Lt. Fiscale, singer
Pc:2   War Captain, Fiscale, singer
Pc:3   Fiscalito, dancer
Pc:4   Dancer (sporadically)
Pc:5   Fiscalito, dancer

Pc:1 and 2 were *Katsina*: I am not sure of any of the others. There is much scope in the patrifamily for the influence of individual personality, and a relatively weak older generation can sometimes fail to 'hold' the younger who succumb to the counter attractions of town and job.

We might pause here and note that the men of the middle generation of these groups have nearly all seen war service in foreign parts. Yet almost without exception they have returned to Cochiti and thoroughly reintegrated themselves into the life of the tribe, particularly the ceremonial life. Elsewhere I have argued that it was because many of these veterans were the 'sons of conservatives' that they were able to take over so effectively the running of the Pueblo and to fit back so easily into the tribal life. Also,

I argued, they did not have to join the societies as these were on the decline. The present genealogies will demonstrate some of the details of this thesis. None of the middle-generation men in fact are society members, although all are *Katsina* and hold various offices, and they encourage their children to participate in the ceremonies. Particularly involved are Ta:6, 7, 8, 9 and 12; Pa:5, 6, 7 and 8; Pb:2, 4 and 5. These represent over half the veterans in Cochiti, and show their position in the ceremonial life quite well.

The groups described so far have been patrifamilies of some strength and cohesion. They have all had absent members, though not many. They are all strongly knit socio-ceremonial groups, unwavering in loyalty and zeal towards their respective *Kivas*. Not all groups are like this, however. A man is sometimes thought to be drawn too much into the affairs of his matrifamily, and to be neglecting his *Kiva* duties in consequence. There is often rivalry between wives, particularly young ones, over the relative merits of their children. Old wives are often very good friends, and this may ripen once their children are independent. As long as the old men of the group can keep a grip on it, however, it usually remains intact. But often when, for example, the old 'father' of the group dies, it will disintegrate. It is at this point that most *Kiva* membership changes occur. Those recorded by Lange were often of this nature. The change of membership sheds the old bitter ties, as it were, and gives the changers a chance to start again. But often the dissidents return eventually to their natal *Kiva* and their original paternal loyalties.

One such group is shown in Genealogy XVI. This includes a man we know already, F:2, and the grandson he raised as his son, Oa:34. I have not assigned these to a *Kiva*, as they have vacillated in membership. Below are their various offices.

X:1    *Flint*
X:2    (Progressive)
X:3    *Flint-Koshare*
X:4    Governor, singer
X:5    *Kwirena, Kiva* head. His wife is *Kwirena*
X:6    Dancer

This was a group of strong-minded men who, rejecting Pueblo values, intended to manage their lives as individuals. They never formed a close-knit ceremonial socialization unit like the others described. Nevertheless, there was considerable feeling between them, which showed itself on the death of a member. The original *Kiva* move was made by X:1, who changed from Pumpkin to Turquoise, but soon returned to Pumpkin. His two sons, X:4 and 5 followed him, but they went back to Turquoise when he died.

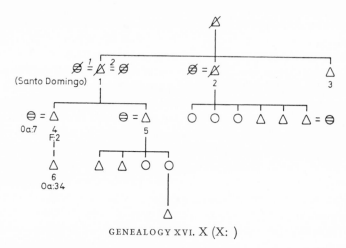

GENEALOGY XVI. X (X: )

On succeeding to the headship of the *Kwirena* society, X:5 had to change again to Pumpkin. The sons simply followed their father in the first moves, but it is interesting that X:4 thought Turquoise was his father's *Kiva*, having been too young to understand the first change of membership. X:2 dropped out of ceremonial life and became a progressive, and shortly after this his brother X:3 changed from Pumpkin to Turquoise and stayed there. Other instances show that while a father is alive his sons follow whatever shift he makes, so that the very business of changing allegiance reveals the strength of the father-son bond. On the death of a father, however, his sons may very well return so as to be with some other member of the patrifamily such as an old influential uncle who is ceremonially *in loco parentis*. Thus the X men remained for a time in Turquoise, until X:2 dropped out and X:5 was forced to change by circumstances beyond his control. It is not even certain that the latter really considered himself to have changed membership. Although he and his wife and children participated in Pumpkin affairs, he would never actually say outright that he was a Pumpkin member, and he never actually asked to be moved from Turquoise. Much *Kiva* changing can be understood only if one knows how the actors view the situation, and this is difficult to assess.

Although X:2 dropped out of the group as regards ceremonial, he was not treated as alien to it and after his death his children continued to associate with the other members. There was some economic co-operation between them, particularly between X:4 and X:5, who were helped by X:6 when he was available. The latter worked outside the Pueblo, but returned as often as possible for ceremonies and baseball. He was typical of the strong individualism of the group and the strong affectual side of personality which characterized them. They did not do things by halves. X:6 felt cut off from his 'Indian' roots because of his education and job (schoolteacher), and this bothered him. So he renounced the Catholic Church, much to everyone's horror, and went so far as to shed his Spanish name and take, legally, as his surname, the Indian name of his grandfather – who was effectively his father. Within all these groups there is strong feeling about the native religion and culture and a strong desire to preserve these.

The importance of the patrifamily must not be underestimated. It is the unit within which develop the strong feelings for *Kiva*, ceremony, *Katsinas* and all the essentials of the native religion. When the 'father' of such a unit opts out of the nativist faction, he carries with him his sons and possibly, in fact usually, their wives. If this were to happen in too many cases, the religious life of the tribe would be lost for ever. The patrifamily, then, is to be regarded as the essential unit of ritual socialization and control.

## V

### BASEBALL RECRUITMENT

We may now consider the relations of baseball teams to kin-groups. I was only able to unravel the affiliations of one team, the Redskins, in any detail. This had twenty-five more or less regular members. I obtained the *Kiva* affiliations of twenty-two, twelve Pumpkin and ten Turquoise. This made it obvious that *Kiva* affiliation as such had nothing to do with membership. Sixteen of the twenty-two appear on the genealogies which I have just presented. These form the resident hard core of the team, including its manager, and, of course, they also belong to the hard core of Cochiti conservatives and nativists. Eleven of the sixteen are members of the Oak lineage, the largest in the village, and eight of these were also members of two patrifamilies connected by marriage with Oa. The four not directly associated with Oa are members of patrifamily Pb. The link with this group is its 'father', who is head of the Water clan, which is so closely linked with Oak in marriage and healing. Full details on all sixteen are given in Table 4. The complete picture can be imagined if one notes that all the members of Oa, and all the members of patrifamilies listed, would be supporters of the Redskins.

TABLE 4. Patrifamily and Lineage Affiliations
of Sixteen Redskins

| | Patrifamily/Kiva | | | | Lineage/Clan |
|---|---|---|---|---|---|
| | Ta | Pa | Pb | X | Oa |
| 1. | 12 | | | | 39 |
| 2. | 10 | | | | 35 |
| 3. | 11 | | | | 36 |
| 4. | 13 | | | | 31 |
| 5. | ★ | | | 6 | 34 |
| 6. | | 9 | | | 30 |
| 7. | | 6 | | | 18 |
| 8. | | 7 | | | 19 |
| 9. | | | 7 | | |
| 10. | | | 8 | | |
| 11. | | | 5 | | |
| 12. | | | 9 | | |
| 13. | | | | | 5 (+son) |
| 14. | | | | | 28 |
| 15. | | | | | 29 |

The numbers are those assigned to these individuals on the genealogies on which they appear.
* 5, for all practical purposes, works with this group in Kiva affairs.

This analysis does more than merely show how a baseball team is recruited. It illustrates the intensity of the kinship and affinal ties created by the sequential marriages of the Ivy and Oak lineages. Numbers one to eight of the Redskins team are the children of such marriages. The intertwining of Ivy and Oak has produced a wider group of lineages, matrifamilies and patrifamilies which is itself a unit in the Cochiti kinship system, and the recruitment of the baseball team is in a sense an expression of its unity as against other (or at least one other) similar meshes. At the height of the season, baseball rivalry is so intense that only such a tight-knit group could possibly make up a team. But as I have argued before, the team hostility is itself a function of hostility between rival family groups. The analysis of the Redskins has shown the nature of these family groups, and above all their lineage basis and the patrifamily-lineage linkage, meeting, in a sense, in the matrifamily.

My material on the Braves team is too sparse to be worth an analysis, but it does not seem that the mesh is quite so tight as with the Redskins. Both *Kivas* are represented in it, and at least two patrifamilies which do not seem connected with those presented above, make up the core of it. It has, like the other team, strong support from conservatives, including the Cacique himself, although he does not actually play now.

If one were to take any Oa member of the Redskins and trace out his membership to the rest, he would seem to be surrounded by a bilateral 'web' of kin out of which the team is recruited. One does not join the team via a lineage or patrifamily, one is just a Redskin to whom other Redskins are related in various ways. Thus, like the *Kivas* and clans, the baseball teams are not conceived of as being units made up of smaller units, which provide members to play. They play as individuals in their own right. But when one examines what 'related' means in terms not of the kin surrounding any ego, but of the corporate groups involved, one can see what produces the common network of kin. Were it simply a bilateral web, it would have no boundaries, but this group has clear boundaries because it is made up of descent groups with determinate membership.

The nine members not accounted for by our genealogies were more casual in their membership, some of them being non-residents who returned for ball games. Two were related patrilaterally to 12 (Pb:9), and one to 14 and 15 (Oa:28 and 29). Another was probably patrilaterally related to Oa:34. Where family feuding did not preclude it, friendship among young men could serve as a basis for recruitment, and at least two Spanish boys participated on this basis.

# 6

# Discussion

So far I have tried to keep the discussion as factual as possible without the intrusion of analysis. I have referred to the 'patrifamily' because this is the group to be observed in action, but, as I mentioned, it might be better to conceptualize it differently for analytical purposes. And really what is at issue here is analysis. Eggan chose to conceptualize Western Pueblo kinship groups in a particular way, and then extended his concepts to the other Pueblos. I have questioned his basic conceptualization, but, even supposing it is correct, we still have to ask whether or not it is adequate as an analysis of Cochiti kinship groups. Here we must remember two things: first, the Western Pueblo type as seen by Eggan is supposed *once* to have existed in Cochiti. Thus, all we can do is to look for survivals of it, that is, ask whether any aspects of the existing kinship groupings still fit the Western model. Secondly, the predominant kinship type now is supposed to be 'bilateral' and to approximate Anglo, Spanish or Tewa models. Therefore we must try to see whether or not this adequately describes the existing kinship groups.

## I

### 'DOUBLE DESCENT'?

We can now try to conceptualize the kinship structure of Cochiti at a more abstract level. In Figure 5, column 'A' represents a 'line' of fathers and sons with their wives, that is, a patrifamily. Column 'B-C' is the opposite line, of mothers and daughters with their husbands, and column 'C-D' is the same mothers and daughters with their 'brothers'. Thus 'B-C' is the matrifamily and 'C-D' the lineage. These are shown juxtaposed at a marriage, which allows us to illustrate the nuclear family.

In column 'A', the patrifamily, the role relationships concerned are those of father-son, brother-brother, and husband-wife, the

main weight, of course, being borne by the first two. In column
'B', the matrifamily, the relationships are mother-daughter,
sister-sister, and again, husband-wife. Column 'B' shows the
important relationship of father-in-law to son-in-law (and, by
implication, brother-in-law to brother-in-law). This is more
important than its reciprocal of mother-in-law to daughter-in-
law in the patrifamily. Column 'C' shows the mother-daughter
axis which is common to 'B' and 'D'. Column 'C-D' is, of
course, the lineage, and 'D' the line of 'brothers', showing the
relation of mother's brother to sister's son, while the whole of
column 'C-D' emphasizes the importance of the mother-child
bond, and by implication that of sister-sister and sister-brother.
'A' and 'C-D' are linked to the wider associations of *Kiva*
and clan respectively.

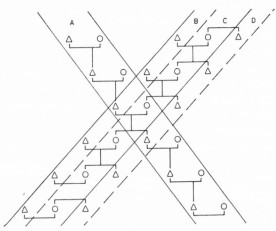

FIG. 5. Relation between kinship groups in Cochiti

Thus the system turns on the two axes of the father-son relationship and the mother-daughter bond. Despite the loss of the 'sisters'
to the father-son line, the system has some of the elements of a
double-descent arrangement, particularly one in which 'sisters'
are effectively lost to the patriline on marriage and wives more or
less incorporated into it.

It might in fact be profitable to consider Cochiti as a double-
descent system. It could be objected that, although the clans are
unilineal descent groups, the *Kivas* are not. There are, of course,

two levels at which this can be viewed: the *Kiva*/clan level on the one hand, and the matrilineage/patrilineage on the other. Let us take the *Kiva*/clan level first. In a sense the composition of *Kiva* and clan is very similar. While the clan is technically, i.e., ideologically, a unilineal descent group, it does not work like one, and for most purposes does not see itself as one. Ideologically, descent from a common ultimate ancestress may be granted – although this is disputed and even denied by some – but, in fact, one simply shares a 'name' with some other people, only some of whom are regarded as real consanguines. With the others one merely shares a mystical bond, but does not trace out genealogical connection. The relationship is, as I have said, a kind of nationality.

Exactly the same is true of the *Kiva*. In the same way as one takes one's mother's clan, one takes one's father's *Kiva*. The issue is perhaps confused because there are only two *Kiva* groups, which puts them in the 'moiety' class, while there are many clans. If there were only two 'clans', or several *Kivas*, then should we hesitate to call this a double-descent system? I think not. The issue of acceptance of common ancestry seems to me to be irrelevant. The membership rules of both clan and *Kiva* are the same; that is, unilineal. One joins one's mother's clan and one's father's *Kiva*.

There is, however, the problem of female membership in the *Kivas*. This as much as anything has made me hesitate to call this a double-descent system. The *Kivas* do not recruit female members by birth but by marriage. But as I have said before, this need not stop us from classifying the system as double descent. As the Cochiti see it, a woman's *Kiva* membership is wholly determined by marriage. An unmarried girl is simply kept in trust until her *Kiva* membership is decided. It is true that she has a 50–50 chance of ending up in her natal *Kiva*, but it is her marriage that decides this. A girl who does not marry stays in her father's *Kiva* by default rather than of right. It may be that the Catholic emphasis on marriage has contributed to this situation, and that before the establishment of the Spanish in the eighteenth century things were different. A young widow can if she wishes return to her father's *Kiva*, but remarriage will fix her membership again. An old widow, particularly one who has no chance of remarrying, will be likely to stay in her deceased husband's *Kiva*. Even some young widows stay and dance with their dead husband's *Kiva* mates. Women, then, do not have 'natural' rights to *Kiva* membership, only 'contractual' rights through marriage. But this is a matter of etiquette rather than formal rule. After all, the position of women in the *Kivas* is peripheral. They hold no offices and only perform such functions as plastering, cooking, and acting as dancing part-ners, which require no formal training or esoteric knowledge. *Kivas* are men's affairs: the women are simply appendages to their husbands.

This is, of course, true of all patrilineal systems in a theoretical sense. In a structural sense women are not necessary to their natal lineages. They are significant, not as 'consanguine women', but as 'wives' through whom their husbands' lineages are continued. In some cases a woman, on marriage, may lose all her rights in her natal lineage and be wholly incorporated into her husband's, even to the extent of worshipping his agnatic ancestors.[1] In other cases, she retains some rights in her natal lineage, and can, for example, return to it on divorce. But *structurally*, in any patrilineal system she is unnecessary to her lineage. As in the Cochiti *Kiva*, she is simply an appendage of her husband.

If, then, we see Cochiti as fitting the above paradigm, the woman's membership in the *Kiva* ceases to matter and the system could be seen as one of 'double-descent'. This is even clearer if we move to the matrilineage/patrilineage level. While neither *Kiva* nor clan can really be described as unilineal descent groups, insofar as this implies at least a fiction of common kinship, they are both, in fact if not in theory, *composed of* unilineal descent groups. A man at least will be a member of a matrilineage and a patrilineage, while a woman will be a member of a matrilineage and be incorporated into her husband's patrilineage.

This view of the matter makes the patrifamily the structural opposite of the lineage, and the *Kiva* directly comparable with the clan – in structure though not in operation. It also means that findings on other double-descent systems can be applied to Cochiti. For example, Harris, following Goody, has argued that a 'merging segmentary lineage system', and the political system that goes with it, are not possible with double descent because great depth of lineage and wide span of relationship between lineages are precluded.[2] In such a system one will be likely to find a political structure in which the officiants are 'peace-priests'. She

[1] Freedman, 1958; Leach, 1957; Fallers, 1957.
[2] Harris, 1962; Goody, 1957.

is, of course, taking only those societies with agnatic residential groups and dispersed matrilineal groups, but her observations are not wholly irrelevant. I have been struck, for example, by the similarities in structure between Cochiti and, say, the village of Umor amongst the Yako, where great weight and power is given to associations and secret societies in the context of double-unilineal organization.[1] Also Harris points to the shallowness of genealogies in double-unilineal systems, a point I have raised regarding Cochiti and the other Pueblos and will take up later.

I am not sure where Cochiti should be placed on Goody's classification of double-unilineal societies.[2] His criteria for deciding what constitutes a 'corporate unilineal descent group' seem somewhat narrow. He uses material property as the criterion *par excellence*. Unilineal-descent groups of a corporate nature so defined are not found in Cochiti. Hence it cannot fit into his classification at all. This seems to me very odd. Perhaps we should add to his scheme a third group of 'full' double-descent systems in which neither group is a property-holding corporation. The 'property' of both clan and *Kiva* is 'incorporeal'. The *Kiva* owns its buildings and paraphernalia, but these are held in common, and do not constitute what I *think* Goody means by property. Again his criterion of a 'name' seems odd. Both *Kivas* and clans are 'named' in Cochiti, but in a sense neither lineage is 'named' in any formal way. What Goody is trying to avoid, I believe, is the calling of societies with one property-owning descent group – say, the agnatic lineage – and a complementary 'matriline' or 'matrilateral kindred', 'double-descent societies'. This is fair enough, but there are meanings to 'double descent' which seem to me to be quite valid other than just that of 'both types of property-owning corporations present'. It is possible to find societies without property-owning unilineal-descent groups of both types (such as Cochiti), which still recognize two types of grouping based on the two forms of unilineal descent. An example of this can be found in Meggitt's description of the Walbiri of central Australia.[3]

[1] Forde, 1964. It is noteworthy that among the Yakö a man can change his patriclan of birth by adoption into another. (See Forde, 1963.) The sentiments and values of matrilineal kinship among the Yako that Forde describes are very similar to those of the Cochiti: fertility, health and peace are strongly associated with matrilineal descent, and their cults are in the charge of matriclan priests.

[2] Goody, 1961.

[3] Meggitt, 1962.

(Note that Goody dismisses the Australians from his 'double-descent' category.) The Walbiri have 'patrilodges', which are totemic ritual groups and which, like the *Kivas*, own only ritual property. Marriage among the Walbiri, however, is arranged by 'matrilines', which convene for the purpose but are not otherwise 'corporate' groups. The structural similarity with Cochiti is quite striking.

I stress these points because it seems wrong to exclude Cochiti from the double-descent category on such a seemingly arbitrary basis, when so much of importance about the society appears to stem from the fact that it recognizes both forms of reckoning and uses them to recruit groups, 'corporate' or not.

At the *Kiva*/clan level, it might be better to speak of 'dual affiliation' than of 'double descent', as common descent is not necessarily implied and is certainly not traced. There is a confusion here between 'unilineal' meaning 'tracing genealogical links in one line' – that is either the male or female line, and its meaning 'uni-sexual' – that is recruitment by a group of the children of members of one sex only.

## II

### 'BILATERALITY'?

The above conceptualization allows us to assess the so-called bilaterality of the Cochiti kinship system. To say a system is bilateral is not, of course, to say very much – simply that kinship can be traced between persons without consideration of the sex of the linking relative(s). It does not say what kind of kin groups exist. It merely states the basis for recruitment to them, that is, they can recruit the children of members of either sex. Basically there seem to be two popular ways of organizing bilateral kin groups: the ego-focused bilateral kindred, and the ancestor-focused cognatic or non-unilineal descent group.[1] In terms, then, of the formation of kin groups on a bilateral principle the Cochiti kinship system is clearly anything but bilateral. It is, however, bilateral in the sense that any kinship system in which a child is acknowledged to be the child of both its parents is bilateral. This is true of nearly all kinship systems. All it says is that surrounding each ego is a circle of kinsfolk traced 'bilaterally'. Thus, the fact that father's mother's parents and mother's father's parents do not

[1] See Goodenough, 1955; Firth, 1963; Freeman, 1961

appear on our diagram does not mean that they do not exist, or that ego does not recognize them as great-grandparents. But it does mean that they are not members of the descent groups of which ego is a member. That is to say, that for purposes of recruiting to kinship groups, Cochiti does not employ the bilateral or cognatic principle, but that from the point of view of any ego, cognates are recognized as relatives. But this is not what has been meant by saying that Cochiti has a 'bilateral' kinship system. (It seems to be clearly the case with Zuni, and is the basis of Kroeber's distinction between 'kinship' and 'clanship'. Fortes makes the same distinction for the Tallensi, and it seems to be what he means by the difference between 'filiation' and 'descent'.[1])

There is a tendency to confuse what Goodenough has called the 'ego focus' in kinship *analysis*[2] with ego-centredness in kinship *systems*. Thus, any kinship system can be viewed in two ways: (a) in terms of the groups of which it is composed (clans, lineages, etc.), and (b), in terms of the way in which ego 'relates' to his relatives. These will only be coincident in the case of 'kindred' organization where groups are *relative to* egos. When groups are 'ancestor-focused' (Goodenough), that is, are descent groups, the two views become distinct. One can analyse the composition and function of the groups on the one hand, and again, one can look at the system from the viewpoint of ego. Thus Cochiti, looked at from the angle of group membership, has not a hint of bilaterality; but ego certainly regards as 'relatives' persons connected by cognatic ties. Each person is the focus of a (possibly peculiar to himself) constellation of groups and categories as follows:

1. Own lineage and clan
2. Father's lineage and clan
3. Matrifamily
4. Patrilineage and family
5. Relatives other than those in descent groups
6. Affines other than in 3 and 4.

Category 5 here includes, for example, all the descendants of ego's eight great-grandparents, because the Catholic exogamy laws require the recognition of these. All these categories never act

---

[1] Fortes, 1949 (esp. Ch. II), 1953, 1959.   [2] Goodenough, 1955.

together on behalf of ego, therefore they do not constitute an ego-focused group, but ego's recognition of his 'relatedness' to them all certainly has a 'bilateral' component in that it involves the recognition of purely cognatic ties as well as agnatic and uterine. This has, however, to be distinguished from a simple recognition by ego of his membership in the *descent groups* of mother and father. Thus Dozier's statement that the Keres are moving from a unilineal to a 'bilateral or equalizing' system seems to mean nothing more than that the father's 'side' is being given the same 'weight' as the mother's.[1] This does not necessarily make the system 'bilateral' in any sense in which this word is a synonym for 'cognatic'. Dozier is, I think, using it as a synonym for 'symmetrical'. And, in any case, as a statement of fact it is wrong. Both father's and mother's descent groups have been recognized, and both principles of unilineal recruitment have been operative, for as long as Cochiti has had the *Kiva* system of patrilineal moieties. Dozier's remark, however, like so many others, was made primarily on the basis of the terminology – although it is expected that this coincides with 'behaviour' – and the point about terminology is that it is of its nature ego-centred. We will deal with this in the next chapter.

Thus, looking at the system from the point of view of the recruitment of kin groups, it is not true to say that Cochiti has 'shifted' from a lineage to a bilateral principle. And it is almost meaningless to say the same thing about any such shift from the angle of the individual ego. As far as kin groups are concerned, Cochiti possesses those outlined above: as far as ego is concerned, from the bilateral web of kin around him, he selects, on the basis of his membership in such groups, certain relatives for specific kinds of interaction based on specific rights and obligations in the various sphere of ritual, marriage, domestic economy, and so on. (It is worth noting that 'kin groups' is used here simply to mean groups *recruiting* members via kinship links. It does not imply that such members claim common kinship – in fact they will often deny it.)

This analysis to some extent overlaps with the Schneider-Roberts treatment of Zuni. However, I have confined 'bilateral' to the kinship context, although I would agree that 'bilateral integration' of the Zuni type is important in Cochiti. Every

[1] Dozier, 1960, 1961.

Cochiti, like every Zuni, may belong to several associations other than those based on kinship. But in Cochiti, because recruitment to the *Kivas* is kinship-based, the kinship groups are more important. The 'bilateral integration' of Zuni occurs because ego is a member of groups not based in kinship. In Cochiti it occurs even *within* the kinship context, because ego is a member of several different kin-groups, as well as the various associations. Like Zuni, however, Cochiti has 'weakly corporate' lineages and clans. They are not multi-functional. Indeed, the whole purpose of my analysis is to show how the various groups – kin and non-kin – divide functions between them. The 'system' is the balance of functions between the groups. What is basic is a state of balance – a lack of overlap and competition – rather than the existence of any one group or principle of grouping.

## III

### CHANGES IN THE SYSTEM

On the prehistory of Cochiti we have some archaeological evidence, that is if it is assumed that such ruins as those in Rito de los Frijoles were inhabited by Cochiti. But it is difficult to infer any sociological information from them. The number of *Kivas* often exceeds two, but without knowing details of their use one cannot infer that there was or was not a dual organization. Since historical times the Cochiti have been on their present site, and have had a social organization composed of the elements we have described – *Kivas*, clans, extended households, societies, *Katsina* cult, etc. It is therefore reasonable to infer that the kinship system described here is the one associated with the social structure of the village from at least the time of its sojourn on the Rio Grande. The distinctive pattern of its institutions from that time may well have been the result of an adaptation to irrigation agriculture, and while the dual division may have been 'borrowed' from the Tewa, the Cochiti could have brought this system with them.

But if the *structure* of the kinship system has been unchanged since this time (and this seems to me plausible rather than provable), this is not to say that the *functions* of the various elements in it have not changed. It is quite possible that within the system itself, for example, some functions of the lineage have 'shifted' to the nuclear family, and that some functions of, say, the clan may have shifted out of the kinship system altogether and on to the community. This would leave the structure intact, but the relative weightings of the various parts would change. This, I think, is the secret of 'shifts' in the kinship system. The total *structure* of the kinship system has not changed from being uni-lineal to something else, but the distribution of functions has changed, and some have been lost altogether. Thus, for example, in the 1890's Bandalier thought the clan was only a remnant of its former self and had been reduced to a 'mere naming system'.[1] Many (including myself) have noted the 'decline' of the clan.[2] But what is remarkable about the clan is not, in fact, its degeneracy, but its resilience. For the regulation and sanctifying of marriage, and for the healing of the sick, it still operates. This, I agree, is not all that much for the clan to do, but it is not for us to decide what the Cochiti should or should not have their clans do. Those who see the clan as declining suffer from two misconceptions. They do not fully appreciate what it in fact does, and they attribute to it too much prominence in the past. Assuming that clans (as in the proto-typical Western Pueblos) *should* be closely connected with ritual and government, they then assume that the Cochiti clans have lost this connection and 'degenerated'. It is true that any govern-mental function the clans ever had, and we do not know about this, has long since disappeared. But they are still there and still impor-tant, and they continue to perform their allotted tasks. If they have lost weight in the spheres of government and economics, their spiritual importance is still real. Within the system, their economic functions, such as they were, have been transferred to the patri-family and the combine harvester.

It is impossible, without adequate historical data, to assess all the changes that have occurred. Plainly there has been a move from extended to nuclear household, with the result that the nuclear family does most of the household work with occasional recourse to the matrifamily. There have obviously been shifts both within and out of the system of various disciplinary functions. All these will mean that, in terms of the amount of activity carried on, some of the kinship groups will be rendered relatively more

[1] Bandalier, 1890a.
[2] Eggan, 1950; Dozier, 1960; 1961; Lange, 1959; Hawley, 1950b; Goldfrank, 1927; White, 1935; Fox, 1960, 1961b.

quiescent than others. It may be that the clan has been stripped of all but its most essential functions, but it remains essential. My own belief is that it never had many more functions than it has now, and that those it has lost were in any case accidental. Much of what Bandalier describes as being done by the 'clan' was probably done by the matrifamily. Its supreme importance is mystical or spiritual, and this persists.

I do not maintain that it will persist for ever. There is plenty of evidence that the number of clan cures, for example, has fallen off in the past three decades. What I am combating is the idea that because they do not conform to the Western Pueblo pattern of integration with the socio-ceremonial system they are a somehow decadent or marginal institution.

I have dwelt at this tedious length on the clan because it is the social group most discussed. The matrilineage and the patrifamily / lineage have not been discussed by other writers, but their position in the system is easy enough to appreciate. I think we can now see that whether the system is *based* on the matrilineal lineage and household is the wrong question. The task we set ourselves was to see what kin groups did exist, and what their functions were, and to consider how these might have changed. What the whole system is 'based on' I would not like to say, except what I have already hazarded, namely: that it turns on the twin axes of mother-child and father-son, linked by the indissoluble bond of husband-wife.

## IV

### ALLIANCE

Whether this latter bond has always been so important I do not know. It may well be a consequence of Catholicism and its ban on divorce, although this does not seem to have affected the other Keres Pueblos in the same way. But evidence on these latter is not of the kind that would enable us to solve the problem. However, even a high turnover of spouses need not significantly affect the system.

The place of marriage in kinship systems has been the subject of some dispute. Much has been made of the difference between 'descent theory' and 'alliance theory' in kinship analysis. I am not sure whether the difference lies at the level of theory – although

Leach may be right in holding that descent has been over-emphasized at the expense of marriage – or at that of fact.[1] Some societies are geared to a 'prescriptive (or preferential) alliance' system; others are not.[2] Cochiti is not, but something less than 'perpetual' alliance is looked on with favour. Lange's simple phrase 'sequential inter-clan marriage' sums it up.[3] The Cochiti do not make this difficult by describing it in terms of marriage with some specified relative, but simply express a preference for sequential marriage between lineages. If a successful marriage has been made in one generation by a lineage member of either sex, this should if possible be followed up by the marriage of a younger sibling and/or someone in the next generation (or both), to clinch the alliance. For example, an 'ideal' marriage sometimes discussed by the members of the Ivy lineage (Genealogy ii) and the Oak lineage A (Genealogy i), was the one possible between Oa:30 and one of the daughters of either I:11 or I:12 (see Figure 6). (See discussion of other cases in Chapter 5).

There is no category of 'potential spouses' and no prescription or coercion. Such a match would be encouraged, and everyone is pleased when it happens. It is not, therefore, a 'structural' feature, but nevertheless, it is important. It leads to the setting up of relatively closed circles of inter-marrying descent groups. Such circles can become bounded, determinate groups themselves, and can act as a unit – as with the Redskins.

[1] I am not sure who coined this distinction, but alliance theory stems from Lévi-Strauss, 1949, while descent theory is well represented in the works of Fortes and Goody already cited.

I think it can be argued that the difference between the theories is indeed theoretical – that alliance theory sees kinship systems principally as sets of relations between groups or categories which serve to 'circulate' spouses in the system; descent theory on the other hand sees them primarily as systems of group formation and recruitment. Some actual societies, however, seem more amenable to analysis in terms of one theory than another. But Lévi-Strauss is quite clear that his theory is meant to apply to all societies. I suppose my analysis here is essentially a 'descent-theory' analysis. This is not because I am more sympathetic to this than to alliance theory, but because the whole argument has been phrased in 'descent' terms. It might be better to re-cast it in alliance terms, and in Ch. 8 I go some way in this direction. Eggan (1964) seems to be wrestling with the same confusion as myself in his discussion of 'alliance' and 'descent' in the Pueblos. He obviously regards the two as aspects of reality, more or less present in a society, rather than as theoretical approaches. Naturally, he chooses 'descent' as the crucial feature of Western Pueblo society. Now that Lévi-Strauss is turning his attention to Crow systems, alliance theory may penetrate the Pueblo field.

[2] Needham, 1962.

[3] See White, 1942, pp. 154–5, for examples from Santa Ana.

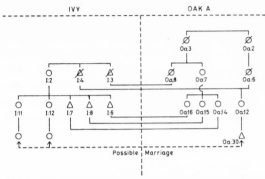

FIG. 6. Sequential inter-lineage marriages in Cochiti

It is therefore interesting to compare this aspect of Keres marriage, noticed by White, Lange and myself, with Eggan's conclusion that descent is more important than alliance in the Western Pueblos.[1] Alliance clearly has an important role with some of the Eastern Keresans at least.

## V

### SEGMENTATION

The matrilineage here is a true lineage, although of shallow depth, and does not seem to be a mere development of the ritual household, although it may well once have been 'based on' the matrilocal household. As I saw it in operation it was a group of close matrilineal kin, the descendants of a common ancestress, and was 'based on' the strong ties between a mother and her children, particularly her daughters, with the sister-sister bond very close indeed, particularly after the mother's death. These latter bonds are, of course, constant features of both lineage and matrifamily, and, as I have suggested, should perhaps be regarded as yet another analytically separate element in the system. They are only lineage bonds when they involve in their activities the men of the lineage (the mother-son, brother-sister ties) for specific lineage tasks.

The shallow depth of the lineage merits some discussion. It may, as Goody and Harris have said, be functionally connected with 'double descent', but it does seem to resemble so closely what we find in the Western Pueblos that it may be correlated with other

[1] Eggan, 1964

factors. As I have argued, if the lineage principle were in fact the integrating mechanism (through time) of the Western system, we should find deeper and more definite lineage groupings. In the east, however, the lineage has little significance for temporal continuity. There is no possible benefit to be gained from the keeping of long genealogies, and this is reflected in the lack of interest in the dead and the possible status designations of great-grand-parents, etc. (see Chapter 7). Ancestors are unimportant: children are supremely important. In this sense, at least, the Pueblos are oriented towards the future and not the past.[1] Miller at Acoma has noted the willingness to give terms for potential children, grand-children, and great-grandchildren, and an unwillingness to bother about ascending generations.[2]

The 'temporal' unit here is the clan, and this has a name and continuing membership which does not depend on the tracing of elaborate genealogical connections. One only needs to know one's mother's clan to be a member of it. The lineage is an 'operational' group. It is the matrilineal kin who, because of descent from a common grandmother or great-grandmother, feel themselves to be close and to have reciprocal obligations to each other. It is rare for it to be more than five generations in depth.

This argues for rapid segmentation and fission, but Schneider has maintained that segmentation is by its nature 'slower' in matrilineal than in patrilineal systems.[3] This, however, depends on the nature of the matrilineal group and the ties on which it is based. If it is based primarily on the brother-sister tie, as with the Trobrianders, then rapid segmentation may be difficult because each generation must wait until the proximate senior generation has died out before it can conveniently split, and then it will have difficulty. It should split into groups of uterine-siblings, but the nature of the property owned by the group may make this diffi-cult. It is hard for such a group to segment rapidly. It cannot break up 'within' a generation, as a patrilineal group can when the brothers simply separate, because, as Schneider sees, brothers and sisters have to be paired.

With the Pueblos, however, a different situation holds. The basic tie here is not between brother and sister, but between

---

[1] Kluckhohn and Strodtbeck, 1961.
[2] Miller, 1959.
[3] Schneider, 1961, p. 27.

mother and child. In the Trobriands the mother role is structurally weak, whereas in the matrilineal Pueblos it is crucial. This stems of course from the female-house-owning/matrilocal-residence syndrome. Unlike the Trobrianders, the Pueblos do not have to overcome the problem of combining corporate matrilineal lineages with virilocal marriage. The lineages, as we have seen, are not strongly corporate and not property owning. Hence, three sisters, for example, might easily set up three separate lineages within their lifetimes. The crucial ties in this case would be those between the sisters, as mothers, and their children. If the sisters had only one brother, he could function in his brother role towards all three. There is no property to be inherited from him; no office of of his to succeed to. No problem of pairing need arise. I would suggest that the analyses of matrilineal systems has neglected the distinction between the brother-sister and mother-child – particularly mother-daughter – relationship, and also the nature of group property.

In practice, in Cochiti, segmentation and fission, and the rate at which they occur, depend entirely on the circumstances of the lineage concerned. A lineage 'leaf' with too few males will cling to its lineage connections longer than a large one in which the sexes are evenly balanced. One that is composed largely of males will seek association over a longer period with one not so handicapped. Where several sisters each have well-balanced families, the foundations for fission are laid. Genealogies III and IV illustrate cases where exact genealogical links between leaves have been forgotten, but the relationship is asserted because of demographic imbalance. The large Oak lineage, A, in Genealogy I, in contrast, is only loosely held together 'at the edges', and on the deaths of the older members is bound to split. Already some of the younger members are showing a lack of interest in what they consider to be 'remote' connections, and join in collective activities at parental insistence rather than out of any sense of belonging. One said to me, 'We must be related to them people because we do things with them. But I don't know how we're related.' Fission can be said to have occurred when we stop doing things with 'them people' whose relationship to us is doubtful. This is at the lineage level. We will still go along with them at the clan level, but we will not initiate activity on their behalf, and this lack of interest will be mutual.

# VI

SUMMARY

How far has this discussion of the conceptualization of Cochiti kinship taken us towards the solution of our problem? We want to know how far Eggan's theory of the state of Keresan kinship in general, and Cochiti in particular, helps us to understand the present situation. We must also ask the converse question how our knowledge of the present state of Cochiti kinship helps us to assess Eggan's theory of the distribution of social types in the Pueblos.

On the first count we can return to Eggan's statements, quoted at the beginning of the previous chapter, which were interpretations of Cochiti kinship derived from his theory. For him the present state of Cochiti kinship was a result of the breakdown of the once prevalent Western Pueblo type, after the rebellion (Laguna evidence). What we should find was a 'bilateral' system on Anglo, Spanish or Tewa lines – or some combination – with traces of a previous matrilineal pattern. I think we have seen that in the sense in which commentators have used the term, the kinship system is not 'bilateral', and it is certainly not an approximation to any of the 'models' suggested. There have in all probability been some Anglo, Spanish and even Tewa influences in the system. Catholic exogamy laws are (more or less) observed, and the indissolubility of marriage is accepted. Also, the nuclear family living in its own house has come to be regarded as the normal household unit. But both these features (and both, of course, may be long-standing) are incorporated into a complex system of kinship groups making up a structure that is not 'bilateral' in any sense of the term. The matrilineal elements of this system belong logically to it, and do not look like wilting survivals. There may have been a time when the only system operating was a matrilineal one – we will take up this theme later on – but even if this is so, the present system cannot readily be interpreted as resulting from the breakdown of such a system in which 'the various manifestations of the lineage principle have been replaced by a "bilateral" principle of grouping'.[1] It seems more likely that the matrilineal elements might have been incorporated into a wider system, which is not bilateral as far as 'principles of grouping' are concerned.

[1] Eggan, 1950, p. 248 – on Acoma.

We can reserve consideration of the wider question until we have examined the terminology. Much emphasis has been placed on this in the analysis of Pueblo kinship, and terminology is often invoked to 'prove' things about changes in the system. So we must turn to Cochiti terminology and see if the chronological hypothesis – Crow terms first, followed on breakdown by bilateral – fits the facts.

# 7

# Kinship Terms: (1) Meanings

We have seen in the last chapter that we cannot really regard the Cochiti kinship system, as it stands, as a bilateral replacement for a matrilineal structure. The structure is more complex than this, and while it has undoubtedly changed in many ways over the centuries, it is not clear that this has been the simple process assumed in the 'running-down'theory. The patrilineal elements seem too well integrated to be recent 'borrowings', and to complement rather than replace or challenge the matrilineal.

Now much of the evidence for the simple process is thought to lie in the kinship terminology. This, like the kinship system itself, is said to have changed from Crow to 'bilateral' – the latter approximating 'Anglo, Spanish and/or Tewa models'. The chief evidence for the kinship change lies, as we have seen, in the 'decline' of the clan; on what does the terminological evidence rest?

The most influential statements on this change for the Keresans as a whole have come from Leslie White, although Parsons, Hawley and Kroeber had similar ideas. They have been echoed by Dozier, Goldfrank, Lange and others, and Eggan naturally embraced them, since they fitted perfectly with his hypothesis.[1] Let us take White's most explicit statement. This is a general comment derived from his Zia data (White, 1926):

'Thus we see that the kinship terminology is in a process of transition from one of a Crow type to a bilateral and generational system: father's sister is classed with mother and mother's sister; both maternal and paternal cross cousins are called "brother" and "sister" by some informants. Of the features of the Crow terminology, only the relationship between mother's brother and

[1] Curtis, 1926; Dozier, 1960; 1961; Eggan, 1950; Goldfrank, 1927; Hawley, 1950b; Kroeber, 1917; Lange, 1959; Parsons, 1932b; White, 1935, 1962.

sister's son, m. sp., remains and even it is giving way in the usage of some informants. The terminology has undergone more change in ego's father's lineage than in his own.

'The reasons for believing that the change is in the direction toward a bilateral system and away from Crow-type terminology, rather than the reverse, are: (1) Some of the earliest observations of kinship terminology among the Keres give terms of the Crow type rather than of a bilateral system. (2) The change from a Crow terminology to one of bilateral type would be the result of a breakdown rather than of development, and the culture in general is tending to break down. (3) There are indications that the influence of clan and lineage organization upon kinship terminology, which would tend to produce Crow features, is diminishing. (4) The influence of Spanish and American usage has been in the direction of bilaterality.'

There it is in a nutshell. 'Bilateral' is used as though synonymous with 'generational', although it is difficult to see the Anglo or Spanish 'model' in *this* development. The change is a result of 'breakdown' – primarily of the clan and lineage organization; acculturation to Spanish and American usage has completed the process.

White finds in Zia many examples of what all observers have noted: confusion and disagreement on the use of terms. All the recorders of Cochiti kinship terms have also noted this feature. In Zia, the last remaining Crow feature – the 'special term' for mother's brother – is 'giving way *in the usage of some informants*' (my italics).

I draw attention to White's wording here because I feel it is a question what exactly the *usage* quoted consists of. Keres kinship terms have been 'collected' by field workers who did not know the language, and by the use of the 'genealogical method': that is, 'informants' sitting at a table and presented with their genealogies have been asked 'what do you call so-and-so?', and so on. Sometimes they have even been asked in the abstract 'what is your word for. . . ?' They never seem to be able to agree. Some informants even contradict themselves. Lange's tables are the most extensive for Cochiti, and show that his informants are at odds with each other and with the informants who supplied previous collectors. The answer is obvious: confusion results from breakdown, and other 'models' intrude. Indeed, when starting my own work on this problem I used this method and got the same results. But one thing soon became clear: amongst themselves the Cochiti had no difficulties and confusions. They conversed on kinship matters happily and with no seeming lack of communication. The failure of communication was obviously between the Indians and the anthropologists. I was slow in seeing the implications of this point. I even wrote a lengthy report which explained the 'confused usages' in terms of acculturation and change on the basis of the accepted Crow-to-bilateral theory. It was only when I hesitantly began 'trying out' kinship usages on the Cochiti that I realized my errors.

The fact of the matter is that 'usage' has never been explored. Even my brief exploration showed quite clearly that the so-called 'kinship terms' were not simply abstract labels for genealogical relationships, but were used in a very general way to indicate status relationships. When actual persons were specified, they would always be qualified in some way. Now the status relationships which link any person to another in a small but complex society such as Cochiti can be many and various. As a consequence they can be variously described. Sometimes the usage is loose and sometimes highly formalized: but the question 'what do you call so-and-so?' is meaningless unless one adds 'when meeting him in the street; when asking for help; at a council meeting; at a wedding or healing; in the *Kiva*; during a dance; when he is fasting. . .?' One should add, I suppose, 'when talking to an anthropologist who is asking questions about kinship terms', but I don't think the Cochiti have settled on a formal usage for this situation.

Some usages are relatively fixed in all contexts. Thus the usages for primary relatives are constant. Whether this should lead us to view other usages as 'extensions' of terms for primary relatives I do not know. It seems to me, for example, that classifying the mother's sister with the mother and the father's brother with the father does not imply 'extending' these terms, but I do not want to get involved in this argument. I am only concerned with the terms as they are used. All I know about the terms is how the Cochiti distribute them, and hence the basis of discrimination in use. This basis is not simply genealogical; the 'genealogical context' in general is only one context in which the terms are used, and within it there are several others.

Thus the terms can be used in a very general way to address or refer to anyone in the society, and even to supernatural objects and powers; a study of this wide distribution will give us the most general connotation of the words. Within this wide context, however, there are several more particular contexts, of which the genealogical is the most important. The terms may be distributed in a simple sex-generation way for general purposes, or used in Crow fashion when lineage membership is the crucial component. On some very formal occasions these usages are relatively fixed, but on most occasions the actual usage will depend on how the people involved perceive the situation. For example, the more insightful of them would describe how when one was 'friendly and easy' one term was appropriate, while on other occasions one was 'respectful and quiet' and would use another. Thus one could work out a series of contexts: subordination and respect; subordination and friendship; equality and joking – and so on. These were not purely a matter of subjective states. They were culturally defined: one knew to whom one should be subordinate and respectful and on what occasions. But sometimes a situation was not well defined, and a judgement was called for. 'Mistakes' were made – by children and anthropologists, for example – and these were laughed at and commented on. Thus I learned, as I thought, that *náwa* was the 'term' for mother's brother, and tried to show off my knowledge of correct 'Crow' usage by calling one of my classificatory mother's brothers by this term at a party. Everyone laughed. But was it not the term? Well, yes it was, in a way, but it 'sounded funny'. I should, I was told, have really called him *umu* ('father'). Here I imagined, was a clear example of the Crow-to-bilateral (i.e. generational) process actually at work – especially when they added that *náwa* was an 'old word'. But on another more formal occasion, when I called the same man *umu*, I was quietly told that this was 'not polite'. I should have used *náwa*. It was by this means – stumbling around with the terms in differing contexts – that I learned that *náwa* was not really a 'kinship' term at all, but simply a term of respect for those in authority in certain contexts. It really was the equivalent of 'sir' in many ways, as we shall see, and was by no means confined in its use to 'mother's brothers'.

I do not pretend to be able to give anything like a complete account of this lexicon of status. I may even have made serious mistakes in interpretation. But I do believe that what I have found

out casts doubt on the simple hypothesis stated by White and sup-
ported by Eggan – at least for Cochiti. I am sure that Crow-type
usages are not as prominent as they might once have been, and in
this White, Eggan and the others are probably right; but for their
hypothesis to be true, Cochiti and the Keresans must have once
been wholly Crow and have succumbed to bilateral influences.
I doubt very much if this could be so even on the evidence as they
present it. White gives us only two alternatives: Crow to bilateral, or the reverse. Eggan writes in a similar vein. Neither
alternative seems to me to fit the facts as I know them. As with
the kinship system itself, several contexts are intertwined. There
is absolutely no reason why Crow, generational and many other
'types' of usage should not sit side by side in the same system.
Indeed in one as complex as the Cochiti we should expect it. The
terminology alone cannot, therefore, settle the chronological
problem, as White's point three acknowledges. It is 'bilateral or
generational' only in some contexts; it is not necessarily breaking
down.

To sum up then: the White-Eggan theory suggests that the
'confusion' we find in Cochiti and Keres kinship terminology is
a result of the breakdown of a Crow system which ends in terminological chaos (at worst), or a 'bilateral or equalizing'
terminology on Anglo/Spanish/Tewa lines (at best). Thus a
combination of breakdown and acculturation accounts for the
present system – or rather lack of system.

In reply to this I would claim that the system is not necessarily
confused or breaking down. It is only when the anthropologist
imposes alien conditions on informants that confusion appears – it
does not appear in 'usage'. I doubt very much, for example, if any
Cochiti isolates a 'pure' genealogical or kinship context in his use
of most terms, except on very special occasions. After all, every
Cochiti is related to every other by ties of kinship and marriage.
He will sometimes stand in several alternative relationships to
another person. Thus everyone is in his 'web of kinship', and as a
rule has more than one definable genealogical relationship to him.
He does not, of course, always choose to recognize these, and he
defines some people as 'non-kin'. But to pin down all his usages
in terms of where the referent stands in this genealogical web
would make nonsense of the words used. In very many contexts
the word will be used not with a 'kinship' connection in mind at

all, but in accordance with its meaning as a general status term denoting a certain type of relationship (nurturant, authoritative, equal, etc.) between the parties. Within the various kinship contexts, of course, the terms will be distributed in accordance with their meanings as general status terms. Thus one would not use a 'subordinate' status term for a 'superordinate' kinsman and so on. Which of these two general contexts is 'primary', and quite what this could mean, I should not like to say.

If one can show that there is a 'rational' distribution of terms and explain the principles on which this distribution rests, then even if the chronological hypothesis is true, the terms do not prove it. There is no reason why they should not be alternate sets within a system which has grown up over the centuries. This, we have seen, is what I have concluded for the kinship system as such; it should be equally true for the terminology.

Perhaps we should take heed of the general warning issued by Hymes, which fits the Cochiti case with uncanny accuracy:

'It is essential to resist the temptation to assign an aspect of a native culture too easily to a familiar category, by either not investigating its full range, or by explaining discrepancies away as due to confusion, or ignorance, or breakdown of an old system, or intrusion of a new one. Such may be the case, but often enough the difficulty is failure to discern a principle or system actually in use, one which makes the full range of variation intelligible.' (Hymes 1964, p. 96.)

## II

I will present here a straightforward account of the kinship/status terminology as I found it in Cochiti in 1958-9. There is often a distinction between terms used by male speakers and terms used by female speakers for the same referent. Also, a term used by both males and females can be applied by each respectively to a referent of different sex. Table 5 shows the thirteen most common status terms. The left-hand column shows the sex of the referent, while the right-hand column shows the most usual English kinship term by which they are translated. This is, of course, purely ethnocentric, and merely reflects the fact that when presenting an informant with a genealogy and asking for terms, the person that one comes across to whom the term, say, *yaya*, is first applied will be the informant's own mother. A better approach might be to ask, 'To what range of referents is this term applied?'. I will now attempt to give at least a partial answer to this question for the thirteen terms listed. It should be noted that only in two cases (1 and 2) is the term of reference different from the term of address, and in case 1 the terms are obviously cognate. In the other cases the term of address can be sometimes simply the root, or the root with a suitable first-person pronominal prefix. With some terms

TABLE 5. Cochiti Kinship Terms

| Sex of referent | Man Speaking Address | Reference | Woman Speaking Address | Reference | Usual Gloss |
|---|---|---|---|---|---|
| 1. M/F | yaya | -naya | yaya | -naya | 'mother' |
| 2. M | umu | -nashtyu | tata | -nashtyu | 'father' |
| 3. M | s'atyum | -tyum(she) | -meme | -mem | 'brother' |
| 4. F | -meme | -meme | satá'o | -tá'o | 'sister' |
| 5. M/F | s'aúshe | -'ushe | s'aúshe | -'ushe | 'child' |
| 6. M | -náwa | -náwa(she) | -nyenye | -nyenye | 'mother's brother' |
| 7. M | -mumu | -mumu | -papa | -papa | 'grandfather'/ 'grandson' |
| 8. F | -papa | -papa | -t'aó | -t'aó | 'grandmother'/ 'grand-daughter' |

the pronominal prefix is obligatory; where this is the case the word is shown in full: where the prefix is optional, the root is shown preceded by a hyphen. In the case of reference, the pronominal prefix will, of course, vary according to the nature of the reference. These prefixes are complex, and I am not sure of the precise meanings of them all. Sometimes the nominalizing suffix -she is added, but this is highly variable. These variations will be discussed as each term is dealt with.

A proper account of these words ~~would deal with their gram~~matical status. Those that I have loosely called 'referential' come into the class of 'inflected words'. Davis, quite rightly, classifies them as 'verbs' because they are inflected exactly as verbs are.[1] Thus naya has a future tense (nanayasi – first person singular), a subjunctive mood (atanaya), and so on. In a sense, then, they could be said to refer to activities rather than objects; 'mothering' rather

[1] Davis, 1964, pp. 75 ff.

than 'mothers'. Neither my knowledge of the language nor my feeling for the implications of this fact are sufficiently profound to allow me to elaborate on it, and if I tried I should probably only confuse the reader. I shall leave it aside therefore.

*yaya* (*-naya*): These terms are obviously cognate, and it may be that the referential term is simply the form of *yaya* for use with affixes. For example, while I have heard *tata* used with affixes, I have never heard *yaya* so used. Sometimes it is shortened to *ya* in address. In general, the term refers to those beings and objects which are nurturant and fertile, or promote fertility. In a sense, of course, it is true that for any individual the prototype of such a person or object is his own mother; and in trying to explain the term to Anglos, Cochiti will often draw the analogy with the mother. Thus, for example, the Cacique is called *yaya*, as is his stone fetish, but Cochiti baulk at the suggestion that he is called *yaya because* he is 'like' a mother. The 'being like a mother' is a useful way of explaining the concept – it is not the reason for its use. 'We call him *yaya*', one put it to me, 'because he *is yaya*'. (When I suggested this was because he was 'like a mother' they laughed and pointed out that he was in fact a man.) He belongs to the same category as mothers proper. Also in this category are the medicine men 'when they are fasting', the corn-ear fetishes of the medicine men, the female heads of clans, and the chief female deity, *Iatiku*. Father Dumarest gives extended examples of the ceremonial use of the term.[1] As regards its application to females generally, it could be applied to any mature female (i.e., one who had borne a child) older than ego, as a term of politeness. The usual connotation is of a 'related' woman who is one generation older than ego. This relationship can be ceremonial; thus godparents and women of a 'healing' clan would be *yaya*. Affines could be, but this would depend on how 'close' one felt. With close relatives, the term would often be followed by the personal name of the relative. With more distant and ceremonial relatives, it would be used alone, or followed perhaps by a clan designation. This latter would be the case between ego and an older woman of one of the 'little' clans that had healed him. All women of the right age in ego's own clan would be addressed as *yaya*, as would those of the father's clan.

As we have seen, while some of these usages are fairly fixed,

---

[1] Dumarest, 1919.

there is an optional air about others. The general connotation of the term as it applies to females is 'someone, usually related, who stands in a senior but nurturant relationship to me'. Some persons are 'automatically' in this category, some are on the borderline, while others are not automatically in it, but can be placed in it out of 'politeness' or respect or affection. I have recorded instances of the term being withdrawn from some persons because of bad feeling – stepmothers, for example. Normally a stepmother would be in this class, but one man insisted on using the term for 'relative-in-law' for his. I doubt if one could withdraw the term from mother's or father's sister whatever one felt.

It is perhaps worth mentioning here that the distinction between address and reference terms is not rigid. If one is feeling 'very respectful' one can use the 'referential' term in address. If one used it otherwise, it would be odd but not outrageous, either semantically or socially. Alternatively, *yaya* can be used in reference (plus personal name), if one is not employing inflections.

*umu/tata* (*-nashtyu*): *umu* is the man's, and *tata*[1] the woman's term of address, and *-nashtyu* the term of reference for both sexes, for males usually of the proximate ascending generation who are held in respect, but not awe. The connotion of *umu/tata* is an older male held in affectionate respect, although it can simply be a polite term for any older male. Again there are some people who automatically fall into this category: one's close male relatives in the senior generation; fathers, uncles, and the male cousins of these; male members of the father's clan generally, and those of one's own clan. It would also apply, particularly for men, to the appropriate senior generation males of the *Kiva*. Certain *Katsinas*, and of course the Sun, are also *umu/tata*.

Outside this compulsory range, there is the same variation as with *yaya*. Ceremonial relatives would come under the term, and for a woman her husband's *umu* would be her *tata*, but I have heard deviations from this usage. In its most general sense, it can be taken to mean 'male of proximate ascending generation', and could be so used out of politeness. But its overtones of affectionate respect mean that it is not lightly used outside its more restricted context.

Again, the reference term can be used in address, and particu-

---

[1] *tata* is of course the baby term in Spanish for father. Somehow I think this is a coincidence, but we can't be sure.

larly when used in collective address – *kuchnashtyu* – 'our father'. The 'reference-address' distinction here is perhaps the wrong one, except that I have heard *tata* used with prefixes, although never *umu*.

The prototype relative here is one's own father, but the term as applied to other men is in no sense an 'extension' of 'the term' for father. A father's brother is an *umu* absolutely in his own right. He is not a kind of pale reflection of one's real father. Both these men are *umu*, as are many others.[1]

*s'atyum* (*-tyumshe*): This is a man's term for male status equals. It is reciprocal, but only if both sides of the relationship see each other as equals. Thus A always addressed B as *s'atyum*, but B addressed A as *umu*. A was B's father-in-law and was held in affectionate respect by the latter, but both were officers and council members. Thus A called B *s'atyum*, 'out of respect', but B could not bring himself to reciprocate, and always replied with *umu*. It would not have been the least improper for him to have used *s'atyum*, in fact it would have been 'correct', but his sensitivity led him to maintain that A was 'always my *umu* first'. In council meetings, however, if the two had to converse, then they both used *s'atyum*. That was quite different, and the formality of the occasion sanctioned the usage.

Automatically coming under this term are one's own siblings and cousins, and males of the same generation in one's *Kiva* and clan. Outside this limit, males who are recognized as status equals will be *s'atyum*. Age equals come under this heading.

For reference, the suffix *-she*, is always added, but again, usage is loose and this suffix is often retained in address.

*-meme*: Man's term for female status equals; woman's term for male status equals; reciprocal. Age equality is usually the governing factor here, as status differences between males and females are

---

[1] Goldfrank (1927) gives *nactuc* as the 'woman's term'. She does not mention *tata* in her discussion of kin terms, but gives *dada* a single reference as the 'vocative' of *nactuc*, in an appendix. Curtis and Parsons – contemporary with Goldfrank – both record *tata*, and Curtis has *(s'a)nashtyu* for both males and females, although Parsons does not have *(s'a)nashtyu* for males. Bandalier (1890b) and Dumarest both write as though *nashtyu* (*nashtio* or *narshtia*) were the joint property of males and females. It may be that *nashtyu* is the older term once reserved for females and that *tata* has replaced this, but it may also be that the anthropologists' notion of a dichotomy between 'terms of reference' and 'terms of address' is confusing both themselves and their informants. The real dichotomy, I believe, is simply between inflected and uninflected forms. Only texts or the actual observance of conversations will, of course, reveal this.

largely a matter of age. Any man or woman of roughly the same age-group, could address each other as *meme*, out of politeness. But again, some would come under this term automatically, some optionally. Automatically included would be own siblings and cousins of opposite sex, members of clan and *Kiva* of opposite sex.

It is, I believe, in origin a Tanoan word, and crops up all over the Pueblos, serving various functions. Parsons uses the graphic expression 'rover term' to describe it.[1]

*satá'o (-tá'o):* Woman's term for female status equals. As with all women's terms, this has a more limited distribution than a man's term, the number of statuses open to women being more restricted. Sisters, cousins and clan members of the same age-group can come under this term, as can sisters-in-law, although again this is variable. It is subject to the same limitations as *s'atyum* for males.

*s'aúshe (-úshe):* Male and female term for status inferiors, generally seen as being of the proximate descending generation. This is a very variable term. It is applied consistently to all children (much in the way that a word like 'sonny' might be to boys in England), but it can be applied to any young cousin. It is interesting that a number of people who applied one of the 'status equal' terms to parallel cousins, rarely did so to cross cousins, but used *s'aúshe*. We shall discuss this later. In reference, particularly in the plural (*s'awishe*), it would usually be taken to mean own children, or children of a person referred to, unless qualified. Its general connotation is a younger person, usually of the next generation down, and a status inferior.

*náwa:* This, strictly speaking, is a man's term for an authoritative male, held in respect, not to say awe. It is the complement of *umu*, in that it indicates respect, but not necessarily affectionate respect. Rather it suggests obedience, deference, and status inferiority. As a term of address it could perhaps be best translated as 'sir'. Outside a strictly kinship context, which we will discuss later, it is used by women also as a term of respect. It is due automatically to several males such as heads of societies, *Kiva* heads, heads of clans, and older male members of one's own clan and particularly lineage. Older male members of one's father's clan can be so addressed out of politeness, although this is not invari-

---

[1] Parsons, 1932b. On the other hand, the root *-me* in Keres means 'same' or similar', and the prefix *me-* is an intensifier.

able. If one's father's own brothers or his father's brothers are important ceremonial people, one can address them as *náwa* out of respect.

Etymologically, *náwa* simply means 'old', or 'elderly', and can be used adjectivally: *náwayatsa k'atruche* – 'it is an old house'. Sometimes it was explained to me that people were called *náwa* 'because they were the oldest' (in the society or clan, for example). This was often patently not true in terms of years, but, in many languages, 'old' connotes 'respected 'or 'revered'; therefore to address someone as *náwa* is to imply that he is deserving of reverence in the way that an old man is. (There is quite another descriptive term for 'old man'.) Translation is always slippery, and it is perhaps unwise to try to find half-a-dozen equivalents in English in order to convey the subtleties of the one Keres word. Knowing the full connotation of the word, however, we could well translate the 'titles' *shrutsuna náwa* or *Shikame náwa* as 'old fox' or 'old Shikame', for example. (Davis records *náwaiy'a* as 'middle aged'. He was working with a single informant, and obviously did not explore further.)[1] The term *wawa* has sometimes been glossed as 'little uncle' for the Keres,[2] and Miller has '*áwá'áwá* in Acoma as a term of address between a woman and a man in the *nawé* category. He thinks it might be a 'baby term'.[3] Goldfrank recorded *awa'wawa* in Cochiti.

In any child's life the first and probably thenceforward prototypical *náwa* would be the male members of his lineage. These *umu* (senior-generation males) would be the *náwa* who were most prominent in his life as opposed to the more nuturant *umu* on his father's side. They would be the people that his mother would turn to in case of the need for discipline and guidance, etc. But the term in no sense 'means' mother's brother, even if this is the person to whom it is earliest and most readily applied. Nor, for that matter, is the mother's brother in all his relations with his sister's children invested with a *náwa* quality. He is just as often *umu*. Similarly, heads of societies are, in different contexts, both *yaya* and *náwa*. The Cacique, however, never seems to be addressed by this term.

It sometimes takes the suffix *-ya* or *-y'*, the meaning of which I did not ascertain, but is perhaps a pluralizer ('singular' and 'plural' usage is not rigid), and is, like *s'atyum*, used as often with

[1] Davis, 1964, p. 167.   [2] Hawley, 1950b.   [3] Miller, 1959.

the suffix *-she* as not. It has its other form *wawa*, which I was told also meant 'medicine' or 'power', and which logically might seem to have borne the same relation to *náwa* as *yaya* does to *-naya*, that is, an uninflected form used in address. It is rarely used now, but seems to be thought of as a kind of diminutive of *náwa*. Thus, the children of someone addressed as *náwa* may be addressed as *wawa*. It indicates, I think, a slight distance socially from the person so addressed – a kind of reserve; but it is rarely resorted to. (See Chapter 8.)

I believe that some ceremonial objects are addressed as *náwa* but I was unable to pursue this line for obvious reasons. White, however, provides a clue to this usage when he speaks of his difficulties in understanding the concept of *ho:nawaiaiti*.[1] He describes this as 'the name of an order in a curing society' and says that it seems 'definitely to pertain to the magical curing function of societies'. His informants found it difficult to explain. The prefix *ho:* – is an intensifier: thus *chaianyi* 'medicine man', and *ho:chaianyi* 'Cacique' or 'great medicine man'. Thus if *náwa(ya)* means 'old' with the connotation of 'revered', then *ho:nawa(yaiti)* should mean something like 'that which is very old and venerated', which fits very well the 'magical curing function of societies', and ties up with the use of *náwa* to address ceremonial objects, and *wawa* for 'medicines' – the old, venerated and powerful instruments of the doctors.[2] (Father Dumarest notes, in a song text, the term *honawa*,

[1] White, 1962.

[2] White asks whether or not there is a relationship between *ho:nawaiaiti* and his other problem word *nawai* which he translates as 'the head of a curing society' – although he elsewhere had recognized another meaning: 'old man' (see 1932, p. 56). Clearly there is such a relationship, but here a problem arises. All the Eastern Keres have a 'respect' term like *nawa* (*nawai, nawaya, nawai'*, etc.), but only in Cochiti, Santo Domingo and San Felipe, does this seem to be the exact pronunciation of the term which is used in the kinship context. At Zia and Santa Ana the term is more like *nawe, nawi* or *nowe* – although Hawley has *nowa* for Zia. We are faced here with a variety of phonetic recording systems, but the more consistent reports (even though these are usually based on only one or two idiolects) show the word ending in a high front vowel rather than a back rounded vowel. This is also the case in Laguna and Acoma, and reinforces the likeness of these to Santa Ana and Zia. (With respect to the congruent woman's term, however, there is a clear three-way division: Santa Ana and Zia – *wa'a*: Western Keres – *muiti*; Eastern three – *nyenye*.) Hawley (1950) summarizes the data extant at that time, although this has to be supplemented by later work. (Davis, 1964; White, 1964; Lange, 1959; Miller, 1959; Mickey, 1956.) (Parsons' *naishdye* for mother's brother in Santo Domingo is a clear case of only one alternate being obtained. The Santo Domingo, like the Cochiti, call the mother's brother both *nashtyu* and *náwa*.)

which he glosses as *chaianyi* (medicine man).[1] I never heard this term used spontaneously, but Cochiti knew of it 'in songs' and suggested it was an old usage for medicine society heads.)

In general, then, as a status term it connotes authoritative, disciplinary males; men who, because of their high status, are held in awe and respect, not to say veneration. The Cacique, despite his awe-inspiring position, is not a disciplinarian; he is a nurturer, and hence wholly *yaya*, and a little *umu*.

*-nyenye* (sometimes pronounced *nenye*): This is an interesting term in that it is the woman's equivalent of *náwa*, but not in all contexts. It seems to be confined to a kinship context.[2] Thus within the circle of a woman's kin, she would call *nyenye* those people whom her brother called *náwa*. Outside this context she would use *náwa*. As the term applies primarily to matrilineal kin, this may reflect the very great importance of these kin in a woman's life. She is, in a sense, much more restricted to the kinship context than a man, and hence her terminology may be subject to a similar restriction.

If we accept the *náwa/nawe* dichotomy for Santa Ana and Zia, how is it to be explained? I do not know the answer except to say that the dialect differences between these groups are often quite marked. It may be that in the internal affairs of the villages – as for example with kinship – differences of dialect have prevailed, but that because of ceremonial co-operation between villages the *náwa* form has been retained for 'society heads' and other officials. We lack information that might help us to solve this problem, but a clue is provided by Miller's work on Acoma. Here he found a 'vocative' of *n'a:ya* which was *n'a:ye*; it could be that something similar is the case with *náwa*, and a 'vocative' form has been retained in Santa Ana and Zia while the 'nominative' has become the 'international' term. The apparent similarity of culture between the Western Keres and Santa Ana and Zia might have reinforced this.

I questioned a man who was born and raised in Zia, but whose mother was a Cochiti. He returned to live in his mother's village in his early teens. He said these were 'all the same word' and maintained that at Zia he could call his senior clansmen, for example, either *(sa)nawi* or *(sa)nawa*, it made no difference. The Cochiti agreed, but added that all the other Keres 'talked funny' anyway.

[1] Dumarest, 1919, p. 156.

[2] I do not know the etymology of this term. It is used as a reciprocal at Cochiti, Santo Domingo and San Felipe. (The reciprocal term at Santa Ana and Zia is *(sa)wa'a* – obviously related to *wawa*.) An ingenious but perhaps improbable derivation would be from the Spanish *niño* – 'male child'. Applied by a woman to her mother's brother it would be similar to the usage in the Western Keres where the mother's brother is called *muiti* (*mu:ti*), 'son'.

The question then is: what was it substituted for in Cochiti? The answer is obviously (following the Western Keres lead) *múti*, which is one of those words which now have a range of meanings like 'son', 'boy', 'fellow', 'lad', 'chap' etc. This is a speculation, but it makes sense, as later discussion may confirm. (See Ch. 8.)

Both *náwa* and *nyenye* are, in the kinship context at least, self-reciprocal terms which may seem to militate against my interpretation. If *náwa* in address simply means 'sir', what sense does it make for the senior user to address it to the junior? It in fact makes very good sense. It used to be common in English usage for two persons to use 'sir' to each other when being angry or haughty, or icy, or in some way distant. Thus a schoolboy always addressed his master as 'sir', and the latter might well do the same to the schoolboy, although this usage could mean either haughtiness or amusement. I think we might interpret this reciprocity not, as anthropologists have been prone to do, as implying equality, but as conveying mutuality. The two people concerned are saying 'we are standing to each other in a "sir" relationship'. It is an acceptance of the formality of the situation, that the two are in the same boat. I think the reciprocity here rather emphasizes the interpretation of *náwa* as 'sir'. As a noun used in reference, of course, we would usually translate it differently, but colloquial English usage sanctions the use of 'sir' as a noun, anyway.

*-mumu:* This word is, I believe, a cognate of *umu*, and is the man's term for a male two generations removed (usually) in either direction, or of considerable age difference.[1] This, of course, automatically makes it reciprocal. It connotes a higher degree of affectionate respect than *umu*, with the emphasis on the affection. The prototype is again one's own grandfather(s). The Cochiti explained the relationship by saying that an old man does not live long enough to discipline his grandsons or be harsh to them. His relationship is purely friendly and encouraging. The term is very freely used between people who see themselves in such a relationship, regardless of generation.

*-papa:* Man's word for a woman, and woman's word for a man, who is two generations removed in either direction, and for a person of opposite sex who is younger, or older, and who is seen as standing in a very friendly, indulgent, kindly and affectionate relationship. The prototypes are, of course, grandfather-granddaughter, and grandmother-grandson. Again, the term is widely used between people not in these kinship categories but who see themselves as being in the friendly, indulgent relationship des-

---

[1] It is likely that *umu*, *mumu* and *tyum* are cognate. A plural form of *tyum* – *s'awatyumishe* is used simply to mean 'my relatives'. For Laguna, Parsons (1923) notes a similar term as 'my clanspeople'.

cribed above. (Several women of the clan of which I was an honorary member called me *papa*, although *meme* or *s'aúshe* would have been more correct in terms of generation. However, they saw the relationship as being one of kindly indulgence with a joking element and considered *papa* more appropriate. Proximate generation terms, for example, would have had a faint air of restraint which is lacking in this one.)

*-t'aó:* This term is superficially like *-tá'o*, but in fact the initial consonant is glottalized, and the final vowel rather than the medial vowel carries the stress and also a rise in tone, both of which prolong the *-o*. The pronunciation is, however, somewhat variable, and the words are undoubtedly cognate. It is the complementary term to *-mumu*, being a woman's word for a female two generations removed in either direction, or of an age difference that suggests a two-generation remove. It is subject to the same use and variation as *mumu* and *papa*, but outside a strict kinship context it is also used by men as a term of respect, or just of general address, to very old ladies. I get the impression that it has more overtone of respect than *mumu* or *papa*, or can be used in this way. Generally, one can say that the really indulgent relationship is *papa*, which is cross-sex, while *mumu* is similar between males, but not as familiar, and *t'aó* between females has more of an air of respect, which is accentuated when used by males. But none of these terms suggests authority or deference or anything approaching it. They are essentially friendly terms.

Both men and women use *pihya* for female affines, and *wa'ti* for male. These simply mean 'male/female relative-in-law', and can be applied to anyone married to a cognate, including people married into one's clan or patrilineage. They generally have an overtone of reserve, and if one wants to indicate respect or affection, or to stress, say, generation difference, one would use one of the other status terms as appropriate. They are very often used as reference terms (with or without inflection) but always followed by the personal name of the referent. Another term often used is *comp'ar'i*, the Keres version of *compadre*, again followed by the personal name of the *compadrino*. There are also old words for 'son' (*múti*) and 'daughter' (*mák*) that are not used often today (see note 13), and two roots for 'spouse': *-ku* = wife ('woman'); *-trushe* = husband.

We should note that there is no variation in the use of these status terms for primary relatives. Thus one's own mother is always *yaya*, father *umu/tata*, brother *tyum/meme* and sister *tá'o/meme*. Thus, if one wished to refer to someone's actual mother's brother descriptively, *k'anaya k'ameme* (his/her mother, her brother), would be quite unambiguous.

## III

I have dwelt at some length on these words in order to emphasize my argument that these are general status terms, not simply 'kinship' terms. But as kinship statuses loom so large in Cochiti social relations, they are obviously going to play a large part in determining how the status terminology is used. Before discussing any further the general aspects of the status terms, we should turn to kinship statuses and see how the terms are distributed within the kinship system. First, however, let us look at some features of terms in relation to each other. One simple way of organizing them is shown in Table 6. Here we will assume that a male and a

TABLE 6. Status Terms for Sex-generation Distinction:
Male and Female Ego

Male Ego

| | Males | Females |
|---|---|---|
| +2 | *mumu* | *papa* |
| +1 | *umu* | *yaya* |
| 0 | *tyum* | *meme* |
| −1 | *s'aúshe* | |
| −2 | *mumu* | *papa* |

Female Ego

| | Males | Females |
|---|---|---|
| +2 | *papa* | *t'aó* |
| +1 | *tata* | *yaya* |
| 0 | *meme* | *tá'o* |
| −1 | *s'aúshe* | |
| −2 | *papa* | *t'aó* |

female Cochiti wish to divide up their social world simply on the basis of sex and generation. If this were so, the status terminology would be as arranged. All males, for example, of ego's own generation would be *tyum* for a man and *meme* for a woman. All females of the first ascending generation would be *yaya* for both, and so on. But the world is not so simple, and every ego wants in fact to make more distinctions than this. He may wish to circumscribe more closely the people to whom he applies the terms, by, for example, singling out affines for special attention instead of including them under the general sex-generation scheme. He may also wish to indicate those in authority over him by a special term of respect. Anyone not coming under these headings, and not addressed by one of the sex-generation terms, would be addressed

TABLE 7. Composite Table of Status Terms for Male and Female Ego

Ms Male speaker or subject
Mr Male referent

Fs Female speaker or subject
Fr Female referent

by a special title, if he held an office which bore a title, or by a personal name or clan name. Those within the scheme may be addressed and referred to by a combination of term, title and/or personal name. Table 7 is a composite table of terms used by both male and female egos. Outside the persons covered by this terminology lie those covered by titles, personal names, friendship terms, clan names etc. One cannot know exactly where any individual will draw these boundaries, or, figuratively speaking, which persons he will put into what box. All this tells us is what kind of distinctions are made in the vocabulary of status, and on what basis one term is distinguished from another. We have seen that sex, generation, affinity and authority are important, and the table makes it clear that the relative sexes of speaker (subject) and referent are important as well. What is impossible to show is that the terms for generations +2, −2, and −1 can be used without generation restriction, like the authority and affinal terms, and also that *náwa* and *t'aó* are not subject to rigid restriction in terms of sex of speaker. In fact, there is no rigid generation restriction in use, and, of course, it is more often than not relative age that guides usage rather than generation in the strict sense.

The only context in which the restrictions by generation would be automatically observed is the 'kinship' context as it affects lineal relatives and some collaterals. One of the components of meaning that each of these terms carries is that of generation difference or relative age. But this is not the only component, and not necessarily the decisive one, except with lineal relatives. With these, the crucial distinction is that of actual genealogical generation position *vis-à-vis* ego. Thus no man would ever call his own sister *papa* no matter how friendly and indulgent he felt towards her. She must be *meme*.

## IV

Let us now turn to the kinship context. As we have seen, the terms allow for certain distinctions by generation, sex of subject, sex of referent, affinity and authority. How are these distributed in the kinship system, and how do they tie up with the other components of meaning we have previously discussed? Taking generation as our reference point for the moment, we can see that the distinctions implied in the terms suggest the following:

+2 and −2: The relations of males to males and females to females are distinguished from each other and from the relation of males to females.

+1: The relation of junior males to senior males is distinguished from the relation of junior females to senior males, and both these are distinguished from the relation of junior males and females to senior females.

Ego's generation: As for +2 and −2 above.

−1: The contemporary reciprocal of +1 makes no distinction as to sex of subject or referent. Members of the proximate junior generation have much the same relationship to the senior regardless of sex. The words for 'junior male' and 'junior female' do not seem to be used very much.

With the authority relations, the relation of male to male and female to male is distinguished.

Let us then narrow down the field to the kinship system in terms of the groups of which it is composed and of which ego is a member. These group memberships define certain status relationships for ego and we might expect the terminology to 'fit' them in some way, or at least not be inconsistent with them. Generation −1 we can ignore, as no distinctions are currently made in it. We will leave +2 and −2 on one side for a moment, and concentrate on the proximate generations of ego and +1. Let us start with ego's own generation and his more immediate relatives. Here the terms consign brothers to one sphere and sisters to another, but allow a sphere in which brothers and sisters are merged. We might represent this as on Fig. 7.

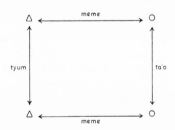

FIG. 7. Sibling terms

Now where, in the kinship system, is the sister-sister relationship distinct from the brother-brother: that is, what are the groups to which brothers but not sisters are automatically consigned, and vice-versa? The answer is clearly that brothers are members of the patrifamily, and sisters of the matrifamily. In fact, these two sets of relationships can be viewed as the 'base' of each group. If we add generation +1, then, we get the following, as in Fig. 8.

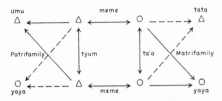

FIG. 8. Sibling and parental terms
(Double-headed arrows indicate self-reciprocal terms.
Single-headed arrows indicate non-self-reciprocal terms)

This suggests that the 'mother' is constant, but that the 'father's' relationship with his daughters is different from that with his sons. Now the relationship of boys to their *umu* in the patrifamily/*Kiva* organization is, of course, quite different from the relationship of girls to their *tata* in the matrifamily/household. Their mother, however, is equally a member of both. Thus the constant term for 'mother' makes sense.

This is, however, only part of the kinship context. We are left with the *meme* relationship. Where in the system is the 'base' of a group the brother-sister relationship? The answer is, in two places: the lineage and the family. While brothers and sisters must necessarily split between matrifamily and patrifamily, they are united as members of the same lineage/clan, and as members of the same nuclear family (Fig. 9).

With the lineage, again, the mother is the same, and the authority terms are used for her brothers. This assumes the lineage actually functioning in lineage/clan affairs. A man may call his mother's brothers *umu*, i.e., 'senior-generation male', in other contexts (see Table 6), but in the strictly lineage context the authority term would be most appropriate and would commonly be used. The woman's term is interesting here, in that it suggests that the relation between a woman and her lineage males (senior) is different from that of a man, and that it is a 'special' kinship relationship. The term is not used by a woman outside this context. I have occasionally heard a woman use it for a related man whom her brother calls *náwa*, but this is rare unless he is of the lineage/clan of the woman. She would be more likely to use *tata*. This again makes sense, since women are less involved than men in the ceremonial and governmental life of the Pueblo, and a woman is much more confined to the kinship context, and particularly the context of matrifamily and lineage/clan.

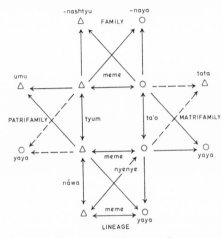

FIG. 9. Terms for own and first-ascending generations

The case of the family is even more interesting. I have deliberately put the reference or inflected terms here rather than the vocatives. In the case of *-nashtyu* this was inevitable. It is the only term for 'father' shared by brother and sister. Thus, when facing outwards as it were, brother and sister can refer to their father by the same term, but when facing inwards and addressing him, they have to diverge. To complement this I have used the referential *naya*, but this is only the inflectional equivalent of *yaya*.

This latter point is very significant. As we saw in the kinship system, the only 'constant' member is the mother herself. She is the only person who automatically belongs to all the groups that a male ego belonged to. Terminologically she is constant too. Wherever she appears she is *yaya*.

The nuclear family I find hard to explain. Internally it is split between the matrifamily and the patrifamily 'wings'. But when facing 'outwards' to the outside world and talking of itself, it is united. It is also a unit to those talking of it. This does, I think, make sense in terms of my analysis of kinship, but I am not sure how to express this meaningfulness except to say that 'internally' the family is not a unit, while 'externally' it is.

It will be obvious that various cousins are covered by one or the other of the above rubrics. Thus, all a man's parallel cousins, except his father's brothers' daughters after marriage, will fall into one of his groups. Within the system they will be classed with his siblings, and the father's brother's daughter will be so classed as well, probably out of consistency, i.e. she is the sister of someone called *s'atyum*, even though after her marriage she is lost to the patrilineage. If she marries within the *Kiva*, the term *meme* will be reinforced in application to her. For a woman the situation is different, as her father's brothers' children may have no connection with her. She will still be inclined, however, to call them *meme* and *satá'o*, because her own brother addresses them by the corresponding terms. This is, however, variable, and I have heard 'cross-generation' terms used between a woman and her father's brother's daughter (*yaya*, for example, or *s'aúshe*).

For cross-cousins the usage is as varied as are the relationships between cross-cousins. I think it is fair to say that any of the terms listed can be used. It all depends on how they are seen. If they were seen as age mates, they would come in the *tyum-meme-tá'o* category. If the relationship was seen as friendly and indulgent, they would be *mumu-papa-t'aó*. If they were seen essentially as 'children', as the children of a mother's brother would be in their role as 'children of a lineage member', they would be *s'aúshe*. The son of a mother's brother might be seen as sharing the awesomeness of this figure and addressed by the authority term (rarely) or more likely its diminutive form – *wawa*.

There is also a sense in which the use of a term for one person will determine the use for a relative of that person, and this is particularly so with cousins. Thus if, for example, the mother's brother is viewed as *umu* (senior-generation male), the *generational* criterion is operative, and this will apply to his children, who will be addressed as generation equals (*meme-tá'o-tyum*). If, on the other hand, he is seen as a *lineage* authority (*náwa*), his children will be, as we have seen, 'children of the lineage', and addressed as *s'aúshe*, or, rarely, by the terms for 'son' and 'daughter'.[1] Thus there is

---

[1] Strictly speaking, if ego calls his mother's brother's children *s'aúshe* they should respond by calling him – their father's sister's child – *umu* or *tata* (*yaya* if ego is female). This is the Crow usage and does in fact occur on some occasions.

a 'triadic', not simply a dyadic, determination at work here. The number of combinations that could occur is doubtless finite but it is certainly large, and it would differ as between male and female egos. The invariant terms are those for lineal relatives, because these relationships are in a way invariant. This applies to certain collaterals of generation +1 also. Thus the father's sisters are inevitably *yaya*, as are the mother's sisters. The mother's brother, in the lineage context, is definitely *náwa*, but outside this he is *umu*. The father's brother is usually *umu*, but could well be *náwa* when viewed as an authority.

We have to deal yet with the +2/−2 generation. The terms here are not distributed according to the social categories we have outlined above, but simply convey for lineal relatives what they convey as general status terms, i.e., that the relations of a boy to his grandfathers and a girl to her grandmothers are different, while the relations of grandfathers and granddaughters, and grandmothers and grandsons, are more or less the same. In other words, same-sex relationships are different from each other, while cross-sex relations are the same. Grandparents, as we have explained, are thought to be too far in age and experience from their grandchildren to be much involved with them in any but a friendly way, no matter where they stand to them in the kinship system. While a boy may well see his mother's mother's brother as *náwa*, he would not usually see his mother's father as such, at any rate in the kinship context. He may see his father's father as an authority figure, but this would be rare, for however authoritative this grandfather was in village life in general, he would be kindly and indulgent with his grandson; he would, however, guide and teach him, and hence there would be a little restraint in the relationship which would be completely lacking between a boy and his grandmother (father's mother). Similarly with a girl; she would be under the guidance and tutelage of her grandmother (mother's mother), but completely free in her relationships with both grandfathers equally. Both boy and girl would show respect towards their maternal grandmother, but this would be in the form of kindly actions towards her rather than a show of deference. Thus

But these 'reciprocal' usages are not rigid, and *s'aúshe* is very often – outside the lineage context – used as a self-reciprocal term. Thus cross-cousins call each other *s'aúshe*. In fact this is rare, and, as we shall see in the next chapter, when the 'status equal' terms are not used for cross-cousins in ordinary conversation, it is the 'alternate generation' terms that are used.

grandparents are not, as it were, drawn into the web that ties proximate generations together in a complex of system-determined relationships. The main feature, then, that comes out of this distribution of terms is the generation difference, and the difference between cross-sex and same-sex relationships.

The usage for generations + 3 and − 3 varies, but within narrow limits. For non-kin the same terms as for + 2 and − 2 are used, but for kin, or at least lineal kin, the generation criterion is again the most important. Thus the + 3 / − 3 generations are often, though not always, distinguished by using for them the + 1 and − 1 terms. Another usage is to add the prefix *tsei-* 'first' to the + 2 terms for generation + 3. The repetition of + 1 and − 1 terms gives an 'alternating' pattern for the generations which is found elsewhere among the Keresans, and which always seems confined to lineal kin, or very close kin.[1] Thus the Cochiti seems to see his lineal kin as extending in both directions like a ladder in which alternating rungs are equivalent. Non-kin or distant kin, on the other hand, simply merge after + 2 and − 2 into an undifferentiated past and future.

$$\text{Lineal kin} \quad (-1)\ (-2)\ (-1)\ (0)\ (+1)\ (+2)\ (+1)$$
$$\text{Others} \qquad\ \ (-2)\ (-2)\ (-1)\ (0)\ (+1)\ (+2)\ (+2)$$

The equation of + 3 with 'senior generation (proximate)' people may seem strange, but it is reckoned that between such generations relations may in fact be more restrained than between alternate generations. Cochiti were not much interested in these categories of relatives; 'You don't live that long', I was told. There would not be very many people in these categories. Occasionally they are referred to by Spanish terms or even hybrid terms.

## V

There is another 'kinship' context in which an interesting distribution of the terms occurs. In any formal situation involving ego in a relationship with his own and his father's lineage/clan, when these groups act as units – legal persons – on his behalf, for example, at a wedding, healing or naming, he will address all the male members of his father's clan as *umu*, and all the female as *yaya*,

---

[1] Acoma and Laguna for example: see Eggan, 1950, and Miller, 1959. Also Zia and Santa Ana: see White, 1962 and 1942.

collectively and individually. Conversely, he will address all the male members of his own clan as *náwa* and all the females as *yaya*. Children of male members of his own clan will be *s'aúshe*, children of male members of his father's clan *s'atyum* and *meme*, although in the ceremonial situation these latter usages are less necessary and not always strictly observed. I noted this usage at the wedding ceremony I attended, without, at the time, fully understanding it.[1] Later I questioned the more knowledgeable of the men who had been there, and they agreed, on reflection, that it was the proper usage but was not always rigidly observed. In a situation such as a wedding, they agreed, all the men of ego's (bridegroom) father's clan were his *umu*, and all males of his own clan *náwa*. As one man put it, 'It's like they [his own clan males] decide for him. They say what he's to do; they ask for the girl and tell her folk what he wants. He has to do as they say. His father's people, they all come along to help him and give him advice. Even the little ones help him, just coming along'.

Now the distribution of status terms in this context is pure Crow, at least for males. Even the use of *yaya* in this way follows some patterns recognized as Crow,[2] and the use of terms for children of male members is perfectly Crow. This makes excellent sense when one knows the context, and were this the only context in which kinship operated, and were kinship the only status system, then Cochiti would have as pure and unadulterated a Crow system as ever existed. But it is not the only context or the only relationship system, and hence not the only determinant of the use of terms.

This, I think, can apply to the other Pueblos as well. Clearly Zuni is struggling with both a generational and a 'lineal' context in its use of terms. Neither is more 'basic', nor, in all probability, earlier in time. Each is equally valid, and an observation of range of use and context would probably reveal that the notorious 'alternate uses' in Zuni were quite consistent with alternate contexts, and not necessarily a result of acculturation. In Laguna these

---

[1] In the thesis on which this book is based I failed to note this point. It was buried in the mass of notes I had on the wedding ceremony and which I did not comb over in detail when preparing the material on kinship terms. This only goes to show that field notes should be treated with the same care as historical documents – and with the same circumspection, of course.

[2] Lounsbury, 1964. It is in fact the pattern followed by the Crow Indians them selves.

alternates are clearly present, although Eggan dismisses them as 'unimportant'. For Acoma, Mickey found that the 'alternates' discovered by Kroeber, which ran along generational lines, still operated, but she still thinks that the 'lineal' system is older, and that the alternates were 'already' being applied in 1917.[1] Miller remarks that the change from 'lineage to bilateral' in Acoma is not borne out by his data.[2] What is probably at work here too is a system of shifting contexts which the 'genealogical method' will not tap, used as it is in a curiously artificial context with one or two informants.

White, in his monograph on Santa Ana, offers his well-known demonstration that this Pueblo has changed from Crow to generational in terminology.[3] He found two patterns of which he says:

It might be well to emphasize the fact that these terms do constitute two patterns, not merely a variety of designations. If an informant gave 'uncle' for mother's brother, he always gave 'son' and 'daughter' for his children, never 'brother' and 'sister'. If the informant gave 'father' for mother's brother, he always gave 'brother' or 'sister' for his children, never 'son' and 'daughter'.

This is the pattern that we have seen in operation in Cochiti. But White goes on to say:

It is our considered opinion that the pattern in which mother's brother is called 'uncle' and his children 'son' and 'daughter', which is characteristic of the Crow type of terminology, is the earlier of the two patterns. We believe that this pattern is breaking down and giving way to the pattern in which mother's brother is called 'father' and his children 'brother' and 'sister'. We believe that we have sufficient reason and evidence in support of this view, but we must reserve discussion of it to another time and place.'

As far as we know, this reason, evidence and discussion have not appeared, and, although we cannot answer for Santa Ana, it will be obvious that our considered opinion on Cochiti is much more cautious than this. Both patterns are present – and White is perfectly right in saying that they are two patterns – but whether the Crow pattern is declining in favour of the newcomer is more doubtful. This view, of course, fits perfectly with the Eggan theory, and we have already seen that this is dubious on other grounds. What I would say for Cochiti is this: both patterns exist in different

[1] Mickey, 1956.      [2] Miller, 1959.      [3] White, 1942, p. 159.

contexts and both are perfectly intelligible once these contexts are known, but it may well be that the amount of clan/lineage activity is on the decline and that the usages of this context are less active. But this does not make the 'generational' or 'bilateral' use of terms a *replacement* for the Crow or lineal use as the result of inter- ference from Spanish, Anglo and/or Tewa 'models', or 'patterns'. What it means is that, of two *already existing* patterns, one is now followed less frequently or consistently than it used to be.

This view fits my notion of the development of Cochiti kinship, which sees it as the gradual development of a double-descent type with ancient roots. In so far as Cochiti ever had 'monolithic multifunctional' lineages/clans (matrilineal), then it had, perhaps, a pure Crow terminology. But evidence for this must rest on facts other than those of the language itself.

It will be obvious that my conclusions are very similar to those of Schneider and Roberts on Zuni. They relate the failure of Zuni to produce a clear-cut Crow pattern of kin terms to the fact that the *role-designating* function of the terms dominates the *classifying function*, and this in turn, they argue, is the outcome of an ego-centred integration pattern and the absence of multifunctional lineages. I am not sure that I fully grasp the significance of their distinction, but I agree with their general position. Clearly the matrilineal pattern of grouping relatives is important as *one* deter- minant of the structure of terminology, but my point – and I think it is the point of *Zuni Kin Terms* – is that it is only one of a number of determinants, some of which may dominate the kin- classifying function. I add to this the simple suggestion that the use of terms will differ in different contexts, but that they will be distributed in accordance with their meanings as general status terms.[1]

[1] Lounsbury's analysis makes the assumption (and it is only a useful logical assumption in his case although he writes as if he were describing an aspect of reality) that the terms in a Crow system have *primary* reference to 'kin'. This may be so, but it cannot be assumed *a priori*. Even where they do not have this primary reference, however, they have to be *distributed* in the kinship system and this may well be done in a Crow fashion, whereupon Lounsbury's analysis could be ap- plied. I do not think there need be any conflict of views here except on the location of the 'primary' reference of the terms, which I regard as variable and prob- lematic.

In Cochiti, as we have seen, the Crow determinants operate in some contexts but not in others. Buchler (1964) says graphically that 'the "Crow" principle is a code which imposes logical rules upon the genealogical network'. Lounsbury, the cryptanalyst, has cracked the code, thus, 'allowing us to decode genealogical information with all the intellectual certainty of a native decoder'. But with the use of status terms in Cochiti, I am arguing, there is *more than one code at work*. (Parsons seems to see this when she speaks of the 'clash' of principles at work within a system, as opposed to Eggan who only sees one principle effectively at work – with 'exceptions'. Whether or not the principles 'clash', except in the mind of the anthropologist, is an empirical question.) The genealogical network, then, is only one field in which these terms operate, and here they operate variously according to context. To be as certain in usage as the native decoder, we must add context to our decoding repertoire.

The major problem with all 'componential analyses' – other than those difficulties presented by Burling (1964) – seems to be this definition of the *domain* covered by the lexical items at issue. In most analyses of 'kinship terminology' this seems to be prejudged on ethnocentric grounds. (Hymes – 1964, pp. 105–6 – makes a similar point in a more general argument.)

# 8

# Kinship Terms: (2) History

## I

In the previous chapter I was concerned with the contemporary 'meanings' of kinship terms, and have been content to show that they cannot really be interpreted as evidence of a declining Crow system, any more than can the kinship system itself.[1] I have tried to outline the general connotation of each, and to show that the use of the terms for close kin is not inconsistent with the more general use of them as status indicators. The 'fit', however, is not perfect, and some features of the terminology have led me to look for a possible historical explanation. Clearly the system of terminology has a history, and in one sense the 'meanings' of the terms are a residue of historical associations and usages. The current meanings have, of course, no conscious reference to these derived meanings, and Cochiti will often rationalize a hiatus between the structure of usage and that of society with a skill that rivals the anthropologist's. Sometimes, however, they invoke historical explanations: 'That's an old word; we don't know why we use it that way.' 'I guess it doesn't make sense, but that's the way with us; that's the way the old people said it.'

In short, terminological structure and status structure do not necessarily change at the same pace, and I think we can be sure that language is more conservative than society. It may be that some features of usage are what they are because they carry a residual meaning – one that at some time in the past had a direct reference to the status structure but has now simply become a *feature of the language itself*. I doubt whether such usages could persist indefinitely if they absolutely contradicted their social referents,

---

[1] I have throughout this chapter used 'Crow' to mean both the system of terminology and a social system based on exogamous matriclans. This is not really correct, as 'Crow' should pertain simply to the terms; but I think in the present context it is clear what I mean, and it is a useful shorthand way of referring to the kinship system-*cum*-terminology.

and I think we can see some cases where they may be in process of change; but it may be that they only clash in *some contexts*, and in consequence they tend to survive even though they are puzzling in terms of the total system. In other cases they may be neutral to the system; then no easy explanation of their structure is possible unless one knows their history.[1]

Bearing this in mind, let us examine some features of the terminology that might give us a clue to the historical development of the system.

1. There is a tendency to identify or merge alternate generations.

2. There is a tendency to self-reciprocal terminology (which includes the above).

3. There is a tendency to classify parallel cousins with siblings and to distinguish these from cross cousins.

4. There is a tendency, in some contexts, to identify MB, MBS and MBSS with the use of the term *wawa*; this term can be used reciprocally.

5. There is a possibility that all the words with the *-mu* root are cognate. (*umu, mumu, tyum, múti.*)[2]

6. There is a possibility that the term *nyenye* (*nenye*) is derived from *niño*, and has been substituted for *múti* by female speakers. (See note 13 to chapter 7.)

The first two statements are self-explanatory. Point 3 means that parallel cousins are frequently classified with siblings in the 'status equal' categroy. Cross-cousins, on the other hand, can be, and often are, placed in this category, but may also be placed in

---

[1] To follow this out would take us right into the heart of the debate on the 'determinants' of kinship terms. In the debate between Kroeber, Rivers, Lowie and Radcliffe-Brown, I find myself in agreement with everyone. (Kroeber, 1909; Rivers, 1914; Lowie, 1932; Radcliffe-Brown, 1941; see the summary in Eggan 1950.) 'Linguistic conservatism', 'psychology' – in the sense in which Kroeber used the term, and 'sociological factors', all contribute to the generation, maintenance and change of kinship terms.

[2] It can be seen that there are two possibilities:

| 1 | 2 |
|---|---|
| (mu) *-mu* | (m-) *umu* |
| (u) *-mu* | *umu* |
| (tyu) *-mu* | (ty-) *umu* |
| *mu* (-ti) | (u) *mu* (-ti) |

With *tyum*(*u*) the final vowel is indeterminate, appearing in compounds as a long (vocalic) *-m-*, (*s'atyum:she*), sometimes as an *-i-*, (*s'awatyumishe*) – and so on. I am inclined to accept *mu* as the original root, but it makes little difference.

others, and the latter usage is, if anything, more likely. The most popular category for cross-cousins is the *mumu-papa-t'ao*, or '+2/−2 generation' category; next comes the 'status equal' category; and then the 'junior generation' category (*s'aúshe*). If this last usage were strictly reciprocal, one would, of course, be calling a cross-cousin by a 'parental generation' term (*umu-tata-yaya*); but it is not inevitably reciprocal – one can reciprocate with other terms than the 'parental'. The next candidate for cross-cousins is *wawa*.

FIG. 10. Use of the term *wawa*

*Wawa* is a curious term. It has, as we have seen, been glossed as 'little uncle', and is used by a man to address (and sometimes to refer to) his mother's brother's son, and his mother's brother's son's son, in some contexts. It is technically reciprocal, and hence one could say that the patrilateral cross-cousins were so 'addressed' (FZS and FFZS). But in fact it is usually the matrilateral cousins who are 'addressed' as *wawa*, and it is 'reciprocal' in the sense that they return the compliment. Thus it is usually initiated by the FZS to, for example, his MBS. The circumstances under which it might be used can be illustrated by an example. (See Fig. 10.)

A wished to consult his mother's brother on some matter and went to the latter's house. Here the mother's brother (B) was making drums with his son (C$^1$) and his brother's son (C$^2$) and a grandson (D), a small boy. They were sitting outside the house, and as A approached and saw them, he called out *kowatsina wawa* – 'hello *wawa*'; C$^1$, who looked up first, answered simply *kowatsina*. A volunteered *kuwetsitikut'e'* – 'how are you all?' to which B replied *rawa'e rawa'e wawa* Nat – 'fine, fine, *wawa* Nat'. After this opening they used *wawa* freely, but then A asked if he could talk to his mother's brother alone on an important matter; the old man agreed and got up to walk with his nephew, and A immediately thanked him with *wo'e* (thank you) *sanawashe*. This was the longest conversation in which I heard the

term used, and is fixed in my memory because I took the opportunity to question the two men who remained behind. These
were very conservative men who were particular about correct
form. Their impression seemed to be that any other usage would
have been improper under the circumstances. A had wanted them
– a working patrilineage – to suspend their activities and release
their leader for consultation on a grave matter. He had therefore
been 'very polite' and proper in speaking as he did: young people,
of course, didn't always remember their manners these days and
some young men would have said 'anything'. In the normal
course of events – meeting on the road for example – what would
A and C have called each other? That was different, *mumu*, or
*s'atyum:she*, perhaps. (To refer back to an earlier point: When a
younger brother of C¹ got married, at the ceremony and the
negotiations the C's (as they reported to me) addressed A as *umu*,
and he called them *s'awishe*.)

As we have seen, *wawa* can be used for the mother's brother,
and hence by reciprocity, for the sister's son, but it is rarely used
for the mother's mother's brother. It is generally said to be an
'older' term than *náwa*, and in some sense the 'true' term; it has
the strange occult overtones mentioned earlier – it means 'medicines'. I have said that it might bear a relation to *náwa* similar to
that which *yaya* bears to *naya*. It may be that these two words are
related, but *wawa* does not merely operate as a kind of vocative of
*náwa*; it has an independent existence. Thus it can only be substituted for *náwa* in the immediate MB-ZS reciprocal – not beyond
this range. Otherwise it seems confined to being a term of address
(which is reciprocated) for the mother's brother's son (MBS), and
his son's son (MBSS). Now this is curiously unlike Crow terminology since it stresses the *patrilineal* identity of these men in the
opposite – Omaha – fashion. The fact that it is a reciprocal term
suggests that this patriliny should be linked to an exogamous-
moiety organzation, simply designating 'men of the opposite
moiety' (up to a certain degree). (Goldfrank notes its reciprocal
use between MBSS and FFZS, but she seems to regard this as a
'recent extension'. She does not comment on the *náwa/wawa*
distinction.) *Wawa* (with, perhaps, *nenye*) is really the only true
'kinship' term in Cochiti; i.e. one that has 'primary' – indeed
exclusively – genealogical referents. It is not used as a general
status term in the way the others are.

The point about the -*mu* root words (point 5) is that they could themselves be seen as marking out ego's *patrilineage*, i.e. as genera-tion-specifying variations on the root -*mu* which could mean 'man of my lineage/moiety'. *Mumu* applied to the +2 and −2 generations would in fact apply 'across the board', and not just to ego's own moiety; but this is not incompatible with a dual organization, since these generations are often seen as being 'out-side' the reciprocal exchange pattern, either as having finished with marriage or as not having started it yet.

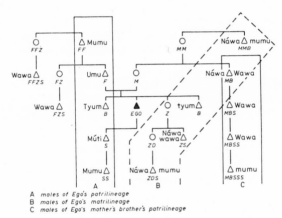

A   *males of Ego's patrilineage*
B   *males of Ego's matrilineage*
C   *males of Ego's mother's brother's patrilineage*

FIG. 11. Terms for males of ego's patrilineage, matrilineage, and mother's brother's patrilineage

Let us first get the picture of this aspect of contemporary (or near contemporary) usage – (I have kept the old word for 'son'). Figure 11 shows how the terms are used today and were in the recent past. I did not adequately explore the *wawa* usage, but I am convinced that it is used when ego sees himself in a relationship with his mother's brother's patrilineage as a collectivity – much as he uses *umu* for his father's clansmen when they act collectively for him. In this context *náwa* serves primarily to mark out the males of ego's matrilineage, and the -*mu* root words to mark out his patrilineage. *Tyum* occurs in both matrilineage and patri-lineage, but a brother always falls into these two groups, and, as we shall see, the identity of parallel cousins and siblings in a moiety system underlines the patrilineal meaning of -*mu*. Indeed it is these 'equations' that all add up to the suggestion of a moiety system. Thus alternate generations are merged in *mumu*; ZS = MBSS, FZS = MBS, MB = FFZS (by the *wawa* reciprocal); siblings = parallel cousins. All this adds up to a 'bifurcate-merging' pattern of terminology based on exogamous patri-moieties, with matriclans as a later addition.[1]

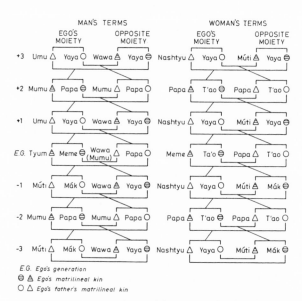

FIG. 12. Reconstruction of former Cochiti kinship terminology

This is eminently plausible, since Cochiti has in fact two patri-moieties. They are not now exogamous, but exogamy could easily have shifted to the clans, if they were a later development. In fact, the more I look at Cochiti terminology the more this explanation appears to be the only reasonable extrapolation from current usage, and the less plausible the argument that a Crow system has degenerated to a bilateral one. I am prepared to hazard the conjecture that ancient Cochiti had a bifurcate-merging, reciprocal-exogamic, patrilineal-moiety system of terminology. (See Fig. 12.) Clearly the terms need not have been exactly those shown, since there must have been changes and substitutions; it is

[1] I am using 'bifurcate-merging' in the sense employed, for example, by Service (1962), to mean a terminology distinguishing sex, generation and moiety membership.

the general pattern that matters. Perhaps we should spell out some details:

*Male ego:* most of the terms are straightforward, apart from that for 'father's sister', which I have given as *yaya* in accordance with current usage. A true bifurcate-merging system would have a separate term to designate 'women of my moiety' (within a certain degree, that is), and 'true' Crow would have a distinguishing term for father's sister and 'women of my father's lineage'. But even Crow systems do not always differentiate this category. In ancient Cochiti the men might have been strongly differentiated whereas the women were not. The men perhaps lived and even slept mostly in their respective *Kivas*, while the women – not much involved in *Kiva* affairs – were distributed about the apartment blocks. The woman's *Kiva* membership would not be so prominent. A man needed, as it were, to distinguish his '*wa*' males from his '*mu*' males, but women were not so strongly distinguished. This would be true for older and younger generations, but for women of his own generation whom he might marry one might expect a special term. Judging by current tendencies, however, I have given these 'cross-cousins' (women of opposite moiety and own generation) the 'grandrelative' term – *papa* – as this seems to be the most popular, and, what is more, fits exactly the symmetry of the alternate-generation scheme. *Yaya* would be logical for the sister's daughter (see Murdock 1949, pp. 170–1).

*Female ego:* the same problems with the 'father's sister' term occur here, with the same solution. The interesting terms are *múti* (see point 6) and *t'aó/ta'o*. I have put in *múti* rather than *nyenye* (*nenye*) because the logic of this scheme seems to lend itself to such an interpretation and it may help to solve the problem of the use of the term *muiti* at Laguna and Acoma. From the point of view of a female ego in this scheme, her son is a 'man of the opposite moiety'; the term *muiti* or *múi*, then, means simply this, as it applied to proximate and then alternate generations. Thus it applies logically enough to the mother's brother and sister's son. That a woman should call women of the opposite moiety of her own generation by the 'grandrelative' term – *t'aó* – follows the logic of male usage and the alternate generation pattern. It emphasizes the resemblance of this term to the 'sibling' term, and as a female ego does not seem particularly concerned to distinguish female roles in this system at all, it perhaps underlines the common root of these two words. Perhaps we can propose a proto-Keres *tao, which became differentiated over time. The classification of the spouse is exactly the same as with the male – indeed the term *papa* would be reciprocal between potential spouses. If it *is* true that *nashtyu* was once exclusively a woman's word, then maybe *tata* was a later substitution. I have hazarded *nashtyu* as the woman's term.

This is not a thoroughgoing 'bifurcate-merging' scheme, but then it is probably only in the distant past that Cochiti (or rather the proto-Keres) had a patrilineal exogamous-moiety system untouched by other influences. If they developed matriclans in the eastern San Juan, the functions of exogamy were probably at some time shifted to the clan. To this end the terminology shifted also, but the fact that the moiety still existed, even though no longer exogamous, led to a continued influence of the moiety on the use of terms. Thus *náwa*, however one glosses it – 'elder', 'sir', 'lord' – was distinguished from *wawa* and used to defer to the men of ego's clan when they acted in the role of clansmen towards him. It did not rob the word of its wider meaning and more extensive application, or pin it down to mother's brother. *Wawa* continued to link ego to three generations of patrilineally related males descended from the mother's brother. This was, however, no longer a very necessary distinction now that the moiety had lost its exogamic functions, so the term wavered and was used as an alternate, and when one wanted to identify the MBS and MBSS with the MB (as one often might, since the *patrilineage* continued to be important). It also, because of its association with the old system and its connotations of 'them' – the men of the other *Kiva*, the mysterious ones – slipped into ritual usage and notions of strangeness, ancientness and power. The clan system meanwhile penetrated the terminology to some extent, producing the Crow usages we have discussed. In this sense, 'extensions' may well have occurred. Thus a man may well have applied the term *umu* to his father's matriclan males, because they were males of his *father's* matriclan and he called his father *umu*. (This does not make *umu* 'mean' father; but it does mean that Lounsbury's technique may have some relevance to an understanding of Crow systems without contradicting this analysis, even though his premises and interpretations differ sharply from mine.) Matrilineal classification is, of course, 'built-in' to any bifurcating-merging scheme, and some peoples (e.g. the Australian Aborigines) have utilized this tendency to produce 'section' systems, matrimoieties etc. In fact, what I am proposing for Cochiti is a version of the 'Kariera' system.[1] This built-in matrilineal classification will have automatically reinforced some features of 'Crow' usage for Cochiti. Thus ego's father's matrilineage males would in any case have been alternately *umu* and *mumu* even on the existing classification; a female ego's matrilineage males would have been *múti* and *papa* – and so on. To get the full significance of this, let us look at Laguna usage and compare it with Cochiti.

## II

Eggan (1950, pp. 268–71) discusses the Laguna problem of alternating-generation and self-reciprocal terminology. While recognizing that further research will be necessary to explain these deeply ingrained usages in Laguna, he regards them as 'subordinated to the lineage principle' and of relatively minor importance. They may, however, be associated with 'both lineage and generation structures', he says. It is a short step from this to saying that they may be associated with 'lineage-generation' structures which themselves have their roots in an exogamous-moiety system. He agrees that cross-cousin marriage may well *once* have been a pattern amongst the Keres, but he does not accept Parsons' suggestion that this is the reason why spouses call each other *papa*. This is put down to a joking relationship between a man and the women of his father's clan on the Hopi model. *Papa* is reciprocal between MBS and FZD: and, of course, the 'key' equation in a reciprocal-exogamic system is cross-cousin = spouse. Furthermore, Parsons suggests that Laguna was once based on a moiety system which broke down in favour of the clans, but it is not clear what kind of system she envisaged. She did not put her facts together, but had she done so and added to them the alternating-generation and self-reciprocal terms, she might have concluded that she was dealing with a system of exogamous patrimoieties. The *Kiva* organization of Laguna is not altogether clear, informants mentioning one to four *Kivas*. In the 1870's there were two. Children, however, joined the father's *Kiva*, and women the husband's, as in Cochiti.

[1] Radcliffe-Brown, 1931.

I here set out a reconstructed patrimoiety scheme for Laguna (Fig. 13). This can be checked against the Cochiti scheme and against Eggan's 'lineage' arrangement of the terms, which I would see as a later partial adjustment to Crow usages – utilizing some elements already present and changing others.

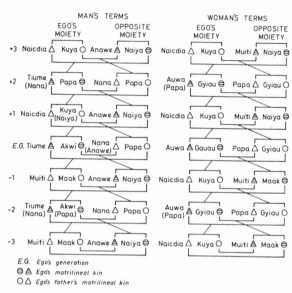

FIG. 13. Reconstruction of former Laguna kinship terminology

In many ways the Laguna scheme is more satisfactory than the Cochiti, and there are several interesting parallels. The women's terms *gyiau* and *gauau* parallel the Cochiti *t'aó* and *ta'o*. They differ from each other in a similar small detail of pronunciation, and are similarly obviously cognate. The rendering *-auau* is probably intended to convey much the same sound as my *-aó*. *Naicdia* (our *nashtyu*) is used by both men and women, but this does not throw much light on Cochiti. The elusive 'father's sister' term – *kuya* – is very neat, although it seems that 'generation' influence leads to *naiya* as a possible alternative here. The *nawa* term seems not to be challenged by any *wawa* alternative, although it may be that the latter was simply unnoticed. The *wawa*-like 'baby-term' recorded by Miller at Acoma is suggestive, but then so is the woman's 'brother' term, *auwa*. But since the two languages divided 700 years ago, one cannot push comparison too far. What is remarkable is that there are so many correspondences and suggestive parallels.

To show how the 'shift' to Crow usage might have occurred, I have set out some of the terms used in Laguna in accordance with Eggan's 'lineage' diagram (Fig. 14). I have taken a woman's own and her father's lineages for the sake of illustration. These are the people respectively shaded and unshaded in Fig. 13. By comparing these we can see how easily the terms for own lineage in a Crow system as used at Laguna could be taken over from the classification of matrilineal relatives in the exogamous-patrimoiety scheme.

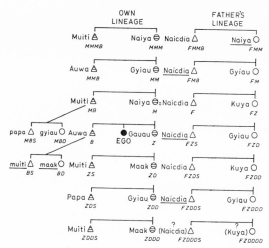

FIG. 14. Terms for own and father's matrilineages
in Laguna: female ego

(The hypothesized modifications are underlined)

In ego's father's matrilineage, the permanent substitution of *naicdia* for *papa* has taken place, as might be expected (this is the only really radical change), but note that the *women* of this lineage continue to be classified exactly as they might have been under the older system – in terms of alternate generations. Even more significantly, the members of ego's *own* lineage continue to be classified in *exactly the same way* as they would have been under a moiety scheme. Thus, as far as the internal classification of the lineage was concerned, no change was needed to produce a 'Crow' system: the matrilineal classification was already there; the clan appeared and fitted exactly into it; the moiety exogamy fell away, leaving the clan neatly classified by the old terminology. The major changes have come in the terms for children of clan members, for example, as these would no longer be 'automatically' classified as 'kin' when the older system ceased to operate, and new classifications would be needed. But the mother's brother's son and daughter are still *papa* and *gyiau*, and spouses are still *papa* to each other.

We can compare this with the hypothetical situation in Cochiti (Fig. 15). I have extrapolated from Fig. 12 the same two lineages

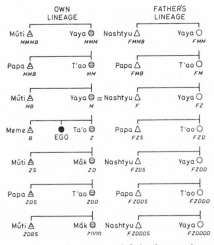

FIG. 15. Terms for own and father's matrilineages in Cochiti: female ego

for a female ego as in the case of Laguna (see Fig. 14). Again we can see that the classification into matrilineages was implicit. The men whom a woman called *múti* were in any case those who were matrilineally related to her; those whom she called *nashtyu* were men of her *father's* matrilineage. To produce a more Crow-like system she would have at least to drop *papa* and substitute *múti* in her own lineage and *nashtyu* in her father's. (In Cochiti, we conjectured, *nyenye* and *tata* replaced these two for women.) Now in Cochiti what has happened is that for some purposes and on some occasions these substitutions are in fact made; namely, on clan and lineage occasions. But they are not made all the time, and the older classification prevails in other contexts. The generational principle is also very much 'built-in' to the old pattern, and it is perhaps easy to see how generational usages such as have been shown on Table 6 came into use.

There may be another and more plausible hypothesis to account for the present system and its peculiarities in Cochiti and Laguna. One cannot, of course, present any observed 'facts' to prove or disprove such hypotheses. My argument has been largely logical, and the only hard facts we have are the *Kivas* themselves. My logic may very well be completely wrong. If it proves to be so it will be a great pity, since it produces such a neat solution to the problem. But we must experiment with all possible combinations of social and linguistic elements if we are to find the correct solution.

## III

Eggan ends *The Social Organization of the Western Pueblos* (p. 324) with the suggestion that his arguments should be examined in the light of the theories of Lévi-Strauss and Murdock. *Les Structures Elémentaires* and *Social Structure* were published almost simultaneously with Eggan's book. In the following sections I will attempt, very tentatively, to follow up Eggan's suggestion. This can be no more than an introduction to the possibilities of such an examination. So many intriguing questions arise that to answer them would require another book. I offer my suggestions in the same spirit as Eggan offers his: as hypotheses that might well be wrong.

If the ancient system was an 'elementary structure' in the sense in which Lévi-Strauss uses the term, we possibly have here an example of the problematical 'passage aux structures complexes', to borrow the title of his chapter 28.[1] A complex structure is one in which there is no category of 'potential spouse'; any regularities will be of a statistical nature, and will not stem from the rules of exchange. One of Lévi-Strauss's problems was to explain how 'elementary' structures turned into 'complex' structures. The place of Crow-Omaha systems in this process, it seems, is crucial. His earlier statements on these systems were particularly obscure, and if interpreted literally did not make sense,[2] but lately he has

---

[1] Lévi-Strauss, 1949.    [2] Lévi-Strauss, 1949, p. 576; 1958, pp. 73–4.

said that Crow-Omaha systems are in a sense 'half-way' between elementary and complex structures.[1] They involve more widespread prohibitions than complex structures do, and these prohibitions apply to social groups (own clan, father's clan, mother's father's clan/phratry etc.), but they are 'complex' in that the selection of a mate is left to chance factors – there is no category of 'prescribed spouse'. They are, however, less open to chance selection than our own complex system, because, in a sense, a man's choice of spouse will be circumscribed by the previous marriage choices of the clans to which he is related. These will in fact leave him with a 'category' from which to draw a wife. This category, however, is not preordained by the *normative rules* of the system, but by the statistical rules under which it operates.

Now if what I have postulated for Laguna and Cochiti is correct, we have here a process by which an 'elementary' system of direct or restricted exchange moved some way towards becoming a Crow system with modifications. These examples seem to me doubly interesting in that Cochiti in particular, and to some extent Laguna as well, have only gone part of the way to a Crow system. The 'remnants' of the 'elementary' system are still very evident, and, as we have seen for Cochiti, there is no particular rule of exogamy applying to any clan other than one's own. In fact sequential inter-clan marriage is looked on with favour, a marriage into the mother's father's clan, for example, being particularly well received. There is no evidence of exogamic rules extending beyond own clan in Laguna either. This contrasts with the more thoroughly Crow system of the Hopi where the phratries of mother, father and mother's father are banned.

My theory for Cochiti, and by implication for the Western Keres, is that they never went the whole way towards a Crow system. The Crow elements were partly integrated into the system but never came to dominate it. They still do not dominate but they are still there; thus they cannot be said to have declined significantly. I believe this reinterpretation of the terminology and its possible history makes very much more sense than the theory of degeneration from a Crow to a bilateral system, which begs too many questions, and is forced to ignore or explain away too much of the data.

[1] Royal Anthropological Institute, Huxley Memorial Lecture, 1965. To be published in a forthcoming issue of the Institute's proceedings.

## IV

How exactly the dual-exogamic organization of the Keres came to be transmuted into the present system is a mystery that will probably never be solved. That something like this happened appears to me reasonably certain, but by what mechanisms it happened I cannot tell. As I see it, the Keres could have been hunters and gatherers who were organized in bands and developed (probably but not necessarily) through reciprocal band exogamy, the moiety system that is compatible with such an organization. (See Service, 1962, chs. 2, 3.) The move into the San Juan led to a modification of residence patterns, and matrilocal settlements grew up, but the moiety system remained intact, and brides were still exchanged between moieties. These might have broken down completely but for the fact that the Keres then began to move into larger settlements. This aggregation both preserved the moieties and allowed for the development of the clans. That the two are compatible we can see from the terminology. A man would not in any case marry matrilineally related women, since they would be either of the wrong generation or of the wrong moiety; hence clan exogamy would be automatically observed. For some Keres, clan and moiety remained in balance, but exogamy was lost to the moiety while remaining for the clan. When the number of clans increased and, for example, exogamic bans were placed on father's and mother's father's clan, the moiety system could not survive as a marriage regulator, and the system would be pushed in a Crow and 'complex' direction. (This is probably what happened with the Hopi. That they and their Shoshonean relatives and forebears practised bilateral cross-cousin marriage seems certain, but now they ban marriage with the father's and mother's father's clans and phratries.[1]) The Western Keres seem to have institutionalized the clan more effectively than the Eastern, and it is more prominent in their system; in consequence, their kinship usage is more heavily 'skewed' in a Crow direction.

In Cochiti, exogamy does not seem to have been lost to the moieties as a result of bans on father's and mother's father's clans. It was probably a result of the exodus from the San Juan and the wanderings that followed. Under the pressures of demographic

[1] Titiev, 1938. See also Eggan, 1964.

imbalance that probably accompanied these journeyings, the 'bride-exchanging' function of the moieties may well have collapsed, leaving the clans as the sole exogamic units. The moieties, however, retained their ceremonial importance.

This is, of course, simply guesswork, but something *like* this must have happened. Service thinks that some such process was more or less universal in the change from band to tribal structure during the course of social evolution. The following passage describes quite graphically the process I have been outlining.

In some cases where lineages and clans are strongly corporate, the widespread bifurcate-merging terminology undergoes further specific change. Clan and/or lineage membership may become such an important aspect of social interaction that the status of a person of ego's affinal group—his father's clan or lineage in a matrilineal society, the mother's in a patrilineal society—becomes more importantly a matter of group membership than of the more individualized, more specific, egocentric relationship. Thus *the bifurcate merging type of egocentric nomenclature remains characteristic of ego's social relationship to members of his own clan and lineage*, with whom he has close and frequent interaction, but in dealings with members of the affinal lineage or clan the terminology normally used is sociocentric, meaning something like 'male (female) of the such-and-such clan (or lineage)'. Generic names have been given this overriding of the egocentric terminology by a sociocentric term in situations like the above: 'Crow system' when the affinal group is father's (i.e. a matrilineal society) and 'Omaha system' when it is mother's (a patrilineal society). (1962, pp. 132–3). (My italics.)

There are many difficulties in this passage. I have never myself grasped the distinction between 'sociocentric' and 'egocentric' in relation to the Crow and Omaha systems, but it clearly refers to the kind of development which I suggest has taken place in Keres. The phrase italicized fits the Laguna case exactly. It was in ego's own lineage/clan that the terminology of the old system remained unaltered, while that of the father's clan was adjusted.

It is interesting that White – a prominent exponent of the theory of the degeneration of a Crow type of terminology – should have put forward a very similar argument to Service's. When trying to account for the development of Crow-Omaha systems he says, 'When the clan system is young and weak the kinship system will be of the Dakota-Iroquois type, regardless of the sex in which descent is reckoned. As the clan system develops, however, and comes to exert its influence more and more upon the social life of the tribe, the Dakota-Iroquois terminology will be transferred into the Crow type in a matrilineal society and into the Omaha type in a patrilineal society.' (1939, pp. 569–70.) The kinship terms of the proto-Keres system as I have reconstructed them would certainly be classified as 'Iroquois' by Murdock. The essence of White's theory is that the Crow system is the most highly developed form of matrilineal organization. It is thus a plausible deduction from his theory that Cochiti (and by implication the other Keresans) represents a partly developed Crow system which retains many Iroquois features. This is not precisely how I would like to characterize the present system, but it is probably nearer the truth than the theory of the degeneration of a Crow system.

Murdock does in fact classify contemporary Cochiti as 'Normal Iroquois' on the basis of Goldfrank's evidence (Murdock, 1949, p. 244). Had this evidence stressed the patrilineal elements of the Cochiti system then Murdock would have had to classify it as 'Duo-Iroquois' – a category that includes the Kariera and other Australian tribes. This must strengthen my contention that the Cochiti system is derived from a Kariera-like structure. (He classifies Acoma – his only Western Keres example – as 'Bi-Crow', which accords with my theory that the Western Keres have a more fully developed Crow system.) He describes all the Duo-Iroquois systems as having 'patrilocal residence'. He says they are derived from matrilineal structures as a result of a change of residence rule from matrilocal to patrilocal and a consequent development of patrilineal kin-groups. This is almost the reverse of the sequence I have proposed for Cochiti. It is not quite the reverse, because I have suggested that the two sets of institutions, matrilineal and patrilineal, developed together in the Cochiti system.

The possibility that matrilineal institutions in Cochiti were earlier than patrilineal should be explored. It would be consistent with the hypothesis that the Keresans developed clans at an early stage and then 'borrowed' the moiety system from the Tanoans. But it would still not accord with Murdock's theory because there was no change in the rule of residence at marriage from matrilocal to patrilocal. I do not think that this is a very serious difficulty for two reasons: (a) the classification of the Australians as 'patrilocal' may be wrong since recent evidence suggests that residence is 'mixed', (b) the theory that a particular form of residence rule is a *necessary* cause of the development of unilineal kin-groups is not satisfactory. Patrilineal kin-groups in Cochiti are not connected with any rule of residence at marriage, although it is true that men may have 'resided' for long periods in the *Kivas*.

Murdock's overall scheme probably needs revising, but in classifying Cochiti as Iroquois rather than 'dubious Crow' he showed great insight. He maintains that Normal Iroquois changes to Normal Crow, and it thus follows that in his view Cochiti is not yet a fully-fledged Crow system. White too maintains, as we have seen, that Iroquois changes to Crow, but he does not apply this insight to the Keres data. By insisting that the Keres must have had, at one time, a fully-fledged Crow system, he allows himself no alternative but the inadequate theory of a degeneration from this type.

In the light of this we can look at Murdock's reconstruction of Cochiti evolution. He sees the Iroquoian system as a successor to a Hawaiian system, the chief characteristic of which is, of course, generational terminology. 'Hawaian' usages in contemporary Cochiti are therefore vestiges of a former system, according to him. Again, while this is not exactly how I would analyze contemporary Cochiti usage, it accords more closely with my theory than with White's.


V

The Kariera-like bifurcate-merging terminology that I have suggested for the proto-Keres can, of course, occur without unilineal descent groups or a dual-exogamic organization. A rule of bilateral cross-cousin marriage would be sufficient to produce something very like it. The Dravidian terminology, for example, is very similar; it lacks only the reciprocal alternate-generation terms (Dumont 1963). Lévi-Strauss is quite correct when he says that it is a mistake to infer a pre-existing dual organization from such a terminology or such a rule. In fact the reverse is more likely; the rule comes first and if it is consistently followed it leads to the development of both the special terminology and, when unilineal descent is recognized, the dual organization. This could be a matrilineal dual-organization, as with the Iroquois themselves. I have explored this possibility with the Keresan terms, but it seems highly unlikely. If it were true the present moiety system (except perhaps at Santa Ana) would be a complete freak.

I have assumed throughout this argument that ego would apply the terms 'globally' to his own and his affinal moiety. This need not have been the case. We have to allow for the possibility that the terms embraced only ego's genealogically defined kin, and that he sought a spouse within this circle of kin, that is, a 'real' MBD/FZD. If he failed to find a wife within this category, then he would, to use Radcliffe-Brown's expression, marry an 'equivalent' woman. She would be a woman of the same generation but opposite moiety. There is no evidence from the Keres to suggest the existence of patriclans, so there would be no smaller named unit than the moiety in which ego could find a classificatory cross-cousin. There may have been an institutionalized system of patri-lineages, and these, rather than the moieties, may have been the 'alliance units'. We cannot know, however, whether the terminology was global, but nothing is lost by assuming this for the sake of argument.

The whole subject is fraught with difficulties, and I have been able to do no more than give a sketchy outline of what might be involved. What is needed is a thorough review of Aztec-Tanoan and Keresan linguistic and social systems, in conjunction with archaeological findings, and an examination of the results in the light of the theories of Lévi-Strauss, Murdock and Service.

## VI

To return to the discussion at the beginning of this section, we have seen how certain aspects of Cochiti kinship terminology might be explained as linguistic features with a primarily historical explanation. Self-reciprocity is the most obvious of these, since it is readily explicable in terms of an exogamous-moiety system, but is not always easy to correlate with modern status realities (even if it is not altogether incompatible with them). Still other usages – the *wawa/nawa* syndrome, for example – seem to have residual features which show signs of strain in the current system.

Cochiti usage in this perspective can be seen as the outcome of a change from an exogamous-patrimoiety system to a non-exogamous-moiety system with exogamous matriclans. This changed situation has persisted for some time, and usage has to some extent

fallen into line with it, but has also been subjected to other influences. For a start, under the ancient system everybody was 'kin'
to everyone else; there was no differentiation between kin and
affines. Under the new dispensation this was no longer true, and
terms for affines, for example, had to be introduced.[1] The status
terms, however, could still cover the *whole* society, just as they
might have done under the ancient system, but they covered it in
simple sex-generation terms, as shown on Table 6. This gives the
'bilateral or equalizing' usages. (How could anyone imagine that
these derive from Anglo or Spanish models?) Thus we have three
historical influences on the terminology: the inherited features of
the ancient system, still to some extent bolstered by the continuing
existence of the patrimoieties and their constituent patrilineages;
the sex-generation classification, inherent in the ancient system
and extended to the whole society when the moiety division
becomes non-exogamous; and the Crow elements introduced by
the advent of matriclans, which utilized elements already built
into the system and introduced others – notably the importation
of the word for 'elder' or 'sir' as a means of addressing and referring to matrilineage males.

In the absence of the *Kivas* other explanations might be equally
valid. However, the combination of these with the other features
cited cannot be a mere accident. Any one of these would not be
enough to support my theory, but the combination of them with
the *Kivas* is overwhelming. Thus the discriminations that, as we
have seen, are built into the vocabulary of status can be viewed as
products of an evolution from a dual-exogamic system through
a lineage-generation system, to the present system. Their distribution in the present system is, of course, not simply a historical relic.
The discriminations provide the Cochiti with categories, and they
decide who or what is placed in each category on criteria that may
be very far removed from those on which the terms were originally based. In some cases, as we have seen, the facts of contemporary life sit uneasily with the inherited category system. In yet
other cases, new categories have been invented – the affinal terms,
for example, and possibly the use of *nashtyu* and *t'ao* by both men
and women.

---

[1] It is perhaps interesting that the terms *múti* and *wa'ti* have a similar construc-
tion. If *múti* = *mu* + *ti* = 'son', then *wa'ti* could equally be *wa* + *'ti* = 'son-in-law', or
'relative-in-law' generally: that is, a '*wa*' person, or male affine.

But even if my analysis is completely wrong, I am content to rest on the negative case. This system cannot be described with any plausibility as a Crow system in a state of decline following the inroads of alien bilateral models. Several models are inherent in the system, and others are still emerging: these wax and wane as the groups and statuses to which they refer wax and wane. If anything can be seen as 'declining' it is the usages derived from the exogamous-moiety system. The Crow usages are more or less latent, but they do manifest themselves on the appropriate occasions, while the 'generational' usages are fairly constant.

There is a reasonable degree of 'fit' between this analysis and my analysis of the kinship system proper. There are some loose ends, but these rather depend on the time-perspective adopted in analysis – a point I will take up in the concluding chapter.

# Conclusion

## I

Let me briefly summarize the argument again. Eggan interpreted the present distribution of social systems in the Pueblo group by a theory of the degeneration of a universal type. This, according to him, was the Western Pueblo type, based on a matrilineal system, which once prevailed throughout the area. It has survived in the west, but in the east has largely disappeared, having been replaced by a 'bilateral' system. A subsidiary theory, the 'time of arrival: length of survival' theory, explains why different groups in the east show different stages of this decline. The Eastern Keresans, as the youngest of the groups, while having gone some way towards a bilateral system like the others (the Tanoans), retain faint overtones of their matrilineal organizations. This is thrown into relief by Laguna, which was founded after the rebellion by Eastern Keres refugees, and is therefore a preserved version of the true Eastern type. Among the Eastern Keresans, Cochiti represents the most acculturated towards 'Anglo and/or Tewa models'.

We can quickly discount the Laguna evidence in the sense in which Eggan employs it. If Laguna shows a resemblance towards the Eastern Keres, it is because it shares a common origin with them, and has gone through a similar process of development up to a point, and not because it is an Eastern Keres colony. As far as the Tanoans are concerned (with the exception of Jemez), the theory that they are the most degenerate and therefore the most 'bilateral' of the Eastern Pueblos, having only vestiges of clans remaining, is probably totally wrong. The weight of evidence is that they are not from the San Juan at all (this is the home of the Keres), but from some other dispersion point (north-west or south-west – more probably the former), and that they never had clans. Much more work needs to be done on the re-interpretation of their development, but I think we can take the negative case at least as established.

This leaves the Eastern Keresans. Have they, at any rate, a declining Crow system? For Cochiti at least I think I have established that this is unlikely. The evidence for this contention has rested largely on the so-called 'breakdown' of groups, norms and language in the face of acculturative pressures. I have maintained (how successfully the reader may judge) that this rests on a misinterpretation of the present state of kinship. The present system is *not* a bilateral imitation of Anglo, Spanish or Tewa models; it is an intelligible system in its own right, based on a form of double descent and dual affiliation, and an organization of extended families. I have conjectured that this system in its outlines has characterized Cochiti since the move to the Rio Grande about 700 years ago. Changes have occurred in the relative 'weightings' of the parts of the system, but the clans have never been the dominant institutions and have not significantly declined; they continue to perform their allotted tasks.

It is impossible to emphasize too strongly that interpretations of the present state of Keres social structure must depend on historical assumptions. If one assumes that the Keres must have once had 'strong' clans as in the west, the only conclusion one can reach is that the clans have 'lost' their importance. If, on the other hand, one looks at the relation between clans, lineages, maternal extended families and paternal extended families, the 'fit' between these becomes obvious. Each has its functions, which complement but do not interfere with those of the others; and a simple addition of the functions makes up a kinship system as adequate and 'strong' as any in the area. The division of functions between the various kin groups is certainly different from that in the west, where the clan is not complemented by other kin-groups such as are found in Cochiti. The place of the clans in the general structure is simply different in the two cases. Similarly with the terminology – if it is assumed that this 'must be' determined by the lineage principle, any deviance from this principle is hailed as evidence of decline and confusion. But it is not clear that Western Pueblo terminology is 'determined' solely by this principle – and the Cochiti status terms are clearly not even 'determined' by the kinship system as a whole, much less by one principle in it. They are clearly influenced by the kinship system, and again this influence is understandable and rational, and in conjunction with the other determinants makes sense of the terms as used. This is taking the system on its own terms; to take, as some authors have done, the view that alternative usages must be explained on a chronological basis, assuming the 'Crow' usages are the earliest, is completely to misinterpret the facts.

I have suggested that certain inbuilt features of the terms – in particular self-reciprocity – in conjunction with the *Kivas*, point to an earlier system of exogamous moieties. If the terms are arranged in this way, their development becomes easy to envisage, and the contemporary discriminations which they imply make sense in terms of a gradual change from the original system, through one of the clans with non-exogamous moieties, to that which can be observed at present. I have suggested further that Laguna usage can be analyzed in the same way, and the features that Eggan found inexplicable can then be understood. If this is true, the line of development of Keres society may have been very different from that conjectured by Eggan. Rather than an example of a universal Pueblo process it becomes what my analysis of contemporary Cochiti led me to suspect: a distinct type of system with a developmental progression quite different from that of the Hopi.

Since we have shown that the Tanoan system cannot be explained in terms of degeneration then there is little left of this theory except the Zuni case, which exhibits a system perhaps not as thoroughly Crow as it might be. I would tentatively suggest that Zuni is not very different from Laguna, and that it shows indications of an earlier moiety organization. One might conjecture three lines of development:

1. Hopi: straightforward Crow with very slight modifications.
2. Zuni/Keres:
   (a) Zuni – exogamous patri-moieties
      to Crow and non-exogamous moieties, then to Crow without moieties.
   (b) Keres – exogamous patri-moieties
      to Crow and non-exogamous patri-moieties (the Crow processes being *more* influential with Western than Eastern Keres).
3. Tanoan: patri-moieties (exogamous ?) to non-exogamous (patri-) moieties and bilateral kindreds.

The Hopi present some difficulties. They may well have had cross-cousin marriage, a possibility explored by Titiev (1938). The Shoshone, from whom they are descended, had institutionalized sister-exchange and the resultant cross-cousin marriage, as well as the levirate and sororate. Steward maintains, however, that they never developed patrilocal bands, but Service disagrees, and explains the absence of such bands as a result of the breakdown of the society after its failure to acquire the Horse. (Service 1962, pp. 94–9.) I think it probable that the Shoshonean ancestors of the Hopi never developed an *extensive* system of reciprocal exogamy based on patrimoieties, even though they had the same raw material for it as their Keresan neighbours. Matrilocal residence, and then the dry-farming economy, came quickly to dominate their development, differentiating it from that of the Keresans with their communal building projects and irrigation economy. [Trager supposes that the Hopi-Shoshone simply moved into Zuni villages which had either been abandoned or cleared of their inhabitants. Thus, they were simply settled, matrilocally organized, hunters-cum-agriculturalists.]

As we have seen, some moiety usages can be grafted on a Crow system, and the more fully institutionalized the clan becomes, the more will these be modified, until, perhaps, they disappear altogether. Their presence among the Keresans suggests that it is not very long since the abandonment of moiety exogamy.

But what, in this context, is a long time? The time perspective is all-important. One's opinion as to what is declining depends on where one fixes the base line. Eggan goes back to the Modified Basketmaker period – A.D. 400–700. It may well be that the 'unit houses' of this period housed 'matri-families'. But this might be an ecological adaptation, and not prejudice an already existing moiety structure – amongst the Keresans at least.[1] It may well have been the origin of clans, if they flowered in the Developmental and Great Pueblo periods – A.D. 700–1400. The Shoshonean Hopi, without moieties, had already gone westwards to their mesa-top sites and dry farming, and elaborated their clan organization. Meanwhile, the Keres were involved in large-scale building in

---

[1] It would, however, produce a 'disharmonic' system in Lévi-Strauss's sense: one in which the principles of descent and residence were at variance. Lévi-Strauss regards a dual organization as an answer to the 'problems' created by such a system.

Chaco Canyon and Mesa Verde, and may have been engaged in quite extensive, even if primitive, irrigation work. If, as Wittfogel and Goldfrank suggest, communal activity and a hydraulic economy are conducive to a moiety system, then the pre-existing system may well have been reinforced in these conditions. Whether the moieties remained exogamous at this stage is a moot point.

What happened after the exodus from the San Juan (*circa* A.D. 1250) is difficult to assess. Acoma and Laguna (separating about A.D. 1450) went off to their mesa-top sites and dry farming in the neighbourhood of the Zuni. Here they too intensified the clan system on 'Western' lines, and perhaps lost many features of the moiety organization, except such as remained in the terminology and the overtones of dual organization in ceremony. The evidence on *Kivas* is uncertain, but there are indications of a moiety and *Kiva* system, and the *Kiva* membership was certainly on the Eastern Keres model. The Eastern Keres for their part went to the Rio Grande. Here they continued, as perhaps at Tyuonyi (Frijoles Canyon), to practise communal building and irrigation, and later, on the Rio Grande proper, they intensified their irrigation activities with all the consequences that the hydraulic hypothesis implies for their moiety system. Oral tradition maintains that Cochiti, Santo Domingo and San Felipe shared this experience. Similarities of dialect, custom and structure support this identification, but place Cochiti in a rather independent position. Perhaps the Zia / Santa Ana group moved south like Acoma /Laguna. We should in fact classify the Keresans into three groups:

1. *Western*    Acoma and Laguna
2. *Central*    Zia and Santa Ana
3. *Eastern*    Cochiti, Santo Domingo and San Felipe

The Central group appear to be something of a hybrid.

Whatever the actual history may have been, I think that we can establish at least the negative case: the Eastern Keresans did not have a 'social structure of the Western type until the rebellion'. They had, and still have, a structure of a different type. What forms of this type are to be regarded as decadent depends on where one starts. If my picture of development is correct, one could see 'the social structure' as beginning to decline when the moieties lost their exogamic functions. This might have been during the efflorescence of the Great Pueblo period, or very much later. Perhaps the diaspora destroyed a well-regulated system of exo-gamous-moieties. The groups which left the San Juan might have been demographically unbalanced, so that reciprocal exogamy was impossible. Perhaps it was then that the rules were relaxed. If the clans increased in importance as a result, one could perhaps regard them as having 'declined' again after the move to the Rio Grande had had its full effect and the rebellion had disrupted the social structure. If this is the starting point, we might almost accommodate Eggan's view, though even then it would be diffi-cult to maintain that the social structure was really 'of the Western type'.

## II

I must turn briefly to the problem of the newly named Central Keresans.

As far as I can tell, Cochiti, Santo Domingo and San Felipe are very much alike. They have a strong tradition that they were originally 'one people'. This would accord with the results of dialect studies which place them close together and separate from Santa Ana and Zia, which also show the greatest differences structurally. Zia presents problems in that, in spite of its reputation as one of the most conservative of the Pueblos, it is clearly one of the least well integrated.[1] It suffered a severe population decline, and its end was prophesied several times. In 1881 it had a popula-tion of only fifty-eight, and was in a 'ruinous condition'. (It was even proposed to join it with Santa Ana.) Later it slowly returned to 'normal', but obviously there must have been some discon-tinuities. The two-*Kiva* pattern is found there, but does not seem to be very stable. Informants differ widely as to the basis of re-cruitment, some saying this is decided by one official, others that it is a matter of residence. In either case it would lack the stability of the Cochiti system, and could not really provide for continuity as the patri-virilateral method does. The paternal extended family cannot have the place here that it does in Cochiti. For some time, also, Zia had only one *Kiva*, since the other was burned down during factional fighting and has only recently been rebuilt. A heretical Holy Roller movement made some converts in Zia, and there was much dissension on this issue. Marriage also seems to be

[1] White, 1962.

less well institutionalized in Zia; the number of unmarried is remarkably high, as is the number of illegitimate births. If we had more data on the clan (and possibly the lineage) at Zia, we might know whether or not these facts represented a failure to get back to normal after the nineteenth-century decline, or simply a manifestation of a different type of integration, with a weak *Kiva* and strong clan structure.

Santa Ana, which is closely associated both in dialect and historically with Zia, presents yet other problems.[1] It has the familiar units of *Kivas* (two), clans and societies, but is unique amongst the Keresans in dividing its clans between the *Kivas*. White notes that he checked this information by picking out people at random whose clan affiliation he knew and asking for their *Kiva* membership. In most cases it worked out, but there were 'discrepancies' that he could not explain. (Perhaps in Zia the discrepancies became so many that the clan-based *Kiva* system broke down and membership problems were handed over to the War Captains?) Only Hano, the Hopi-acculturated Tewa Pueblo, follows this system, and its occurrence at Santa Ana is indeed odd, as White says. Possibly his informants described the ideal scheme and the discrepancies reflected the real situation. It does seem, though, that neither in Santa Ana nor Zia has *Kiva* recruitment the same firm patrilineal basis as is found in the three eastern villages. They should perhaps be recorded as '*Kiva* membership problematical'. In any case, a double-descent system of the kind found at Cochiti and presumably at Santo Domingo and San Felipe would be impossible there. It might very well be that the two 'central' villages reached a different form of integration from their eastern cousins, and one that was more vulnerable to change. The uniqueness of each of these villages cannot be overstressed, and this is underlined by the fact that they used to be fairly endogamous. All reports agree that endogamy was either a rule, a strong preference, or a *de facto* certainty. Cochiti were not interested in, and in some cases totally ignorant of, what went on in other villages, and most villages regard the others as deviant versions of themselves. Thus, although the same elements are present, it is not surprising that the social structures are very different.

That integration appears to be greater in Cochiti may simply be a result of our greater knowledge of this Pueblo. But Cochiti

[1] White, 1942.

has been pursuing something of a separate course now for 700 years, and its solution may be unique among the Keresans. In some ways the central groups are more like Acoma and Laguna, and, indeed, Zia may have been a founder member of the composite post-revolution Laguna. I should be inclined to see it as a degenerated version of the Eastern Keresan type.

## III

It only remains to place the Cochiti kinship system in the context of the social system as a whole. As we have seen, the kinship system and the public-ritual and governmental system do not meet except in the determination of *Kiva* membership. In this Cochiti differs from the Western Pueblos, where many of these functions are in the hands of the clans and houses within the clans. Eggan stresses the contribution of this factor to 'vertical integration', and makes the excellent point that the phratry system insures against the dying out of a ceremony or office by allowing it to be transferred from an extinct clan to another of the same phratry. But while the 'lineage principle' – or at least the unilineal principle – has advantages in this area, it also has dangers. It is open to demographic vagaries and crises against which even the phratry system cannot protect it. In a sense, 'voluntary' association is a more flexible and adaptative mechanism for ensuring continuity. Certainly the rate at which clans have died out in Cochiti, and the failure of some to throw up many male members, would have rendered difficult any system of succession to office based on clanship. The weight of the system therefore rests on the *Kivas*, which are large enough to avoid the danger of extinction, and on the societies. These die out only if they fail to recruit members, as has sometimes happened; but this is a response to change, an aspect of the flexibility of the system. Whereas it is hard to throw off an ascribed office, no one is constrained to join the societies, and they can be allowed to fade away without the complications of unilineal inheritance. As long as the community wishes, it can ensure the continuity of society control of the rituals by encouraging the initiation of new members. I do not see that this method is less efficient than the lineage principle; it even seems to have advantages over it.

The system of land tenure and inheritance also does not seem to follow the lines of the kinship system. Here too there is a difference from the Western Pueblos – but Forde has pointed out that the Hopi are by no means rigid in the 'clan' ownership and inheritance of land. In Cochiti many of these matters seem to be centrally controlled by the council.

Thus associational principles and achieved status seem to be more important in the religio-political system of Cochiti than in the Western Pueblos. The functions left to the kinship groups are, roughly, the control of marriage, ritual and other socialization, domestic economy, and healing. One should perhaps add baseball recruitment. The clan controls marriage and undertakes healing; the lineage handles the details of this for its members and deals with some aspects of the socialization of its children; ritual socialization is in the hands of the patrifamily; and the domestic economy is largely the function of the matrifamily and the nuclear family. Some economic enterprises are undertaken by the patrifamily, and the nuclear family is now the household unit.

The only spheres in which functions are shared with the religio-political wing are healing and discipline. There are some offences which are judged by the Pueblo as a whole, and conversely some aspects of socialization are the concern of everyone through the officers. In healing, the clans divide functions with the medicine societies. I am maintaining throughout this analysis that what Cochiti has achieved is a division of labour in which functions do not overlap between the groups. Some observers have argued that this is contradicted by the clan-cure system. They maintain that curing is the prerogative of the societies, and that clans are called upon only by people who cannot afford to pay the exorbitant fees that the societies charge.[1] This is not the case. I have elsewhere examined at length the differences between clan and society cures,[2] but it suffices here to say that the Cochiti distinguish between illnesses requiring different types of cure. The crucial distinction lies in the source of the illness. Witch illness has to be treated by the societies (which also render first aid), but some illnesses are not attributed to witchcraft. These are generally psychosomatic complaints that persist over long periods. What the individual requires in these cases is nurturance, and not 'shock' treatment such as the societies specialize in. The only organization geared to nurturance is the clan. Hence in these cases clan adoption

[1] Goldfrank, 1927.                     [2] Fox, 1964.

is resorted to, and the sick individual is given a store of *yaya* to shore up his damaged psyche.

This, I maintain, reinforces my thesis that the clan is a mystical union. Its 'real' functions are spiritual and nurturant. It has great 'power' – hence the popularity of adoption. The more clans one belongs to, the more spiritual nurturant power one acquires. My figures are far from complete, but I would guess that most adults were adopted members of at least one clan in addition to having the strong 'complementary' relation with their father's. Thus there are at least three clans to which they can turn for succour. That this mystical bond is seen as being like that between mother and child is indisputable on the basis of Cochiti statements and the affect surrounding clanship and its functions. ('Mother' here refers to all female nurturers of the child, whoever they may have been.) Thus for illnesses requiring succour and love in their cure, the essentially male political societies are no good. The 'strength' of the clan cannot be gauged simply on the basis of its political involvement or its use in agriculture. For Cochiti these would be contingent features which the clan might well acquire, but which it might just as easily shed. In the days before the combine harvester the clan would not see a member starve because he could not get his harvest in unaided. But now it is not needed in this sphere. Lange maintains that Cochiti have a poor knowledge of their clan membership and that young people are not interested in it.[1] In fact, Cochiti do not talk freely about clans and clan membership because these are 'personal' matters.[2] Moreover, young people are not a good source of information on these matters. How many young people in any society know or care much about its workings? All I can say is that I never met a young person who could not tell me at least his own and his father's clan when properly approached, i.e., when asked a question which required this in its answer rather than just asking, 'What is your clan?' At all the gatherings mentioned above, all the young people of the clans concerned were present down to the smallest babies, and all participated on equal terms. Whether they fully understood what was happening is doubtful, but this is not peculiar to Cochiti. The ground of a full understanding was being laid down. This may never flower, however, since change is rapidly overtaking Cochiti

---

[1] See Lange, 1959, ch. 10.     [2] See White, 1935, for similar comments.

in many forms. The next generation may well be faced with social upheavals on a scale not so far encountered.

Thus the kinship system can be seen as a complement to the religio-political system, and the combination of the two leads to a complex division of labour, both ritual and secular, between the different groups and institutions. When I say there is no overlapping of functions but a genuine complementarity, I do not mean to imply that there is no rivalry or hostility; simply that structurally there is no obvious clash of interest or purpose. This does not mean that I regard the structure as static and unchangeable, as previous chapters have made clear.

The one exception to this theory of balance is the baseball teams; that is why they are so crucial to an understanding of the direction of change in Cochiti. This is the only case of non-complementarity. Even the factions have settled down to an understanding and a generally accepted division of functions, but the baseball teams puzzle the Cochiti themselves. They see dimly that the problem presented by baseball antagonism is utterly different from any they have faced before. They have no way of channelling hostility of this kind. The only way to mitigate it would be to have the two teams play in different leagues, but this is not possible at present.

The Cochiti social system has two characteristics, complexity and complementarity, which give it flexibility and adaptability.[1] The effect of complexity is that there has always been a variety of groups between which functions could be transferred. The effect of complementarity is that the division of functions is always possible without serious clashes. The result is a structure of great resilience which has, despite numerous pressures, and maybe even because of them, achieved a remarkable degree of integration. Whether it will survive the pressures of the future is doubtful. Television, baseball rivalry, wage work, the vote and a proposed dam on the Rio Grande (which will be exploited as a pleasure resort) all pose new threats. But in the question of American Indian survival, prophecy is notoriously futile.

[1] cf. Fox, 1963.

## IV

It has been put to me that I should not complete this book without explaining and defending my use of 'conjectural history'. In doing so I follow Sir Karl Popper, whose latest book is significantly entitled *Conjectures and Refutations*. All science is conjectural: what matters is that the conjectures should be, in principle, capable of refutation. Now, most of the conjectures of structural-functionalism, it seems to me, are not so capable in practice, even if they are in principle. Very often the same is true of historical conjecture but again, as in all science, we are concerned here with degrees of probability. There is no value in making historical conjectures without any evidence at all; Radcliffe-Brown was quite right about this. But when relevant evidence is available, a historical conjecture is no less, and often a good deal more, scientific, than one concerning the 'functional prerequisites of the system', or the 'maintenance of the system as a functioning entity'. In the same way as palaeontologists know the relations between anatomical structures and behavioural structures, we know the relation between linguistic structures and social structures. Moreover, we can reconstruct linguistic and migrational history from lexicostatistical and archaeological evidence. Of course, this is all 'conjecture', but so are the steady-state theory of the universe and the theory of natural selection. What matters, as I have said, is whether these conjectures (*a*) have relevant evidence available to test them and (*b*) are so framed that they are amenable to refutation (not *verification* as the positivists thought). It seems to me that the Pueblo material meets these criteria. It is the great merit of Eggan's work that he frames his hypotheses in a refutable way. In fact, he is much more cautious in his conjectures than I have been and does not explore the possibilities of the terminology for historical reconstruction. But he clearly saw such possibilities in his recognition of the possible use of Murdockian and Lévi-Straussian analysis on the Pueblo material.

How do we 'test' a historical conjecture? Well, it should be in terms of degree of probability. The 'explanation' should be parsimonious, cover a total system, be logically consistent, and account for as much of the variance as possible. Eggan's hypothesis meets the first three counts but fails, I think, on the last. Of course, we are now in possession of fresh evidence, so that we have more means of testing our hypotheses than Eggan had. On the basis of this, and on the re-analysis of kinship terms in this book, I would claim to have accounted for more of the variance than Eggan was able to do, and hence that the probability of my reconstruction being correct is greater. More evidence and a more correct analysis of terms may lead to the refutation of this reconstruction.

Of course there are always areas of great uncertainty in such reconstructed schemes. We never get more than a broad outline, and essential details may be completely obscure. All we can try to do is to reduce the uncertainty by more consistent or sensitive analysis, and by unearthing more data. To those who ask, then, why I tried 'conjectural history', I can only answer that certain 'historical' facts in the Cochiti linguistic and social structures stared me in the face. They demanded a historical explanation, and I merely followed out their logic, and tried to graft this onto what was known about the South-west generally.

## V

This argument has been an attempt to tackle Eggan's problem of the Keresan Bridge. It rests mainly on the rather narrow basis of inadequate data from one Pueblo, but one that constitutes a crucial case for the testing of his theory. The kinship system of Cochiti has been consistently interpreted as a degenerate form of a universal type. It is an essential consequence of this theory that terms and norms, and the structure of groups and statuses, should be in a state of confusion as a result of the decline of Crow patterns, and should have assimilated to 'bilateral' models as a result of acculturation. Since the system can be shown to be neither chaotic nor bilateral, the theory is suspect. Not only does the system as it stands not support the theory, but it contains clues to a possible historical development which may in fact be general for the Keresans. Other evidence leads us to believe that Eggan's theory is not applicable to the Tanoans.

The two ends of the Keresan bridge, then, represent divergent developments from a basic Keres type which was not that of the Western Pueblos. The Western Keresan form of this basic Keres type has approximated closely to the Western Pueblo model, while the Eastern Keresans have achieved a different solution. The

Central Keresans seem to be a hybrid. About them we must remain in doubt; but that the Eastern and Western Keresans are different developments from a common non-Western Pueblo base is reasonably certain.

This then, if I am right, is the secret of the Bridge.

# The Towa Pueblo of Jemez

After this manuscript was completed, there came to my attention Florence Hawley Ellis's *A Reconstruction of the Basic Jemez Pattern of Social Organization, with Comparisons to Other Tanoan Social Structures* (University of New Mexico Publications in Anthropology, no. 11, 1964). As I have said that Jemez is crucial in reconstructing Northern Rio Grande pre-history, I must take into account what she says. I must first stress that as far as my argument is concerned, these excursions into pre-history are significant only for their bearing on Eggan's historical hypothesis. Hence I do not feel it necessary to decide between divergent archaeological findings (indeed, I am not competent to do so), a task that would involve a thesis in itself.

Ellis maintains that despite Keresan influences the social structure of Jemez is basically Tanoan, showing affinities to both Tiwa and Tewa patterns, but conforming exactly with neither of its linguistic cousins in 'basic' traits. She 'strips away' the overlay of Keresan and other borrowings to reveal a basic or original social system which had two moieties, each controlled by a society (Eagle or Arrow) and using a single *Kiva*; a 'horizontal or bilateral' kinship structure; and, originally, only one society group, which later burgeoned into Scalp, Hunt, Fire (medicine), 'weather control', women's and 'clown' societies. In this scheme *Koshare* are original, *Kwirena* borrowed from the Keres. A Cacique's society elected the Cacique, while the Scalp Society elected the War Priest. The two moieties did *not* alternate in government like those of the Tewa, but were 'continuous', as with the Tiwa.

The Keresan 'overlays' are the second *Kiva* (Squash/Pumpkin) and patri-virilateral *Kiva* membership; clans, and an association of clan with some offices; some additional societies. The two-*Kiva* system is a simple 'borrowing'. It is 'relegated to the mere direct

classification of 'Kiva groups', for which the main function is putting on the Saint's Day dances, all of which are for rain and
growth' (pp. 45-6). The societies likewise are borrowed, and this
conforms with known Pueblo practices. The clans are the result of
persistent intermarriage with Keresans, which made the adoption
of clanship a 'requirement'. This is plausible. So rooted is the
notion of clanship in female imagination among the Keres that
even marriage into a Pueblo without clans would not eradicate it.
The safety and security of a woman's children lies in their having
one or more clans. When an out-marrying woman's children
returned to their mother's village for feasts they would affiliate
temporarily with her lineage and clan. I have heard of cases where
Jemez and Tewa children of Cochiti women returned to Cochiti
for clan cures.

   This does not, however, explain how the clan came to be integrated into Jemez society as a whole. It may be that over time
so many Jemez people had clans through their Keresan ancestresses
that the rest were adopted and fell into line. In associating clan
with office, however, the Jemez follow the 'Western' Eastern-
Keresan pattern. If they are to be classed with Keresans at all it will
perhaps have to be with the central group (Zia and Santa Ana).

   According to Ellis, the two-Kiva pattern is not of great importance. This is borne out by the fact that the Arrow and Eagle
societies which control the two 'initiation' moieties both use the
Turquoise Kiva, and that Katsina initiation is not Kiva-linked as at
Cochiti (at least). Of course, the Turquoise Kiva at Cochiti is
'senior' to the Pumpkin, and is used by both moieties for some
dances. As we saw in Chapter 2, Kiva and moiety are not necessarily linked.

   How does all this affect our view of Jemez in the history of the
Northern Rio Grande? We must first admit that Ellis' evidence is
difficult to assess in the terms of the analysis made here, because
again all we have is a 'formal' or 'customary' view. We do not
know very much about what clanship and Kiva/moiety membership mean to the Jemez themselves. However, we can accept that
the division into Kiva groups is not as far-reaching as in the
'Eastern' Eastern-Keresans. But this does not mean that patrilineal groupings are less important. As Ellis points out, the 'real'
moiety division is that into the two men's initiation societies,
Eagle and Arrow. The division into two Kiva groups overlaps

this. Thus, if my reading of the situation is correct, there are four possibilities of affiliation on the patrilineal side – Pumpkin-Eagle, Turquoise-Eagle, Pumpkin-Arrow, Turquoise-Arrow. Women, of course, simply follow their husbands.

The difficulty in understanding this is that Ellis only gives the 'customs'. We do not know the details of recruitment to the Eagle and Arrow societies. Men 'join one or the other of them'. If this is so, and there is no patrilineal trend here, and a man is as likely to join the opposite society to his father's as he is to join his father's, the basis for a double-descent system would be lacking. The *Kivas* are patrilineal, with the possibility of membership change, but they seem not to be 'formally' important. Women join the husband's *Kiva*, but it is not clear how they fit into the Eagle-Arrow division. I presume they follow the husband, but the information is obscure. Since Ellis is not interested in recruitment and its consequences the vital information is lacking, and it may be unobtainable.

At the formal level, all we can see is that whereas at Cochiti the recruitment of males follows the division into two *Kivas*, at Jemez there are two moieties in addition to the two *Kivas*, and we do not know how the moieties are recruited. It thus seems an amalgam of Tanoan and Keresan structures in their present form. But what of the past? Perhaps in the Gallina-Chaco intermingling phase of Tewa-Towa-Keres history, the one-*Kiva*/two-moiety pattern was common to both (however the moiety was recruited). The Keres developed the two-*Kiva* pattern and associated the moieties with this – and the clown societies; the Tewa stuck to one *Kiva* and alternating moiety government; the Jemez de-veloped a two-*Kiva* system, but failed to associate the moieties with it and therefore evolved a dual-moiety system. Clans *may* have come in at this stage (eleventh to thirteenth centuries) because of intermarriage and ceremonial co-operation.

This interpretation suggests that the association of Towa and Keres is relatively ancient and that Jemez, which represents a unique evolution of combined Tanoan-Keres traits, may be more ancient still.

Ellis accepts Davis's lexico-statistical findings as plausible. Davis had Towa breaking off from the parent stem in a very early Basketmaker phase (*circa* 400 B.C.). This period – or at least the centuries following it – was the seminal phase of Keres development too, and if they were, over these centuries, building a clan system, then it is possible that the Towa – isolated from the other Tanoans – were influenced by the same conditions as the Keres. Thus the clan system could have developed in both groups in the eastern San Juan drainage area, while they already had a moiety system, and a single *Kiva* with society-houses, in common.

If Davis is right and the Tanoans came from the Cochise-Mogollon area, the Tewa could, as I have suggested, have broken off early and come up to the Eastern San Juan (Gobernador area? see Ellis, p. 8) during the period when clans were being formed. There is no evidence that the Cochise or Mogollon cultures produced a lineage organization comparable to that of the Anasazi. More probably the other Tanoans simply went on with their development of moieties (alternating or not) and a bilateral kinship system.

The association of *Kivas* with the original moiety structure amongst the Keres would then be a later development which the Towa did not follow. Clans, however, would be common to both from an early period. If we knew more about the clan in Jemez it would be easier to come to a conclusion. As we have seen, in associating clan with office, at the formal level at least the Jemez have institutionalized the clan more firmly than the Cochiti. Jemez, of course, has been more influenced by Zia than any other Pueblo (counting Santa Ana in with Zia). The influence goes back at least to the thirteenth century in terms of known (as opposed to postulated) relationships (see Ellis, p. 8). In Zia the clan seems to be more institutionalized than in the Eastern group, at the expense of a weak moiety system. Had Jemez been in close contact with the Eastern group, it might have consolidated its moiety and *Kiva* organization.

What all this shows is that we are still very much in the dark about some of the main issues; but at least we know the following:

(*a*) That my assumption that Jemez is just another Keresan Pueblo speaking a different language is incorrect;
(*b*) That the structure of Jemez is neither Keres nor Tanoan but an amalgam;
(*c*) That the origin of this is doubtful, though I would lean towards a theory of the 'common development' of the clan and the

common possession of moieties, and a later intermingling of
societies;
(d) That Davis's scheme of historical reconstruction seems plausible though we have no real proof;
(e) That we need to know much more about Jemez!

[Conclusion (d) will obviously have to be modified in the light
of Trager's reconstructions – (Trager, 1965).]

DOZIER, E., 1954. *The Hopi-Tewa of Arizona*, University of California Publications in American Archaeology and Ethnology, no. 44.

—— 1960. A Comparison of the Eastern Keresan and Tewa Kinship Systems, *Selected Papers of the International Congress of Anthropological and Ethnological Sciences*, 430–6.

—— 1961. Rio Grande Pueblos, in *Perspectives in American Indian Culture Change* (E. H. Spicer, ed.), Chicago.

—— 1964. The Pueblo Indians of the Southwest, *C.A.*, **5**, no. 2.

DUMAREST, Father N., 1919. Notes on Cochiti, New Mexico (Elsie Clewes Parsons, ed.), *A.A.A.Mem.*, **6**.

DUMONT, L., 1963. The Dravidian Kinship Terminology as an Expression of Marriage, *Man*, **53**, art. 54.

EGGAN, F., 1949. The Hopi and the Lineage Principle, in *Social Structure* (M. Fortes, ed.), Oxford.

—— 1950. *The Social Organization of the Western Pueblos*, Chicago.

—— (ed.) 1955. *Social Anthropology of North American Tribes*, Chicago.

—— 1964. Alliance and Descent in Western Pueblo Society, in *Process and Pattern in Culture* (R. A. Manners, ed.), Chicago.

ELLIS, F. H., 1959. An Outline of Laguna Pueblo History and Social Organization, *S.W.J.A.*, **15**, 325–47.

—— 1964. *A Reconstruction of the Basic Jemez Pattern of Social Organization, with Comparisons to Other Tanoan Social Structures*, University of New Mexico Publications in Anthropology, no. 11, Albuquerque.

FALLERS, L. A., 1957. Some determinants of marriage stability in BuSoga, *Africa*, **27**, 106–23.

FENTON, W. N., 1957. Factionalism at Taos Pueblo, New Mexico, *B.A.E. Bulletin*, **164**.

FIRTH, R., 1963. Bilateral Descent Groups: An Operational Viewpoint, in *Studies in Kinship and Marriage* (I. Schapera, ed.), Occasional Papers of the Royal Anthropological Institute, no. 16.

FORDE, C. D., 1931. Hopi Agriculture and Land Ownership, *J.R.A.I.*, **61**.

—— 1963. Unilineal Fact or Fiction?, in *Studies in Kinship and Marriage* (I. Schapera, ed.), Occasional Papers of the Royal Anthropological Institute, no. 16.

—— 1964. *Yako Studies*, Oxford.

FORTES, M., 1949. *The Web of Kinship amongst the Tallensi*, Oxford.

—— 1953. The Structure of Unilineal Descent Groups, *A.A.*, **55**.

—— 1959. Descent, Filiation and Affinity: A Rejoinder to Dr Leach, *Man*, **59**, arts. 309 and 331.

FOX, J. R., 1959. A Note on Cochiti Linguistics, in C. H. Lange, *Cochiti: A New Mexico Pueblo Past and Present*, Austin.

—— 1960. Therapeutic Rituals and Social Structure in Cochiti Pueblo, *Human Relations*, **13**, no. 4.

—— 1961a. Pueblo Baseball: A New Use for Old Witchcraft, *J.A.F.*, **74**, no. 291.

—— 1961b. Veterans and Factions in Pueblo Society, *Man*, **61**, art. 201.

—— 1963. Cochiti Indians of America, *New Society*, **1**, no. 29.

# LIST OF WORKS CITED

*Abbreviations used*

| | |
|---|---|
| A.A. | *American Anthropologist* |
| A.A.A.Mem. | *Memoirs of the American Anthropological Association* |
| A.E.S. | *American Ethnological Society* |
| A.M.N.H. | *Anthropological Papers of the American Museum of Natural History* |
| B.A.E. | *Bureau of American Ethnology, Smithsonian Institution* |
| C.A. | *Current Anthropology* |
| J.R.A.I. | *Journal of the Royal Anthropological Institute* |
| J.A.F. | *Journal of American Folklore* |
| S.W.J.A. | *Southwestern Journal of Anthropology* |

ABERLE, S. D., 1948. 'The Pueblo Indians of New Mexico: Their Land, Economy and Civil Organization', *A.A.A.Mem.*, **70**.

BANDALIER, A. F., 1890a. Final Report of Investigations among the Indians of the Southwestern United States. *Papers of the Archaeological Institute of America: American Series*, **3**, Cambridge, Mass.

—— 1890b. *The Delight Makers*, New York.

BEAGLEHOLE, E. and P., 'Hopi of the Second Mesa', *A.A.A.Mem.*, **44**.

BENEDICT, RUTH, 1928. Psychological Types in the Cultures of the Southwest, *Proceedings of the 23rd International Congress of Americanists*, 572–81.

—— 1931. 'Tales of the Cochiti Indians', *B.A.E. Bulletin*, **98**.

—— 1934a. *Zuni Mythology*, Columbia University Contributions to Anthropology, **21**, 2 vols., New York.

—— 1934b. *Patterns of Culture*, Boston.

BOAS, F., 1938. Keresan Texts, *A.E.S. Publications*, **8**, Pt. 1.

BUCHLER, I. R., 1964. Measuring the Development of Kinship Terminologies: Scalogram and Transformational Accounts of Crow-type Systems, *A.A.*, **66**, no. 4, Pt. 1.

BUNZEL, RUTH, 1932. Introduction to Zuni Ceremonialism, *B.A.E. 47th Annual Report*.

BURLING, R., 1964. 'Cognition and Componential Analysis: God's Truth or Hocus Pocus?', *A.A.*, **66**, no. 1.

CURTIS, E. S., 1926. *The North American Indian*, XVI, Norwood, Mass.

CUSHING, F. H., 1896. Outlines of Zuni Creation Myths, *B.A.E. 13th Annual Report*.

—— 1920. Zuni Breadstuffs, *Publications of the Museum of the American Indian, Heye Foundation*, **8**.

DAVIS, I., 1959. 'Linguistic Clues to Northern Rio Grande Prehistory', *El Palacio*, **66**, no. 3.

—— 1964. The language of Santa Ana Pueblo, *B.A.E. Bulletin*, **191**.

FOX, J. R., 1964. Witchcraft and Clanship in Cochiti Therapy, in *Magic, Faith and Healing* (Ari Kiev, ed.), Glencoe.

FREEDMAN, M., 1958. *Lineage Organization in Southeastern China*. London School of Economics Monographs on Social Anthropology, no. 18.

FREEMAN, J. D., 1961. On the Concept of the Kindred, *J.R.A.I.*, **91**, Pt. 2.

FRENCH, D., 1948. Factionalism in Isleta Pueblo, *A.E.S. Monographs*, no. 14.

GOLDFRANK, E. S., 1927. The Social and Ceremonial Organization of Cochiti, *A.A.A.Mem.*, **33**.

GOODENOUGH, W. H., 1955. A Problem in Malayo-Polynesian Social Organization, *A.A.*, **57**.

GOODY, J., 1957. Fields of Social Control among the LoDagaba, *J.R.A.I.*, **87**.
—— 1961. The Classification of Double Descent Systems. *C.A.*, **2**, no. 1.
—— 1962. *The Developmental Cycle in Domestic Groups*, Cambridge Papers on Social Anthropology, no. 1.

GOUGH, K., 1961. Nayar: Central Kerala, in *Matrilineal Kinship* (D. M. Schneider and K. Gough, eds.), Berkeley and Los Angeles.

HAEBERLIN, H. K., 1916. The Idea of Fertilization in the Culture of the Pueblo Indians, *A.A.A.Mem.*, **3**, no. 1.

HARRIS, R., 1962. The Political Significance of Double Unilineal Descent, *J.R.A.I.*, **92**, Pt. 2.

HARVEY, B., 1963. Masks at a Maskless Pueblo: The Laguna Colony Kachina Organization at Isleta, *Ethnology*, **2**, no. 4.

HAWLEY, F., 1937. Pueblo Social Organization as a Lead to Pueblo History, *A.A.*, **39**.
—— 1950a. Big Kivas, Little Kivas and Moiety Houses in Historical Reconstruction, *S.W.J.A.*, **6**.
—— 1950b. Keresan Patterns of Kinship and Social Organization, *A.A.*, **52**.

HYMES, D. H., 1964. A Perspective for Linguistic Anthropology, in *Horizons of Anthropology* (S. Tax, ed.), London.

KLUCKHOHN, F. R. and STRODTBECK, F. L., 1961. *Variations in Value Orientations*, Illinois.

KROEBER, A. L., 1909. The Classificatory System of Relationship, *J.R.A.I.*, **39**.
—— 1917. Zuni Kin and Clan, *A.M.N.H.*, **18**.
—— 1925. Handbook of the Indians of California, *B.A.E. Bulletin*, **78**.
—— 1938. Basic and Secondary Patterns of Social Structure, *J.R.A.I.*, **68**

LANGE, C. H., 1959. *Cochiti: A New Mexico Pueblo Past and Present*, Austin.

LEACH, E. R., 1957. Aspects of Bridewealth and Marriage Stability among the Kachin and Lakher, *Man*, **57**, art. 59 (reprinted in Leach, 1961).
—— 1961. *Rethinking Anthropology*, London School of Economics Monographs on Social Anthropology, no. 22.

LÉVI-STRAUSS, C., 1949. *Les Structures Élémentaires de la Parenté*, Paris.
—— 1952. Social Structure, in *Anthropology Today* (A. L. Kroeber, ed.), Chicago.
—— 1958. *Anthropologie Structurale*, Paris.

LI, AN-CHE, 1937. Zuni: Some Observations and Queries, *A.A.*, **39**.

LOUNSBURY, F. G., 1964. A Formal Account of the Crow- and Omaha-type Kinship Terminologies, in *Explorations in Cultural Anthropology* (W. H. Goodenough, ed.), Philadelphia.

LOWIE, R. H., 1929. Notes on Hopi Clans, *A.M.N.H.*, **30**, Pt. 6.
—— 1932. Hopi Kinship, *A.M.N.H.*, **34**.
MEGGITT, M. J., 1962. *Desert People*, Sydney.
MICKEY, B. H., 1956. Acoma Kinship Terms, *S.W.J.A.*, **12**, no. 3.
MILLER, W., 1959. Some notes on Acoma Kinship Terminology, *S.W.J.A.*, **15**.
MURDOCK, G. P., 1949. *Social Structure*, New York.
NEEDHAM, R., 1962. *Structure and Sentiment*, Chicago.
OPLER, M. E., 1941. *An Apache Life Way*, Chicago.
—— 1955. An Outline of Chiricahua Apache Social Organization, in Eggan, 1955.
PARSONS, E. C., 1917. Notes on Zuni, *A.A.A.Mem.*, **4**, nos. 3, 4.
—— 1918. Notes on Acoma and Laguna, *A.A.*, **20**.
—— 1920a. Notes on Isleta, Santa Ana, and Acoma, *A.A.*, **22**.
—— 1920b. Notes on Ceremonialism at Laguna, *A.M.N.H.*, **19**, Pt. 4.
—— 1923. Laguna Genealogies, *A.M.N.H.*, **19**, Pt. 5.
—— 1925. *The Pueblo of Jemez*, New Haven.
—— 1928. The Laguna Migration to Isleta, *A.A.*, **30**.
—— 1929. The Social Organization of the Tewa of New Mexico, *A.A.A.Mem*, **36**.
—— 1932a. Isleta, *B.A.E.*, *47th Annual Report*.
—— 1932b. The Kinship Nomenclature of the Pueblo Indians, *A.A.*, **24**.
—— 1933. Hopi and Zuni Ceremonialism, *A.A.A.Mem.*, **39**.
—— 1936. *Taos Pueblo*, General Series in Anthropology, no. 2.
—— 1939a. Picuris, New Mexico, *A.A.*, **41**.
—— 1939b. *Pueblo Indian Religion*, Chicago.
POPPER, K., 1963. *Conjectures and Refutations*, London.
RADCLIFFE-BROWN, A. R., 1931. The Social Organization of Australian Tribes, *Oceania*, **I**.
—— 1941. The Study of Kinship Systems, *J.R.A.I.*, **71** (reprinted in *Structure and Function in Primitive Society*, London, 1952).
REED, E. K., 1946. The Distinctive Features and Distribution of the San Juan Anasazi Culture, *S.W.J.A.*, **2**, no. 3.
—— 1949. Sources of Upper Rio Grande Culture and Population, *El Palacio*, **56**, no. 6.
RIVERS, W. H. R., 1914. *Kinship and Social Organization*, London.
SCHNEIDER, D. M., 1961. Introduction to *Matrilineal Kinship* (D. M. Schneider and K. Gough, eds.), California.
SCHNEIDER, D. M. and ROBERTS, J. M., 1956. *Zuni Kin Terms*, University of Nebraska: Laboratory of Anthropology, Notebook 3.
SERVICE, E., 1962. *Primitive Social Organization: An Evolutionary Perspective*, New York.
SIMMONS, L. E. (ed.), 1942. *Sun Chief: The Autobiography of a Hopi Indian*, New Haven.
STEPHEN, A. M., 1936. *Hopi Journal*, Columbia University Contributions to Anthropology, **23**.
STEVENSON, M. C., 1889. The Sia, *B.A.E.*, *11th Annual Report*.
1904. The Zuni Indians, *B.A.E.*, *23rd Annual Report*.

STEWARD, J. H., 1937. Ecological Aspects of Southwestern Society, *Anthropos*, **32**.

—— 1938. Basin-Plateau Aboriginal Sociopolitical Groups, *B.A.E. Bulletin*, **120**.

—— 1955. *Theory of Culture Change*, Urbana.

STRONG, W. D., 1927. An Analysis of Southwestern Society, *A.A.*, **29**.

TAX, S., 1955. Some Problems of Social Organization, in Eggan, 1955 (first published in 1937).

TITIEV, M., 1938. The Problem of Cross-Cousin Marriage among the Hopi, *A.A.*, **40**.

—— 1944. *Old Oraibi*, Peabody Museum of American Archaeology and Ethnology, Papers, **22**, no. 1.

TRAGER, G. L., 1951. Linguistic History and Ethnologic History in the Southwest, *Journal of the Washington Academy of Sciences*, **41**, 341–3.

—— 1965. The Tanoan Settlement of the Rio-Grande Area: A Possible Chronology, Ms. to be published in *Studies in Southwestern Ethnolinguistics* (D. H. Hymes, ed.).

WENDORF, F., 1954. A Reconstruction of Northern Rio-Grande Prehistory, *A.A.*, **56**.

WENDORF, F. and REED, E., 1955. An Alternative Reconstruction of Northern Rio-Grande Prehistory, *El Palacio*, **62**.

WHITE, L. A., 1932a. The Acoma Indians, *B.A.E.*, *47th Annual Report*.

—— 1932b. The Pueblo of San Felipe, *A.A.A.Mem.*, **38**.

—— 1935. The Pueblo of Santo Domingo, New Mexico, *A.A.A.Mem.*, **43**.

—— 1939. A Problem in Kinship Terminology, *A.A.*, **41**, 569–70.

—— 1942. The Pueblo of Santa Ana, New Mexico, *A.A.A.Mem.*, **43**.

—— 1962. The Pueblo of Sia, New Mexico, *B.A.E.*, *Bulletin*, **184**.

WHITMAN, W., 1947. *The Pueblo of San Ildefonso*, New York.

WHORF, B. L., 1956. *Language, Thought and Reality*, Cambridge, Mass.

WHORF, B. L. and TRAGER, G. L., 1937. The Relationship of Uto-Aztecan and Tanoan, *A.A.*, **39**.

WITTFOGEL, K. and GOLDFRANK, E. S., 1943. Some Aspects of Pueblo Mythology and Society, *J.A.F.*, **56**.

WORMINGTON, H. M., 1956. *Prehistoric Indians of the Southwest* (3rd ed.), Denver Museum of Natural History, Popular Series, no. 7, Denver, Colorado.

# INDEX

*Italic figures indicate principal reference*

# LONDON SCHOOL OF ECONOMICS
## MONOGRAPHS ON SOCIAL ANTHROPOLOGY

Titles marked with an asterisk are now out of print. Those marked with a dagger have been reprinted in paperback editions and are only available in this form.

1, 2. RAYMOND FIRTH
 *The Work of the Gods in Tikopia*, 2 vols. 1940. Second edition, 1 vol., 1967.

3. E. R. LEACH
 *Social and Economic Organization of the Rowanduz Kurds*, 1940. Available from University Microfilms Ltd.

*4. E. E. EVANS-PRITCHARD
 *The Political System of the Anuak of the Anglo-Egyptian Sudan*, 1940. (Revised edition in preparation.)

5. DARYLL FORDE
 *Marriage and the Family among the Yakö in South-Eastern Nigeria*, 1941. Available from University Microfilms Ltd.

*6. M. M. GREEN
 *Land Tenure of an Ibo Village in South-Eastern Nigeria*, 1941.

7. ROSEMARY FIRTH
 *Housekeeping among Malay Peasants*, 1943. Second edition, 1966.

*8. A. M. AMMAR
 *A Demographic Study of an Egyptian Province (Sharquiya)*, 1943.

*9. I. SCHAPERA
 *Tribal Legislation among the Tswana of the Bechuanaland Protectorate*, 1943. (Revised edition in preparation.)

*10. W. H. BECKETT
 *Akokoaso: A Survey of a Gold Coast Village*, 1944.

11. I. SCHAPERA
 *The Ethnic Composition of Tswana Tribes*, 1952.

*12. JU-K'ANG T'IEN
 *The Chinese of Sarawak: A Study of Social Structure*, 1953. (Revised edition in preparation.)

*13. GUTORM GJESSING
 *Changing Lapps*, 1954.

14. ALAN J. A. ELLIOTT
 *Chinese Spirit-Medium Cults in Singapore*, 1955.

*15. RAYMOND FIRTH
 *Two Studies of Kinship in London*, 1956.

16. LUCY MAIR
 *Studies in Applied Anthropology*, 1957.

†17. J. M. GULLICK
 *Indigenous Political Systems of Western Malaya*, 1958.